JOHN MILT

Macmillan Literary Lives
General Editor: Richard Dutton, Professor of English,
Lancaster University

This series offers stimulating accounts of the literary careers of the
most admired and influential English-language authors. Volumes
follow the outline of writers' working lives, not in the spirit of
traditional biography, but aiming to trace the professional, publishing and social contexts which shaped their writing. The role and
status of 'the author' as the creator of literary texts is a vexed issue
in current critical theory, where a variety of social, linguistic and
psychological approaches have challenged the old concentration on
wr:
the
ma
ho\
anc
the

Published titles

Morris Beja
JAMES JOYCE

Cedric C. Brown
JOHN MILTON

Richard Dutton
WILLIAM SHAKESPEARE

Jan Fergus
JANE AUSTEN

Paul Hammond
JOHN DRYDEN

W. David Kay
BEN JONSON

Mary Lago
E. M. FORSTER

Joseph McMinn
JONATHAN SWIFT

Alasdair D.F. Macrae
W. B. YEATS

Kerry McSweeney
GEORGE ELIOT (MARIAN EVANS)

John Mepham
VIRGINIA WOOLF

Michael O'Neill
PERCY BYSSHE SHELLEY

Leonée Ormond
ALFRED TENNYSON

George Parfitt
JOHN DONNE

Gerald Roberts
GERARD MANLEY HOPKINS

Felicity Rosslyn
ALEXANDER POPE

Tony Sharpe
T. S. ELIOT

Gary Waller
EDMUND SPENSER

Cedric Watts
JOSEPH CONRAD

Tom Winnifrith and Edward Chitham
CHARLOTTE AND EMILY BRONTË

John Worthen
D. H. LAWRENCE

Forthcoming titles

Ronald Ayling
SEAN O'CASEY

Deirdre Coleman
SAMUEL TAYLOR COLERIDGE

Peter Davison
GEORGE ORWELL

James Gibson
THOMAS HARDY

Kenneth Graham
HENRY JAMES

Philip Mallett
RUDYARD KIPLING

Ira Nadel
EZRA POUND

Angela Smith
KATHERINE MANSFIELD

Grahame Smith
CHARLES DICKENS

Janice Thaddeus
FANNY BURNEY

John Williams
WILLIAM WORDSWORTH

Barry Windeatt
GEOFFREY CHAUCER

David Wykes
EVELYN WAUGH

John Milton

A Literary Life

Cedric C. Brown
Head of the Department of English
University of Reading

MACMILLAN

First published 1995 by
MACMILLAN PRESS LTD
Houndmills, Basingstoke, Hampshire RG21 6XS
and London
Companies and representatives
throughout the world

ISBN 0–333–42515–4 hardcover
ISBN 0–333–42516–2 paperback

A catalogue record for this book is available
from the British Library.

10   9   8   7   6   5   4   3   2   1
04   03   02   01   00   99   98   97   96   95

Printed in Hong Kong

Contents

List of Abbreviations   vii

Introduction   ix

1   Education: the 'Vacation Exercise' and Early Latin
     Poetry   1

2   Cultivating the Self: the 'Nativity Ode',
     Petrarchism, and the Social Poet   19

3   Occasions, Impulses, and the Sense of Vocation:
     from 'Arcades' to 'Lycidas'   35

4   Italy, Politics, and the Voice of Authority   59

5   Cultural Renewal in a Time of Free Speaking   86

6   Servant and Defender of the Commonwealth   118

7   Prophet to the Commonwealth   134

8   *Paradise Lost*: Spiritual Strengthening for Adverse
     Times   155

9   Last Days: Patience and Monuments   182

Further Reading   208

Index   210

List of Abbreviations

The following abbreviations are used in references in the text and in the notes:

1645   *Poems of Mr John Milton* ... (London, 1645). Milton's first collection of occasional poems. It has been reproduced several times in facsimile in modern times, and can also be found in F below.

1673   *Poems, &c, upon Several Occasions* ... (London, 1673). Expanded and revised collection of occasional poems; can be found in F below.

C   *The Works of John Milton*, general editor F. A. Patterson, 18 vols (New York: Columbia University Press, 1931–8).

CF   *The Poems of John Milton*, ed. J. Carey & A. Fowler (London: Longmans, 1968; revised 1971).

D   *The Early Lives of Milton*, ed. Helen Darbishire (London, 1932).

F   *John Milton's Complete Poetical Works in Photographic Facsimile with Critical Apparatus*, ed. H. F. Fletcher, 4 vols (Urbana: University of Illinois Press, 1943).

LR   J. Milton French, *The Life Records of John Milton*, 5 vols (New Brunswick, NJ: Rutgers University Press, 1949–58).

MQ   *Milton Quarterly*

P   William R. Parker, *The Life of John Milton*, 2 vols (Oxford: Clarendon, 1968).

TMS   *John Milton, Poems, Reproduced in Facsimile from the Manuscript in Trinity College, Cambridge, with a Transcript* (Menston: Scolar Press, 1972).

VC   *A Variorum Commentary on the Poems of John Milton*, various editors, 4 vols to date (London: Routledge, 1970–5).

Y   *The Complete Prose Works of John Milton*, ed. D. M. Wolfe and others, 8 vols (New Haven, Conn.: Yale University Press, 1953–82).

Unless otherwise signified, texts of the poems are taken from CF and prose from Y.

Introduction

This book is an introduction to the whole literary work of Milton in the context of his life. I hope it is of practical value in that way, all the more so since there is I believe no such comprehensive one-volume, affordable volume on the market. One must say, to begin with, however, that there is an embarrassment of materials: Milton's literary output was very large and this book does not simply offer an introduction to the famous poems often studied or anthologised. Some ninety poems find mention (but some only as groups) as well as some thirty prose tracts (although some only briefly) and there is also use of letters and unpublished documents. What is more, his life is unusually well documented for a seventeenth-century writer, in fact splendidly documented when compared to a case like that of Shakespeare. The potential scale of this book was very large and some means of selectivity have had to be found for a study of relatively modest nature.

I should also make clear that this is not a traditional 'life and works'. Milton's career as a writer is treated historically, both in the sense of recovering something of the range of Milton's writing as it appeared during his lifetime and also in the sense of treating the works in their historical context. Throughout, texts are treated as acts of persuasion to their contemporary audiences and are located within the discourses of the time. The further matter, of how the meanings of Milton's texts were constantly reformed by readers of later centuries, is unfortunately beyond the limits of this study.

Despite the fact that Milton's stated intention was to furnish writings 'doctrinal to … [his] nation' (Y i 815) and that his writings are most often encountered within the context of the academic study of English, this book is not limited to works in the English language. When Milton wrote to an academic audience as a young man or when in his mature years he championed the English Commonwealth on the stage of European scholarship, he composed in Latin; when he wrote to some literary friends he used Italian, to others, again, Latin; and very occasionally he revived his Greek composition. Here, works are treated according to what seems to have been their significance at the time, in whatever language they were first written. Translations of quotations are provided.

Restrictions of range should also be explained. For example, although the concept of the profession of the writer is broad enough that brief mention can be made of Milton's editing and publishing of others' texts (like the so-called Racovian Catechism in 1652 or a book attributed to Sir Walter Ralegh which he published for the public good in 1658) and passing mention is made of official writing he had to do as Secretary to the Commonwealth government, I have not been able to take on any of Milton's (sometimes disputed) documents in State Papers. Also, needless to say, some works have not received the coverage they are due and I am painfully aware of the arbitrary nature of some choices of emphasis.

For all that, the wide range of texts has permitted some unusual emphases, if one compares this with more selective accounts of Milton's career. For example, for all that they are rarely studied, sets of psalm paraphrases are given some prominence, the Italian sonnets are read as a series having to do with a love affair with Italian culture, and accomplished Latin poems, like '*Ad Patrem*', '*Mansus*', and '*Epitaphium Damonis*' are given full weight for their urbanity as well as their revelations of literary ambition. It will also be noticed that I give large prominence to Milton's very accomplished and varied sonnets, especially those written in his middle age. The sonnets usually have well-developed significance as self-presentational documents and they often make important statements at key moments of personal or national decision.

Nevertheless, the familiar major works find their due place, often by being highlighted within the more general or comprehensive coverage of a chapter. Individual works or groups of works are encompassed as follows. The first chapter, covering the writing up to 1628, features at some length not only the well-known early verses 'At a Vacation Exercise', but also the whole college entertainment of which it formed a part, because this student work gives definition of a sense of an individual 'career' or vocation, and also demonstrates even at this early stage many facets of Milton's arts of self-presentation. The second chapter, following the years 1628–32, gives special place to the obviously vocational 'Nativity Ode' at the beginning, and the twin poems 'L'Allegro' and 'Il Penseroso' are used as a touchstone of the art of the social poet, at the end. The Italian sonnets are treated in the middle. The two entertainment texts written for the aristocracy, 'Arcades' and the Ludlow masque, feature in Chapter 3, with some attention paid to the way they negotiate with present occasions and to the way Milton's vocational statements are made in them. 'Lycidas' is also considered in the light of its occasion and for its statements about vocation in the context of ecclesiastical reform and this chapter ends by characterising the year of its composition, 1637, as one of crisis for reforming spirits, because of the dealings of church and court. It is claimed that this sense of crisis helped to trigger Milton's first major publications at that time. The fourth chapter, centring on the Italian journey and the period immediately afterwards, first treats Milton's poems to Italian humanists, then his ecclesiastical pamphlets. Concerning the period from about 1642 to 1649, the fifth chapter covers the divorce tracts, *Of Education, Areopagitica* and *The Tenure of Kings and Magistrates* and is the first of the three chapters making definitive use of English sonnets, as well as discussing the psalm paraphrases of 1648 and historical and geographical works being composed at that time. The next two linked chapters cover the 1650s, and a good number of sonnets are given prominence in them. The first of these chapters features *Eikonoklastes* and the *Defences*, whilst the second features in the context of growing disillusion with the Cromwellian regime, the psalm paraphrases of 1653, the *De Doctrina Christiana*, and the political and ecclesiastical tracts of 1659–60. *Paradise Lost* is given a chapter to itself, not however in the form of a general critical account, but rather in that of an essay speculating about its method of speaking to the times in which it was published. An underlying, difficult question here is one concerning possible conditions of censorship in an adverse situation for the writer. Finally, the ninth and last chapter, as might be expected, comes to rest with *Paradise Regained* and *Samson Agonistes* and a review of late publications, but less expectedly perhaps takes some terms of definition from *Of True Religion.*

As will quickly be apparent, the book has various recurrent themes, which give particular colouring to the discussion of works. Not surprisingly, education is a constant concern, both because of the rich documentation on Milton's own distinctive education and also because many major works in verse and prose were designed to be instructive and show great resourcefulness in their instructive modes. Milton himself was involved in various ways in writing about education, which he saw as a key factor in national renewal. The theme of education gives definition to many chapters, especially perhaps to the schemes for regional colleges in Milton's tracts on the eve of the Restoration.

It may also be of little surprise that political dimensions of many works are discussed. There is of course explicit political function for the many prose tracts written in persuasion to Parliament or to other bodies, but a more diffuse sense of political function is also entertained for other works. So, for example, political dimensions are suggested for more very early poems than are usually recognised as having any kind of political expression, and the three great poems published in the last part of his career, *Paradise Lost, Paradise Regained,* and *Samson Agonistes,* are considered as they might have spoken, in both political and spiritual instruction, to the readership at their time of publication. Some suggestions of political function are unfamiliar, as, for example, with the writings on marriage and divorce, where it is suggested that public concerns about the role of Catholic wives at court may be as relevant to our considerations as all those conjectures we have long held about Milton's relationship with his first wife, Mary Powell. Although problems are encountered with works which Milton worked on at different times of his life, there is a tendency in this book to assume that, given his high sense of vocation, Milton would have designed books to speak to the moments in which they were published or were intended to be published. Indeed, there is ample evidence that when he reissued works or put into print something which had only existed in manuscript form, he altered or augmented his text in the light of instructional effect on the particular audience he thought he would reach in print. So, for example, the text of the Ludlow masque was adjusted for print, as for a new occasion.

Another feature of the book is the attention paid to matters of authorial self-presentation. The issue must be made plain, because few writers have put so much on record as John Milton about the shape and rationale of his literary career: as a student he freely announced great future plans to the academic community at Cambridge; to the audience of his printed books (often in self-defence) he supplied retrospective, rational explanations of his career, in terms that were heroically framed; and both to his friends and to the world at large (in several countries), in letters, poems, and prose tracts, he announced his calling. It is because such documentation is so full that many years ago John Diekhoff was able to edit quite a large book entitled *Milton on Himself.*[1] A problem here for Milton scholars is that accounts of his career have been all too tempted to follow the terms of Milton's own rationalisations: no writer has so fashioned his own image and career and, thus, controlled public understanding. For this reason the evidence of Milton's own statements is treated, like everything else, as part of a rhetoric of persuasion, as part of an art of self-presentation.

Perhaps less expected is an emphasis on Milton as a social poet. He has not been seen enough in that light, so that some works have been too little appreciated for their social arts. The matter of communication with a like-minded audience is one that Milton himself frequently raises in his own writings. The familiar, cultivated audiences of many of his sonnets and other social poems give one a glimpse of the elite constituency of his writing.

The matter is important; Milton habitually appealed to kinds of fit audience, for without them his kind of humanist discourse could have no effect. There is both a celebration of right audience and an anxiety about right audience expressed, implicitly or explicitly, in many of Milton's works, and the reception of some works drew comments even at the time about the appropriateness of literary mode for effectiveness in their occasions. Milton's was a particularly acute and interesting case of something not unfamiliar to authors brought up in a highly competitive and specially trained humanist education: we know that *Areopagitica* was thought by one witness to be rhetorically splendid, but probably too high-flown for its relevant readership (see below, p. 97); even through the supposedly accommodating jocularity of a college entertainment we can see Milton as presenter putting a distance in understanding between himself and many of his coarser-grained fellow students; he wants his readers to know that he found better audience in literary academies in Italy than he did in English society; we can see how various major publications and projected publications sought a discriminating European readership; and so on. His elitism has sometimes been read as a symptom of class attitudes, but it is also a product of particular kinds of educational training and of modes of self-presentation which come with that training. It will be noted that I have frequently used the term Horatian to signal the celebration of an eloquent writer–reader relationship; at the other extreme, the eloquent writer is ignored or Orpheus is dismembered by the barbarous.

And yet vocation demanded finding the right mode in which to communicate, to be useful to his nation and the causes he served and there are indeed signs that some lessons were learned, as, for example, in the trimming back of his scholarly presentation in the ecclesiastical tracts and elsewhere, and no-one could question the huge effort that went into the rhetorical design of Milton's publicly instructive works. Such will often be commented on, especially in connection with the larger poems and the prose tracts.

The whole question of a literary 'career' must in fact be accommodated to the religious sense of vocation, expressed so often in Milton's own writings about his literary output. There is a sense in which Milton was one of the progenitors of a modern sense of a literary career: eschewing patronage obligations by and large, he wrote as a private citizen and claimed simple ownership of his published works. In a 'free commonwealth' of rational interchange and debate, such was part of the responsibility of the educated citizen. Yet when he addressed parliament, he sometimes did so in the phraseology of patronage, and his whole literary career, where it touched public responsibility, was shaped by ideas of using one's talents as God directed, through the workings of inner conviction. The idea of vocation, of being a true 'shepherd' to England, informs many chapters of this book, from early poems, where the shadow of a priestly function is clearly visible, to later works, for which the word 'prophetic' sometimes seems appropriate.

We may perhaps illustrate some of Milton's own attitudes to his career by looking at a famous poem, the sonnet 'When I consider ...':

> When I consider how my light is spent,
>   Ere half my days, in this dark world and wide,
>   And that one talent which is death to hide,
>   Lodged with me useless, though my soul more bent
> To serve therewith my maker, and present
>   My true account, lest he returning chide,
>   Doth God exact day-labour, light denied,
>   I fondly ask; but Patience to prevent
> That murmur, soon replies, God doth not need
>   Either man's work or his own gifts; who best
>   Bear his mild yoke, they serve him best; his state
> Is kingly; thousands at his bidding speed
>   And post o'er land and ocean without rest:
>   They also serve who only stand and wait.
>   (CF 83; punctuation modified)

This poem – one of the splendid sonnets written at key and exemplary moments in his life – was only in an eighteenth-century edition (of Thomas Newton) given the title 'On his Blindness'. It is really about Milton's sense of vocation as conditioned by the onset of blindness. It has become famous because it plays out a struggle to reconcile his incapacity with what he thought his calling and duty in life – to serve God and country through letters – and also because it includes a difficult interpretative crux, usually thought of as a biographical crux. The phrase 'Ere half my days', if taken literally, seems nonsense for either of the favoured dates proposed for the poem: around the end of 1651 or beginning of 1652, at the onset of total blindness, when the poet was forty-four, or around 1655, as the seemingly chronological ordering of the sonnets in the edition of 1673 dictates, by which time he was forty-eight. No-one has satisfactorily explained away Milton's absurdly long life expectancy, according to a *literal* understanding of the phrase. It should probably be regarded, I would suggest, as a dramatic computation, expressed with the intemperate exaggeration of an unreconciled voice at the opening of the poem. It may be that that voice betrays itself by the influence of the last verse of Psalm 55, where the phrase 'half their days' is applied to deceitful men.

Putting that crux aside, however, we might concentrate on the very artful way the service of God is figured in the poem wholly by means of other biblical language. It is not just a question of the parable of the talents (Matt. 25:14 ff. etc.), which everyone has recognised in lines 3–6, but also that of the labourers in the vineyard (Matt. 20:1 ff. etc.) from lines 7 to 9, including the word 'murmur', and all other key terms have biblical resonance, among them 'mild yoke', 'stand', and 'wait'.

The first part of the poem defines dark thoughts, the kind of doubts and fears which produce the 'fond' or foolish question in lines 6–7. When the speaker dwells in depressed fashion on the fact that blindness has denied him the opportunity to witness as fully as he ought in his work, he is made to think of himself as like the least of God's servants, to whom only one talent was granted and who hid it in fear, thus incurring wrath and judgement. He may even think that he has been punished already, in his blindness, though he protests that he wants to be able to serve all day long. But this is a poem enacting Christian stoicism and the primacy of faith and trust, and the parable of the labourers in the vineyard teaches that length of service is not the point, when it comes to matters of the kingdom. The impatient complainant can be calmed by recognising that it is not the quantity of visible work which should be in question –

restless service – but the spirit and quality of work – service in this case by standing and waiting. 'Stand' means not merely being idle (as the complaining labourers thought in the parable) but also to be ready and full of strength of purpose; 'wait' means not simply present inaction but also faithful service and the expectation of the word of the Lord. The capacity to serve has not been taken away, but spiritual discipline has been made more urgent, and beyond the stoic resolution of the moment there may be a chance, indicated in that last word 'wait', that signal opportunity for action may be given, if the readiness is there. That formula, balancing a difficult readiness against the possibility of being called to sudden action, Milton will use many times in explanation of his writing career.

The whole poem links the service of a man of letters with religious discipline and duty. The speaker is conditioned by a cultural assumption that his career must be impelled by a sense of constant service to God and by the idea that like a steward one must keep rendering accounts. In so far as this line of thinking was actually applied by Milton to his own literary works, as would seem to be the case, this set a standard of expectation for service in published works that was hard to sustain, both in quantity and quality, but that kind of pressure was nevertheless always there. I shall take it as symptomatic that, having prepared himself in extremely extended study, Milton often thought that occasions had been given to him, that he had been called to give witness on these occasions, and that such expressions as he makes of this kind are rhetorical devices but also more than rhetorical devices. He frequently expressed doubts, on the one hand, about the difficulties of living in the long disciplined periods of waiting, of constantly preparing for action, of being ready without knowing when the call would come; and celebrated, on the other hand, when occasions seemed to have been given him to witness and he had risen publicly to champion the Truth.

What I do not wish to do is what some critics have done with this sonnet, parochially to limit the idea of vocation and service to the writing of poetry. I do not assume with Verity that 'one talent' means *only* 'poetic faculty' or even with Parker his God-given powers as a poet.[2] It is all the reading, as well as the writing, that a blind man finds so hard to do and it is his witness in all kinds of writing, not just in the great public poems. When he exhorted parliament men to complete ecclesiastical reform or to champion reform in matters of divorce, he was also witnessing. When he acted as educator, in compiling a new history or new Latin grammar or a new reformed theology, he was also witnessing, according to his sense of his talents and experience. When he defended his country as a true commonwealth against foreign attacks on impious regicide, he was also witnessing heroically. And so on. Not even the duties of drafting or translating state documents might necessarily be discarded from this notion of principled witness. It is true that he sensed, rightly, that his greatest talent, the work of his more dextrous hand, was poetry, but later centuries wanted to see *only* the poet, a poet whose career was, as it were, interrupted or distracted by other duties. We have to get a shape of the whole career of the man of letters at the service of his Protestant God.

An implication of this self-imposed understanding of his vocation as a writer is that we must recognise the importance of occasion. Vocation awaited occasion. Such a writer readied himself to speak when occasions demanded or when Providence gave opportunity. Hence the importance attached in this study to the way in which texts were tailored for their occasions, and the attention paid to the way in which texts were sometimes refashioned for new opportunities of dissemination. This is not to say that all is simply topical; it is to try to recognise how the lessons of scripture and history and the arts of eloquent persuasion taught in humanist education could be brought to bear instructively upon the resolutions of the moment.

A study of this kind uses hundreds of references from earlier works of scholarship, only a few of which can be signalled in such an introductory, lightly annotated book. The problem is particularly acute with Parker's massive biography of 1968 (soon to be reissued with a list of corrections). Students will find references to Parker's pages only for specific points and sometimes in disagreement, not step by step through the literary career. Attention is drawn to the system of short references for Parker's biography and other volumes given in the text rather than the footnotes, listed above under Abbreviations.

Finally, a word about translations of passages of Latin and other languages. Although page references are given to standard editions, there are occasions on which the precise wording of translation is my own.

Notes

1.   *Milton on Himself*, ed. John S. Diekhoff (NY: Oxford University Press, 1939).
2.   Cf. VC II (2) 465; P 471.

1

Education: the 'Vacation Exercise' and Early Latin Poetry

'Far from all disgrace ..., I studied for seven years in the usual disciplines and arts, up to what is called the degree of Master, awarded with honours [*cum laude*], in fact'. So declared John Milton of the success of his education in the University of Cambridge, writing in the *Second Defence* of 1654, when he was well into middle age (Y iv 613). Not for the first time had he been the subject of detraction. He was particularly sore about a rumour that he had been sent down for disciplinary reasons as an undergraduate.

There is a lot of evidence especially from the later years that Milton wished to present Cambridge routines as unconducive to solid learning of the reformed kind. For some reason, he changed his tutor after one year, from the celebrated William Chappell to the younger Nathaniel Tovey, but the change is hard to interpret: the two men seem to have shared much in outlook. Milton's reference in '*Elegy I*' to his tutor as being harsh is, as we shall see (p. 15), made in a context of playful irony. If young Milton had difficulties of adjustment, at the age of sixteen, they were much more likely to do with his idealistic sense of what a liberal education should be than with any riotous behaviour leading to rustication.

The focus of this chapter is Milton's writing during the time of his education, at home, at school, and through university to about the time of his finishing his first degree in 1629, after four years at Cambridge, by which time he was twenty. The idea of education was of signal importance for him. Later he was to see the future of the nation as bound up with the quality of education available to its leading men. His own high sense of vocation would make him assume the role of teacher; later, the major poems would all speak instructionally, containing figures of teachers within them; he would offer to instruct Parliament in many of his prose tracts; he would set about writing, though not always completing, specimens of

1

reformed history, geography, logic, a Latin dictionary and a system of theology; and he would act as a schoolmaster himself. He inherited an idealism about liberalising education which was both humanistic and godly. He was proud of some of the more liberal aspects of his own education and deeply thankful to his father for affording him the opportunities. Even allowing for the fact that the testimony is largely his own, the story of Milton's education is one of remarkable dedication and method. We have enough documentation, also, to be able to trace Milton's growing sense of identity as a boy and young man in his relationships with those he found about him in the academy.

Let us take a picture of the young Milton at a moment of triumph in his college as a senior undergraduate, in 1628. There was a custom in Christ's College of presenting an academic entertainment at the beginning of the Summer vacation, when most students were still in residence. Rhetorical skills were demonstrated in the chief orator and everyone let the hair down after term-time routine. The sense of community was nurtured by involving younger students and ribbing college institutions. In 1628 Milton was chosen to present this entertainment (Y i 266–306). It is important to remember that in various ways, in school and university, Milton was bred to competitive performance.

There were several sections, each of different style. First, Milton read an oration, aptly taking up the theme of the benefit of sportive exercises (*exercitationes ludicras*) for occasional use in the philosophic studies of youth. This speech of over twenty-five minutes was delivered in elegant Latin and spiced with all the urbane ironies a nineteen year old could muster. He began with backhanded thanks for being chosen master of ceremonies, acknowledging a sense of honour and his nervousness. More daringly, and in the spirit of social candour, he paraded an awareness of his own image in the college. It would seem that he was sometimes caricatured as a fastidious, serious, and independent-minded student, the opposite of a leader of communal sport, not at all the carefree roisterer. Accordingly he suggested that the task of organising the entertainment had actually been a nuisance to him. He had just come back from his home in London, where he had been feasting, he said mischievously, on city pleasures and had been looking forward to a

period of peaceful study back in Cambridge, when the commission
hit him. The mixture of jocularity and sensitivity about reputation is
interesting. He reminded his audience of a previous academic exercise, when he had won applause despite some previous dis-
agreements about studies. That touch of independence, in choosing
to recall his own principles, is matched by what may be a barbed
comment, this time veiled in excessive humility. How can he perform adequately before a godlike audience, free from all barbarism?
It is doubtful that he thought so highly of the culture of all his peers.

The actual defence of jocularity, which follows, displays a liberal
idea of education. Though he is a serious man, he will not decry
jocularity: only shallow men decry that of which they are ignorant.
He then offers four uses for it: to cultivate a pleasant disposition,
fostering friendship; to guard against the danger of academic communities becoming too dry; to sharpen the mind; and it is the mark
of a liberal spirit. He cites authorities of great men of letters who
dealt in jest: Homer, Socrates, Cicero, Erasmus. Then, more whim-
sically – do you want more *manly* examples, then? – he names some
generals, kings, and brave men. Finally, in support of the specific
occasion, he makes a claim for the progress of learning: as learning
has blossomed from the Middle Ages to the present times, it has
become more humane and liberal in spirit. The enemy to Erasmian
sport is therefore old-fashioned scholasticism, 'metaphysical gar-
garisms'. Besides, the best jocularity is the fruit of study, not the
avoidance of it.

Milton therefore declared himself, within his college, as one who
championed a liberal scheme of education building on the strength
of the individual spirit. To an unusual degree he came up to university aged sixteen with some independent sense of direction and
purpose concerning a course of study. At the same time his defences
of jocularity spoke of a concern for his own image in the community.
The solitary student announced his care for friendship and society
and distanced himself from mere bookishness. Then, to show that
he had not forgotten others, he announced at the very close of his
oration a change of mode, towards festive licence, in the *Prolusio* to
follow. Like the satirical comedian, he asked for applause. The Prolusion, still in Latin, was where the broader fun began.

The Prolusion was based on the idea of the entertainment to
follow as a banquet rivalling a great Roman feast. Since college
catering was sparse, the idea may have had immediate point. The
guests are like heroes; they enter the hall by getting past hellish fire

and they face a feast of fifty boars, fifty oxen, fifty calves' heads, a hundred young goats, parrots, a huge snipe, cranes, many geese, eggs, fruit, and so on. But each course has something wrong with it, and this is a feast of fools. The entertainment dealt in the in-joke, as in an end-of-term revue in a modern school. Thus, the fire at the doors seems to refer to the pipe-smoking porter and his family (named Sparkes), whilst calves' heads without brains, young goats which consort too frequently with Venus, green parrots who flock together, and such like, probably refer to different kinds of student. Milton created a persona for himself as the *comestor*, the Roman gourmand, one who knows the luxurious ways of the world (or who had read books about Rome). He kept ironic distance, whilst giving rein to satirical licence.

The sense of self is visible here too. Why me? asked Milton at the beginning and then supplied an answer by recalling the disgrace of a rival, a boisterous sophister who had got into a scrape by inflicting damage on the town's water supply. As master of ceremonies Milton was called *pater*, father. Fatherhood implies sexual experience. Me a Father? I thought my nickname was 'The Lady' (*domina*). He dwelt on this index of his own image: do they call me that because I am not a roisterer or a bumpkin? Plenty of good orators have been little men. Anyway, I can become a man more quickly than they can become intelligent! At that moment we seem to glimpse an uneasy distance between himself and the average student more interested in masculine self-image than the long-term benefits of education. For all that, Milton had served the needs of the social occasion rather well, and he now turned to introduce his actors, the lads who were his 'sons', and for the first time spoke in English.

The verses which followed – 'Hail native language' – were printed in Milton's revised volume of shorter poems in 1673 and have become well-known, because they make an early announcement of his ambition to become celebrated as a poet in English. But he preserved more than this passage. Wanting to give some sense of the whole occasion, he also printed those following speeches which were composed in verse. These introduced two of the ten other students who appeared with him, those personating Substance and Relation. There was some good-natured fun at the expense of old-fashioned Aristotelianism – Scholasticism was to be the bad fare of the feast. Since Christ's College had a tradition of Ramism, this may have been a joke for the whole community. As presenter, Milton himself stood for *Ens*, Being, the 'father' of ten categories, namely

Substance and its nine Accidents or Predicaments. His 'sons' would have appeared in this order: Substance (the 'king'), Quantity, Quality, Relation, Place, Time, Position, Possession, Action, and Passion. Whether they acted or merely declaimed is not clear.

Substance, eldest son, was given a blessing: 'Good luck befriend thee Son; for at thy birth / The Fairy Ladies danc'd upon the hearth …' The paradoxes of the relationship between Substance and its accidents were spelled out as a Sybilline prophecy, an enigma which the learned audience was then asked to solve. The parody of Aristotelian logic was clever and just as telling was the mischievous association of Scholasticism with superstition, figured in the fairies and ancient prophecy. Both belong to an age of darkness; the present age in Christ's College is one of stout Protestant rationality.

The joke in the introduction of Relation touched communal identity in a different way. His name is played on in several senses concerning connection and kinship and the name of the student playing him (Rivers) is extended into a list of celebrated English streams: 'Rivers arise; whether thou be the Son / Of utmost Tweed, or Ouse, or gulphie Dun …' One or two critics have admired this list of rivers, made in the general manner of Spenser and Drayton; others (VC II i 148) have thought it a parody of the mode. However, on the whole, the play is not so much with literary style as with the idea of relation itself and the wit is community enhancing. Thirteen rivers are named, chosen from throughout the country. As in much ancient poetry, rivers figure regions, or the voices or poets of regions. The foundation of Christ's College was based originally on the creation of twelve fellowships, to which a thirteenth, the King Edward fellowship, was later added. Six of the fellows were to come from the 'northern' counties, six from the 'southern'. Although attendance from the north never equalled that from the south – northerners were usually outnumbered about three to one – the idea was to encourage representation from the whole of England. Milton found a clever way of suggesting the community of England within the college, rivers representing counties or local schools or tutors. The Rivers family came from Kent, their tutor, Robert Gell, from London. Milton played the trick of naming other regions first, until finally the right one is found: '… Or Medway smooth, or Royal Towr'd Thame.' The poet has owned a personal affiliation to the English poetic tradition of Spenser and Drayton, a tradition of proud patriotism, whilst deftly showing how the sons of Christ's College bore relation to the land.

Patriotism and a humanistic programme to promote the native tongue inform 'Hail native Language', which also has a freedom which might suggest that the real John Milton might also at last be found in the sound of English verse:

> Hail native language, that by sinews weak
> Didst move my first endeavouring tongue to speak,
> And mad'st imperfect words with childish trips,
> Half unpronounced, slide through my infant lips,
> Driving dumb silence from the portal door,
> Where he had mutely sat two years before:
> Here I salute thee and thy pardon ask,
> That now I use thee in my latter task:
> Small loss it is that thence can come unto thee,
> I know my tongue but little grace can do thee.
> Thou need'st not be ambitious to be first,
> Believe me I have thither packed the worst:
> And, if it happen as I did forecast,
> The daintiest dishes shall be served up last.
> I pray thee then deny me not thy aid
> For this same small neglect that I have made;
> But haste thee straight to do me once a pleasure,
> And from thy wardrobe bring thy chiefest treasure;
> Not those new-fangled toys, and trimming slight
> Which takes our late fantastics with delight,
> But cull those richest robes, and gayest attire
> Which deepest spirits, and choicest wits desire:
> I have some naked thoughts which rove about
> And loudly knock to have their passage out;
> And weary of their place do only stay
> Till thou hast decked them in thy best array;
> That so they may without suspect or fears
> Fly swiftly to this fair assembly's ears;
> Yet I had rather, if I were to choose,
> Thy service in some graver subject use,
> Such as may make thee search thy coffers round,
> Before thou clothe my fancy in fit sound:
> Such where the deep transported mind may soar
> Above the wheeling poles, and at heaven's door
> Look in, and see each blissful deity
> How he before the thunderous throne doth lie,

Listening to what unshorn Apollo sings
To the touch of golden wires, while Hebe brings
Immortal nectar to her kingly sire:
Then passing through the spheres of watchful fire,
And misty regions of wide air next under,
And hills of snow and lofts of piled thunder,
May tell at length how green-eyed Neptune raves,
In heaven's defiance mustering all his waves;
Then sing of secret things that came to pass
When beldame Nature in her cradle was;
And last of kings and queens and heroes old,
Such as the wise Demodocus once told
In solemn songs at king Alcinous' feast,
Whilst sad Ulysses' soul and all the rest
Are held with his melodious harmony
In willing chains and sweet captivity.
But fie my wandering Muse how thou dost stray!
Expectance calls thee now another way,
Thou knowest it must be now thy only bent
To keep in compass of thy predicament:
Then quick about thy purposed business come,
That to the next I may resign my room.

(CF 23)

These verses have sometimes been read in isolation and rather too straight. The speaker is still the sportful presenter, the context still academic entertainment. 'The daintiest dishes' to be 'served up last' are the lads who personate the Predicaments. Milton's apology to the English language, too, though a kind of dedication, is touched with an extravagance of courteous gesture: 'I know my tongue but little grace can do thee.' The business about new-fangled toys of late fantastics is more likely to refer to the language of academic study than to any supposed school of literature.[1] But if the institutions are parodied in terms of Aristotle or Ramus, self-presentation in the digression about poetry works more in terms of the idea of the *vates*, the poetic seer or prophet, of the 'deep transported mind'. As he celebrates his native tongue, Milton offers himself, proudly, yet with self-deprecating humour, in the role of magician with words.

The digression is daring and confessional. The audience is invited to join the speaker's excitement in his ambitions to write high and heroic literature, on 'some graver subject' than the present occasion can offer. The vision begins with heaven itself, descends to the creation of the world, then to history and myth, in the line of Homer. Then the rapt speaker calls himself back to task, as if he had momentarily lost contact with the realities of the world (as in the similar strategies in 'The Nativity Ode' and 'Lycidas'). Best 'resign my room' to someone else, before I take off in high contemplation again. Blazing self-revelation about his personal ambitions is tempered with wry recognition of the way he may look from without. He is independent, yet acknowledges community; he wishes to be intimate with his audience, yet cultivates a distance. In terms of argument, the choice has its point – who would not prefer high poetry to his scholastic predicament? – and quite an image of the scholar–poet has been projected. He shows himself with his college, yet also wishing to transcend its regular skills. A defence of jocularity has become an early proclamation of the training of free spirits in a reforming state.

Milton had made his mark. To appreciate the fusion of courtesy with independence of mind in this academic entertainment makes it easy to understand why, after he had left the university in 1632, someone chose him to write two entertainments for young people in a great aristocratic family. The Ludlow masque was also to concern education, and its adversary, Comus, was to bear some relationship to the jocular mask of the *comestor* in the Prolusion. Meanwhile, looking back to the years before university, let us review the previous education that had already shaped such a distinctive young man.

Milton came from a family of rising middle-class prosperity in London. His father, also called John, was a hard-working business-man, but Milton was also to inherit from him an active interest in literature and music. In the Milton house thrift and industry were mixed with cultured avocations.

His paternal grandfather, Richard Milton, came from a line of Oxfordshire yeoman. Richard bettered his fortune, but, evidently a man of stubborn principle, was fined for recusancy in the latter part of his life. Milton's father, however, born in 1562, was as determined in his Protestantism as his father had been in his Catholicism. Leaving Oxfordshire and his Catholic home to make a new start in London, he apprenticed to a scrivener about 1583, was in independent business by about 1590, had reached the distinction of being admitted into the Company of Scriveners in 1600, and later became quite prominent in the profession, serving in various offices of the Company. He was a self-made man, who had amassed a sufficient fortune in the business of money itself. His wife, whom he may have married late and who was ten years his junior, came of a respectable family in trade. The daughter of a merchant taylor, she was reputedly prudent, virtuous, and had weak eyes.

Only three children survived infancy: John's older sister, Anne, eventually to marry a legal administrator, Edward Phillips, John himself, born 9 December 1608, when his father was already 46 and his mother 36, and his brother Christopher, seven years younger. This late child was destined to be a lawyer and, finally, at the end of his life, to be knighted.

The Milton family had leased a large house in Bread Street, at the sign of the Spread Eagle, as the seat of their solid prosperity. It was part of a rambling property on five floors and served as shop and home. Several apprentices were usually resident as well. By the time John graduated as a Bachelor of Arts at Cambridge his father was beginning to prepare for retirement, but not before he had taken special care to provide for the continuing education of his son, who was not intended to follow his father into business or even the law but rather to have a higher calling, to be educated in the best way for the ministry in the church, 'to whose service by the intentions of my parents and friends I was destined of a child' (Y i 822). The educational idealism with which Milton was filled was partly infused in him by the aspirations of parents determined to nurture to the fullest their intelligent first son, born to their middle age and singled out for distinction.

John Milton senior was a talented amateur musician, a singer, and composer, presumably an instrumentalist too. (Following guesses in early biographies, scholars have speculated that he received musical training as a chorister at Oxford.)[2] He was well enough known in London musical circles to be invited to join other 'artists of that sublime profession' in various collections of songs: he contributed a madrigal to *The Triumphes of Oriana* in 1601, there were four settings of his in a book of penitential psalms printed in 1614, we have six more unpublished songs in an important manuscript collection dated 1616, and a new version of the old Ravenscroft *Psalms* issued in 1621 contains new settings and harmonisations by him. Four other compositions survive in manuscript, and rumour has it that he

presented an elaborate *In Nomine* to the Landgrave of Hesse during
a visit to London in 1611 (LR i 4; D 10). There would have been
musical visitors to the house as well as clients and business associates. We know that young John sang and played the organ (LR i 22;
D 6). He was later to collect and study music in England and Italy,
and become friend to musicians, and all his life pondered the relationship of the 'sphere-borne harmonious sisters, Voice and Verse'
(CF 47). Poetry complemented his father's song.

Details of lessons given to Milton as a boy are not known, but
there were probably many and the curriculum of St Paul's School
has been the subject of scholarly enquiry.[3] We still have the 1612
Bible he possessed as a boy. We do not know the names of his very
first tutors at home, but we do know the name of a tutor who came
to him when he was about nine until he was about twelve. This was
Thomas Young, a Scots minister of stout Protestant principles and
Presbyterian background. Young, who gave his promising pupil a
Hebrew Bible, was to remain an influence for some years and to
become a friend; he encouraged poetry as well as religion. It was
probably when Young left to go to the English church in Hamburg
that Milton began attending the celebrated St Paul's School, by the
cathedral and not very far from his home. He would have started
with a good grounding in Latin from Young, if not before, and was
probably capable of Latin composition from an early age. At St
Paul's he would have perfected his Latin and reached some facility
with Greek, which he may have started before, to the point of composing short Greek verses, and studied some Hebrew. With tutors
out of school hours he was to pick up French and Italian. (About
Italian there will be more to say in the next chapter.) Later he was to
thank his father for the gift of these five languages.

Young Milton seems to have been consumed with the endeavour
of becoming a true scholar, such as could serve a properly learned
ministry. In later life he probably made a less simple connection
between learning and the office of pastor, but there is ample testimony for the early years of his hard study, including out of school
and into the late hours. He saw the 'ceaseless round of study and
reading' (Y i 891) romantically, as a heroic endeavour. Remembering
his concern in the entertainment to range himself against ideas of
manliness, we might note also his habit of insisting that the pursuit
of true learning is as heroic as any other activity.

If Milton found sympathy and respect with Young, then he probably also found a good deal of reward at St Paul's. The current high

master, Alexander Gil senior, was an eminent educationalist, one who encouraged a lively use of the classical languages and, just as important for young Milton, had a patriotic interest in English and English poetry. Equally fortunately there was as under-usher at the school Alexander Gil junior, the high master's son, some ten years older than Milton. This Gil was a poet, 'one of the best Latin poets in the nation', whose equal, Milton would later say, he did not find in the university.[4] Milton and Gil kept up a literary correspondence for some years. The school syllabus also was wide, in terms of reading. Apart from grammar in Latin, Greek, and some Hebrew and New Testament readings and readings in the Psalms, Milton would have tasted a lot of history and literature in both Latin and Greek in his four years at school: Sallust, Virgil, Cicero, Martial, Hesiod, Theognis, Pindar, Theocritus, Horace, Homer, Euripides, Isocrates, Persius, and Juvenal have been mentioned in the standard work on the current curriculum at the school. It was amongst the best grammar schools in the country and produced a good number of authors.

On the religious side Milton would not only have felt the influence of Thomas Young, encouraging his vocation for the priest-hood and his love of literature, but would also have heard candid denunciations in the sermons of the parish priest, Richard Stock. Fired by the mission of continuing the purification of the church in England, Stock was known to inveigh against Rome and the menace of the Jesuits. (Such attitudes were to be found everywhere: Milton's friend Gil, no puritan in churchmanship, nevertheless wrote a big-oted poem in celebration of the collapse with loss of many lives of the Catholic chapel in Blackfriars in 1623.)[5] Stock and his curate for the years 1624–8, Brian Walton, were both graduates of Christ's College, Cambridge. Perhaps the decision to send John there had something to do with these men.

Milton is unlikely to have found the religious atmosphere of the academy at Cambridge quite so straightforward as the blunt views of Richard Stock. The variety of religious opinions even within a college known for stout reformist teaching may have been as large as the number of its fellows, and we still know too little about it. What is more certain is that in academic studies Milton did not find quite the freedom and stimulation he so ardently sought as a matur-ing student. Both his tutors were Ramists, but many exercises seemed arid logic chopping, a remnant of the Scholasticism of the past, rather than solid learning with humane method. What is more, junior boys shared accommodation, several to a room, all a far cry from the special conditions Milton's family had provided for their gifted son. Then there were quite a few richer students who took their studies lightly, even cynically, flaunting themselves in other ways. How was the fastidious and doubtless self-important young Milton to brook all these disappointments and irritations? How was it that the very institution which ought to foster 'generous and free nurture' (Y i 721) was capable of stifling that purpose?

Yet Milton managed the university in time, met its obligations, and finally came out on top. The records show him to have been as distinguished as any student in his college round about that time. Presumably he would have taken what opportunities there were to follow lectures in subjects like mathematics. Presumably he continued his own programme of reading in several languages. But we know of no Thomas Young from his university years, no teacher with whom he would share his dearest ideals in cultivated letters. Some years later, when he pictured the ideal university, in 'Lycidas', a university truly humane and devout in its ideals, he would show a tutor lovingly encouraging his young charges: joy and affection enlighten hard work, and the expression is poetry, 'song':

> Together both, ere the high lawns appeared
> Under the opening eyelids of the morn,
> We drove afield, and both together heard
> What time the grey-fly winds her sultry horn,
> Battening our flocks with the fresh dews of night,
> Oft till the star that rose, at evening, bright,
> Toward heaven's descent had sloped his westering wheel.
> Meanwhile the rural ditties were not mute,
> Tempered to the oaten flute,
> Rough satyrs danced, and fauns with cloven heel,
> From the glad sound would not be absent long,
> And old Damaetas loved to hear our song.
>
> (25–36)

That is not meant to sound like disputation.

To survey the poetry Milton wrote in this period is to examine evidence of about thirty compositions in Latin, Greek, and English. The great majority of these is in Latin; serious Renaissance poets cut their teeth on Latin verse. When he came to publish his Latin verse in 1645, Milton made a broad division between those in elegiac metre (*Elegiarum Liber*) and a miscellany in other metres (*Sylvarum Liber*).

Selection and ordering for publication are worth bearing in mind. Scholars sometimes write of the development of Milton's verse as if it can all be mapped, but the fact is that we cannot be sure of all that he wrote, especially in his youth. With very few exceptions, what has survived is what he chose to preserve in print and retrospective printings usually have careful self-presentation in mind. In fact, self-presentation is at issue both at the original time of composition, for many poems, and at the moment of publication.

Most of this verse is occasional in character. Deaths were meditated, whether of significance to the family (CF 7), the university community (CF 10, 11), or to church and state (CF 9, 18). Verse letters to scholarly friends were framed (CF 8, 19, 35), with news and greetings, but also as examples of urbane intercourse in the aspiring scholar–writer. Conventional poetic subjects for youth were tried, like the advent of spring (CF 16, 24), with a good deal of panache in Elegy V. The anniversary of 5 November was celebrated, somewhat obtrusively (CF 12–17). As in the Vacation Exercise, Milton was keen to show himself as a master of different literary subjects and modes.

A variety of literary roles is also easy to illustrate. He projects himself as the playful, skilful rhetorician in the two sets of verses made for academic disputation (CF 20, 21); he preserves his boyhood attempts at being the Protestant psalm singer (CF 1, 2) or the enigmatic moral fabulist in the wake of Mantuan and Spenser (CF 6); he plays the worldly-wise epigrammatist, on the theme of the Gunpowder Plot (CF 12–15); he plays Ovid, in sensuous, amorous verse (especially CF 8, but also in all the elegies), or Virgil, the poet of national theme, in his miniature epic 'In Quintum Novembris' (CF 17). The carefully preserved variety presents a precocious character, promising varied capacities not to be simply confined within cloistered seclusion. It is an outward-looking, active engagement with the world that this self-presentation of youth is keen to promote.

This self-image is well illustrated by Milton's seven elegies which span the Cambridge years up to 1629. That he wrote easily in the elegiac metre of Ovid is not surprising: schoolboys of his time were exercised in such models. But Milton was out to show more than customary imitation in his calculated series as he published them, in 1645, not quite in order of composition. They show many of the aspirations of this phase of his career.

Elegy I, a letter to Milton's close friend from schooldays, Charles Diodati, presents the jovial, ironic scholar. Elegy II shows another face of student wit, on the occasion of the death of the university beadle. Elegy III, however, which has an ecclesiastical occasion, the death of the famous bishop Lancelot Andrews, presents the poet as an almost prophetic visionary. Elegy IV, too, though its address and occasion are different (it is a letter from Cambridge to Thomas Young), offers serious comment, suiting an intending minister, on Providence and History. Elegies V and VII present less serious roles, the virile young city dweller, playing the pagan, and the poet–lover. Elegy VI, another letter to Diodati, tempers candid self-revelation with wit, in the role of the civilised, admiring friend. The art of some of these elegies deserves close study, for all their early date. We might look at two of them, each deploying Ovid in quite different ways.

In Elegy I, Milton writes from London, just before he is due to return to Cambridge, perhaps after a vacation. The date is not certain, but he is probably still in his first undergraduate year, aged seventeen. The precocious Diodati is ahead of him in formal qualifications, having already graduated as a Bachelor of Arts at Oxford. Milton confides in his friend, yet may also be conscious of the other's greater maturity and also, here as elsewhere, of a difference in temperament. Diodati seems to have been robustly sociable. Milton, the quiet, fastidious student, seems to admire the social confidence and ease of his friend. The tone he adopts in the letter is one of emulation. In particular, the freshman takes on an attitude of ironic superiority over the university. He likes London. There he can study as he wishes, go to the theatre, even go out in the spring sunshine to the leafy suburbs to watch the girls go by. But don't all these distractions of the town threaten to distract the dedicated student, as Ulysses was tempted to forget himself with Circe? Don't worry, I am about to return to the reeds, marshes, and safe confinement of that university again.

Of course, for all its posturing, the poem registers complaints about Cambridge life: little to rival the attractions of the city, a 'hard tutor' (*durus magister*) and things his spirit will not easily bear, no peace and quiet and, most telling of all, perhaps, since the writer presents himself as poet, *'Quam male Phoebicolis convenit ille locis!* – How badly that place suits the worshipper of Phoebus!' All this is understandable, but student writes to student, from within the system, not expecting to be taken quite straight: there is no good reason to assume that the university rooms were literally 'forbidden' to him as a rusticated exile.

In fact, as has long been realised, the playful idea of exile is a part of the technique of allusion in the poem. Milton alludes to Ovid's exile from Rome at Tomis. A series of teasing comparisons is offered, between young Milton's case and the far more drastic case of the Roman poet. In his letters from Tomis, Ovid lamented the loss of Rome and her culture, in books and theatres; Milton congratulates himself that his 'exile' gives him the culture and distractions of London. Ovid found the landscape of Tomis dull; Milton, from London, remembers Cambridge as flat and marshy. Perhaps the idea that the Circean distractions of London might put young Milton in moral danger is an allusion to the assumption that Ovid deserved his exile from Rome. Would that all exiles ended in nothing more vicious than a university, to which young Milton will soon return, perhaps for his own good! As an early example of Milton's capacity to make literary allusion an intelligent and ironic art (presumably some of the playfulness comes from Ovid, too), this poem displays a degree of sophistication noteworthy in a lad of about seventeen.

Elegy III, on the death of Bishop Andrewes, contains a wealth of Ovidian phrases and allusions. Indeed, its highly coloured language is replete with allusion of all kinds. Much is conventional, but what has raised the scholarly eyebrow is the bold last line: *'Talia contingant somnis saepe mihi* (May such dreams often befall me!)'. That recalls a famous phrase of Ovid – *'proveniant medii sic mihi saepe dies* ('May middays like that happen to me often!'). – in celebration of lovemaking with Corinna in the middle of a memorable hot day. Ovidian writing evidently permits much scope with decorum.

In some ways the Andrewes elegy prefigures the technique of the later great elegies, on Diodati (*'Epitaphium Damonis'*) and Edward King ('Lycidas'). The poem features a single speaker, and it is dramatic in the basic sense that the speaker conveys to the reader a sequence of experiences – vision of general death, by day; lament; new vision of Andrewes' reception in heaven, by night – and also a sequence of emotions – puzzlement at the ways of Providence; lament; consolation and rapt understanding. The consolatory vision of heaven is as highly coloured as was the vision of death: the balancing, cathartic effect of the poem depends upon it. The Providence of Heaven must be *felt* to be as moving as the devastations of death. Hence, perhaps, the bold confidence of that last line, challenging any vision, even Ovid's, to match that which the speaker has just seen.

These two elegies illustrate different aspects of Milton's humanism. If Elegy I shows a vying with the ancients in the urbane eloquence of letter writing, Elegy III assures the reader of Christian vocation, working with the gifts of humanist learning, pagan poets not rejected but redirected in triumph. It is a statement of faith in the power of Truth to assimilate the best expressive means of poetry.

Elegy III may also be used to show Milton's desire to show present history in the perspective of the cause of the Reformation. Milton's early verse may be more politically engaged, if perhaps at a rather idealistic level, than has usually been recognised. The vision of death extends from the disasters of England in 1625 and 1626 to those on the continent in the Thirty Years War. The poem must be set in context. The summer of 1625, after the death of James I and the accession of Charles I, saw a bad plague. One-sixth of the population of London may have died that year. Milton pictures Libitina, goddess of corpses, encamped in England and invading the very palaces of kings and nobility. By chance, and as many writers and preachers noted, many great noblemen died at roughly the same time. The poet George Wither, quick to read a judgemental prophecy, represented the time as a rebuke to England from God, asking the country to renew itself and its true religion in the new reign.[6] In his elegy, also, Milton linked the deaths at home with those of leaders of the Protestant forces in the Low Countries. The years 1625 and 1626 were disasters in the military campaigns: Breda was not relieved, other battles were lost, generals and princes died, some English nobility lost their lives. There has been debate about persons alluded to in Milton's poem, but the general position is clear. Milton has linked the death of a church leader with the state of the Protestant nation and with the whole Protestant cause in Europe. Like 'Lycidas' , it laments the death of the single man and the signs of Protestant disaster.

A good many of the early poems which Milton preserved can be seen to have political significance. Is it a matter of chance that the two youthful psalm paraphrases written between December 1623 and December 1624 (CF 1, 2) have themes which connect with the high patriotic excitement of that time? In 1623, to the shouts of thanksgiving of many citizens of London, Prince Charles returned home from Spain in October without a Catholic bride from the old enemy. Many saw this as a new national deliverance. By the end of 1624 James was to pledge Charles to another Catholic bride, Henrietta Maria of France, promising toleration of English Catholics. The year 1624 was also the year of Mansfeld's visit, and feeling against Spain ran at fever pitch. Milton's Psalm cxiv paraphrase, shot through with the mannerisms of the good Protestant poet Sylvester, rings to the national themes of British Israel. God has taken his people out of bondage and will perform further miracles for them: 'Shake earth, and at the presence be aghast / Of him that ever was, and ay shall last.' The poem reads like a tick list of Protestant rallying calls. As for Psalm cxxvi, 'Let us with a gladsome mind', there is political zeal here, too. It promises God's continuing support against tyranny: 'O let us his praises tell / Who doth the wrathful tyrants quell.' Spain should remember God's part in 1588: 'And freed us from the tyranny / Of the invading enemy.' God's deliverance of his people has been renewed.

The militant mythology about the Armada, Marian tyranny, and so forth, obviously stand behind the short epic '*In Quintum Novembris*'. Deliverance from the Gunpowder Plot is another instance of God's providence towards his chosen nation. It may be wrong to think of such an elaborate piece as merely an exercise; in publication, at least, commitment is signalled in a lad of seventeen to the heroic cause which might form a national subject for epic. Coming near the beginning of Charles' reign, this poem might have functioned as an expression of the need to renew the impetus for the struggle of Protestantism in Europe.

The date of composition of the epigrams on the Plot is not certain. One poem (CF 12) speaks of the event as recent ('*nuper*')[7] another (CF 13) indicates that James is by now dead. If some of these epigrams belong to the opening of Charles' reign, or were then put together as a series, they may also express the desire to see the nation renew its Protestant destiny. Changes of reign could be crucial times of assessment. With a Catholic entourage about the new queen, and Catholic worship condoned at court, many feared that Protestantism in England would be undermined in high places.

Elegy IV, written to Young in 1627, also takes occasion to comment on the state of British resolve. Lamenting that Young, a model pastor, has had to go to Germany to find employment, Milton observes that England is at fault. God did not send such ministers to turn away. And again Milton is aware of what is happening in the religious wars on the continent. He muses that Hamburg is not too far removed from the camps from which some of the Protestant armies mounted their campaigns.

Another kind of political comment may be evident in the Vacation Exercise itself, with which this chapter began. Near the end of the Prolusion, where he is advertising the 'salt', the satirical edge of his performance, he dares to say that he has no wish to give his audience as much salt 'as those soldiers of ours who recently managed to escape from the island of Rhé'. The pathetic failure of Buckingham's expedition to capture Rhé (July–October 1627) is topical, but the the point may also be closer to home. In July 1626, after much controversy and doubtful dealing, which split Cambridge into rival factions, Buckingham, the king's candidate, had been made the new chancellor of the university. The politics of this appointment were complicated, but it is likely that some of the opposition to Buckingham in the university came from those of more militant Protestant views. In the country at large prejudice against the favourite ran high, and Milton's friend Gil was to suffer punishment for his tipsy abuse of the Duke after the assassination. But for young John Milton, an undergraduate of nineteen, to sneer at the ignominy of Rhé was to impugn before his college the chancellor of his own university. That was 'salt' indeed.

Notes

1. As Gordon Campbell has probably correctly surmised, the prosaic Ramists seem to be referred to with absurd irony as 'late fantastics' or, taking a longer cultural view, is it the scholastics themselves who are fantastical?
2. P 4 and 686; rather fancifully, Ernest Brennecke, Jr, *John Milton the Elder and his Music* (NY, 1938), Chapters 1 and 2.
3. Donald L. Clark, *John Milton and St Paul's School* (New York, 1948).
4. Y i 314; Antony à Wood in *Atheniae Oxoniensis*, under Gil.
5. Leo Miller, 'On Some of the Verses by Alexander Gil which John Milton Read', *MQ*, 24 (1990), 22–5.
6. George Wither, *The History of the Pestilence (1625)*, ed. J. Milton French (Cambridge, Mass.: Harvard University Press, 1932).
7. An ambiguity in the Latin: *nuper* can mean either 'recently' or 'formerly'.

2

Cultivating the Self: the 'Nativity Ode', Petrarchism, and the Social Poet

The latter half of the time of Milton's studies at Cambridge, up to his receiving his Master of Arts degree, on 3 July 1632, probably gave him a good deal of freedom. The residence requirement was not strict and more liberal studies included developing plans for poetry. He would have been in London fairly often.

As far as poetry is concerned, the so-called 'Nativity Ode' ('On the Morning of Christ's Nativity'; CF 34) occupies a signal place in this period. When he published his early verse in the volume of 1645, Milton put religious poems first, and of these the very first was this. As the longest of the religious odes it formed a substantial headpiece to the book, but the decision to put it first probably connected also with the idea of the poem. The pretence is that the verses are a gift to the infant at the nativity scene: his Muse is to hasten to present it before the Magi arrive. Thus, the opening poem dedicates his volume, his whole art, to the service of Christ.

There was a further personal significance. The composition date was put beside the title: '... Compos'd 1629'. Milton's birthday was in December and in December 1629 he was twenty-one. This poem, then, marked the birth of Christ and his own coming of age.

Milton's ode is a youthful celebration of victory, resting on a broad doctrinal base. He does not dwell for devotional purposes on the persons of the baby or the mother; rather, the poem is about the inauguration of a new era in the history of mankind:

> This is the month, and this the happy morn
> Wherein the Son of heaven's eternal King,
> Of wedded maid, and virgin mother born,

Our great redemption from above did bring;
For so the holy sages once did sing,
   That he our deadly forfeit should release,
And with his Father work us a perpetual peace.

That glorious form, that light unsufferable,
And that far-beaming blaze of majesty,
Wherewith he wont at heaven's high council-table,
To sit the midst of trinal unity,
He laid aside; and here with us to be,
   Forsook the courts of everlasting day,
And chose with us a darksome house of mortal clay.

(1–14)

The address in these opening stanzas is celebratory, approaching the heroic in style. Pindar's odes in Greece had celebrated victors in athletic games; at some distance Milton's ode is in the same tradition. The syntax of the first stanza shows how the nativity is conceived of as a heroic action: the active verb is not 'born' in line 3 but 'bring' in line 4, signalling the wider impact of the coming of Christ and looking forward to the events of Easter; and just as line 4 looks forward in time to redemption, so line 5 looks back in time to the prophecies of the Old Testament: 'For so the holy sages once did sing.' In the second stanza, also, the doctrinal significance of the incarnation is stressed and the focus is as much on Christ in heaven, triumphant, mystical, as it is on the baby: 'That glorious form, that light unsufferable ...' Despite the humility of the stable the construction elaborates what was 'laid aside' and is a foreshadowing of the ultimate victory of Christ in the history of the world.

In terms of diction and versification, the poem displays an allegiance to native English Protestant writing, to Spenser and the Spenserians. In the closing alexandrine of stanza 2, 'darksome' is a piece of Spenserian diction, as is 'deadly forfeit' in stanza 1. A Reformation subject will be treated partly in the manner of Reformation poets.

The infectious youthful enthusiasm of the poem is expressed in the famous passage about the angelic music at the birth of the child:

Such music (as 'tis said)
Before was never made,
   But when of old the sons of morning sung,

While the creator great
His constellations set,
   And the well-balanced world on hinges hung,
And cast the dark foundations deep,
And bid the welt'ring waves their oozy channel keep.
Ring out, ye crystal spheres,
Once bless our human ears,
   (If ye have power to touch our senses so)
And let your silver chime
Move in melodious time;
   And let the base of heaven's deep organ blow,
And with your ninefold harmony
Make up full consort to the angelic symphony.

For if such holy song
Enwrap our fancy long,
   Time will run back, and fetch the age of gold,
And speckled vanity
Will sicken soon and die,
   And lep'rous sin will melt from earthly mould,
And hell itself will pass away,
And leave her dolorous mansions to the peering day.

Yea Truth, and Justice then
Will down return to men,
   Orbed in a rainbow; and like glories wearing
Mercy will sit between,
Throned in celestial sheen,
   With radiant feet the tissued clouds down steering,
And heaven as at some festival,
Will open wide the gates of her high palace hall.
(117–48)

The celebrant imagines that music can have such Orphic power as
to negate all the disruptive evil in the world and fetch back the
golden age. There is a historical range of reference here, too. In
stanza 12 the music is that sung for joy at the creation, picking up
Job 38: 4, 7: 'Where wast thou when I laid the foundations of the
earth? ... when the morning stars sang together, and all the sons of
God shouted for joy?' Stanza 14 refers back to the innocence of
Adam and Eve, whilst implicitly the whole imagined scene is a

great leap forward in time, to the final return of 'golden' order at the end of the world.

At the same time the imagery is updated. Cosmic harmony sounds as music in church, as between organ and voices. Ideas of cosmic harmony go back to Plato, in the *Timaeus*, but the touch of extravagance is seventeenth-century wit. One might also pick out a line remarkable for its adjectives – 'And bid the weltering waves their oozy channel keep' (124) – where both 'oozy' and 'weltering' belie the old charge that Milton's vocabulary is too abstract. The momentum of the verse is infectious, enacting enthusiasm.

As for the famous stanza 15, the climax of this passage, the return of the golden age imagined there recalls the language of the Psalms and of Virgil's celebrated fourth eclogue, the Pollio. Psalm 85.10 reads: 'Mercy and Truth are met together, righteousness and peace have kissed each other.' The personified figure Justice – 'Yea Truth, and Justice then / Will down return to men' – is the figure Astraea, who fled earth at man's fall from innocence and will return at the return of the golden age. These evocations are not at all unusual; they are Christian humanist commonplaces, the sort of thing school-boys learned in Milton's time. What is remarkable is the blithe ideal-ism and the fact that the whole stanza has been enlivened by being presented as a visual conceit: the return of these qualities is pictured as in a gorgeous court masque, with spectacular machinery. The happy romanticism of this idea is set off by referring to heaven as 'high palace hall' in time of festival.

That fantasy of golden age recovery produces a structure which dramatises the speaker and gives doctrinal significance to the birth. As a reaction to Nativity the festival is premature, because the fancy has flown ahead: ' But wisest fate says no, / This must not yet be so.' Passion and Last Judgement must precede the final restoration of heaven and earth, which he has been tempted to prefigure through the effects of music. As in 'Lycidas', the speaker is given passionate outburst and sober corrective in a way which invites the reader to share the mood whilst finally registering the appropriate doctrine.

What is registered as appropriate doctrine, in the closing sequence from stanza 18, where the poet sets the historical sequence right, is something distinctly Protestant in its militancy. The old dragon Satan may not have been finally quelled but has had much of his influence reduced by the institution of the era of Christ. The final sequence celebrates the advent of Christ by the flight of the false gods which he came to replace. In the narration of the shrines of the gods being deserted, there is a description of a procession of Old Testament idols, then commonly identified with the fallen angels and gods of the Greeks and Romans. (The catalogue of false gods at the end of this ode can be compared with the first book of *Paradise Lost*, where the fallen angels are named as they pick themselves off the burning lake.) The effect of this way of providing the climax of the 'Nativity Ode' is, again, to see the role of the infant Christ heroically; the baby in the cradle conquers the monsters of darkness, as the infant Hercules was said to have strangled snakes –

> Nor all the gods beside,
> Longer dare abide,
>   Not Typhon huge ending in snaky twine:
> Our babe to show his Godhead true,
> Can in his swaddling bands control the damned crew.
>
> (224–8)

So this is a triumphant victory celebrated, a Pindaric in Protestant terms. False worship is banished. The birth of the baby is the victory of Truth and provides the context for the Protestant fight for the proper completion of the restoration of mankind through the church, till 'at last our bliss / Full and perfect is.' The present struggle of the church will be the constant reference of the later writing.

There are plenty of immature things about the ode. Its language is somewhat unstable. There is a mannerism of noun–adjective pairings – 'hostile blood', 'armed throng', 'awful eye' (st. 4) – and a kind of Gothic relish in the description of the deserting gods, not far from high romance. Some lines are simply overwritten: 'Yet first to those y-chained in sleep / The wakeful trump of doom must thunder through the deep' (155–6). Still, a telling shape has been achieved, the militant cause of Reformation has been embraced with youthful idealism and for its occasion the poem seems splendidly right. But the careful note of date in the heading in 1645 also showed that the poet distanced himself from its blithe idealism. It was a poem of good directions but not much experience in the real world.

That Milton wished to document his development in 1645 is suggested by the inclusion in it of the fragment 'The Passion' (CF 36), probably written Easter 1630 as a companion piece to the 'Nativity Ode'. 'This subject the author finding to be above the years he had when he wrote it, and nothing satisfied with what was begun, left it unfinished,' he had printed beneath. The subject was one which Milton was never to take on at length. The fragment seems to establish no clear direction, but it furnishes some parallel features to the other ode. Here too the poet compares his action to courtly pageant and theatre: 'O what a mask was there, what a disguise!', he writes of the Crucifixion, and talks of 'scenes'. The new poem is to put sad music in place of 'ethereal mirth, / Wherewith the stage of air and earth did ring.' The self-conscious language seems to show an ambition to work in the medium of drama. In fact, there is little sense of the real world and at the moment in which the heroism of Christ is announced as Herculean (as in the earlier ode) the poetic vocabulary betrays the dominant literary model for heroic subjects as the outdated if nationalistic one of Spenser: 'Most perfect hero, tried in heaviest plight / Of labours huge and hard, too hard for human wight' (13–14). To find the right language for the new heroic poem would require more study, more experience, and more engagement with the world beyond books.

Young poets were, however, expected to write about love and to these years may be assigned Milton's Sonnets I–VI (with one Canzone: CF 25–32), in which he plays the literary lover, the Petrarchist, and just to prove that he can do it properly, he writes all but the first in Italian. As these poems were arranged in *1645*, the English sonnet to the nightingale was first and served as a headpiece to the Italian series and one can see why, whenever exactly individual poems were written. With more whimsy than passion this poem asks that he may this year for the first time have luck in love, according to the omen in folklore (or more probably from the *The Cuckoo and the Nightingale*, the pseudo-Chaucerian poem) of hearing the nightingale before the cuckoo. The poem also allows the speaker to declare his allegiance to Love and Poetry:

> Whether the Muse, or Love call thee his mate,
> Both them I serve, and of their train am I.

One must realise the force of that twin dedication. The poet tries his hand at love-in-literature. Parker read these poems with wonderfully literal mind, as the story of a second loveaffair (the first he reckoned to have been recorded in Elegy VII):

> When Milton met Emilia (along with some other girls and some
> pleasant young men) her beauty, her manner, and her exotic air

attracted him at once. She was of Italian origin ... Milton, fascinated, begged her to talk to him in Italian ... Flattered by his attention, she complied.   (P 78–9)

Appealing, but more than we know. Milton's Italian sonnets indeed tell a story, but their relation to life is harder to gauge than their embracing of literary Petrarchism.

The sonnets express a new love affair with Italian culture. We do not know when Milton started learning Italian, but since he purchased Della Casa's *Rime e Prose*, a major model, in December 1629, it is reasonable to think that he was developing this new linguistic skill at about this time. Perhaps this also corresponds broadly with the period identified in the famous passage in *An Apology* (1642; Y i 888–93) in which he sketches his reading and mentions that he graduated from the elegiac Latin poets to the virtuous love poetry of Dante and Petrarch, before moving on to chivalric romance (presumably Ariosto and Tasso as well as Spenser). However that may be, it was quite a talent which managed these poems in Italian, without yet having visited the country. F. T. Prince probably had achievement and subject about right, when he said that these poems, 'remarkable as they are, reveal themselves on consideration as a daring experiment rather than as an achieved poetic success' and that they are 'less love poems than slightly amorous compliments'.[1]

Milton must have had a tutor for Italian, more likely in London than Cambridge. In Sonnets II and IV we discover that Emilia sings, so, conventional though this is for ladies in sonnets, it may indicate that the dark-eyed, Italian-speaking lady belongs to a musical circle in London, such as his father would know. Italian is the language of music as well as of love. There were quite a few expatriate Italian families living in London. But the identity of young Milton's Emilia has yet to be found.

What we can study is Milton's self-presentation in these poems. He opens in Sonnet II by playing the witty, courteous lover. His heart is in danger: only Grace from above (*Gratia sola di sù*) may save him from the power of her grace. He strikes a pose as the helpless unworthy aspirant. By Sonnet III he feigns to have fallen from Grace, but, in a humorous pastoral analogy about a young shepherdess watering a strange plant on a hillside in the evening, he reveals that his Fall has been for the Italian language itself, though she of course was responsible in the first place. That she brought about his strange addiction to Italian is confirmed by the Canzone, which shows his peer group puzzled at his affectation. In Sonnet IV he confides his helpless love to a friend, to Charles Diodati, who will of course understand both Italian and playful tone. Is it not unlike me, quips John, who has thus far scorned love? The last two sonnets, addressed again to the Lady, complete the story of his help-less infatuation: in V her eyes are the scorching sun, producing in him the Petrarchist's hot sighs and cold tears; in VI, with perhaps a touch of mock solemnity, the poet finally presents her with his heart and tells her what a thing she has got, a heart long hardened with virtue and given to the Muses, which Love only could soften. The prophecy of Sonnet II has been fulfilled. In the briefest of spaces Milton has recreated a miniature sonnet sequence, but I take it that even in that expected final capitulation the Lady is reminded that the career of John Milton is finally to be shaped more by Virtue and the high kinds of Poetry – the gallant Petrarchist is a youthful mask to be worn in the service of acquiring literary language.

The playful tone of these poems, and the fact that they have Charles Diodati as one audience, should remind us of how much the poetry of these years is in the nature of social poetry, enjoying the varied arts of social address. For if we put aside the 'Nativity Ode' and the fragment of 'The Passion' as promises of vocational intent, then all the other poems of the period of Milton's qual-ification for Master of Arts betray social affiliations of some kind. Of course some poems belong to the university community. The two witty poems (CF 38, 39) on the death of Hobson, the aged London carrier, join dozens of other pieces from the colleges in affectionate tribute to a Cambridge institution. Their patronising tone may raise questions in the modern mind, and the second may be more tediously jocular than the first, but these pieces show that Milton wished to share in community ritual and that he desired to demonstrate that he had done so, by printing them in *1645*.

'An Epitaph on the Marchioness of Winchester '(CF 40) may also instance his willingness to join in some collective project to circulate a collection of memorial verses: many other elegies for her survive, and one manuscript collection of such in the British Library includes a version of Milton's poem. As an epitaph Milton's rather long poem displays several distinctive features. The tetrametre measure was common for such poems and the fact that it develops a little mythological fiction about death-in-birth – 'But whether by mis-chance or blame / Atropos for Lucina came' – may be an attempt to fit its young female subject. At the same time it anticipates characteristic passages of fictional explanation in the Ludlow masque, also incidentally much concerned with youth and young femininity. His mode may have been conditioned by occasion, but he evidently enjoyed it.

In retrospect, and with the great poems of the last years in mind, we tend not to think of Milton as a social poet, but his gifts were considerable in that regard. His poems of friendship to Charles Diodati, for all that they partake of several languages, rate as a remarkable series in literary friendship. In that series, Elegy VI, written in late December 1629, during a period of poetic productivity, deserves special attention.

Milton must have been at home. Diodati had written to him from the country on 13 December a light-hearted letter in verse, suggesting that he was having such a merry time with friends and good wine that his verses cannot be much good. The little that has survived of Diodati's letters to Milton – two undated letters, probably of 1625, in Greek[2] – make it clear that there was much good-humoured teasing between them, as has already been mentioned, and that they caricatured themselves and each other. Charles played the sanguine, outgoing social man; John the more introspective, serious-minded student. In Elegy VI Milton takes up the jocular tone and poses as starving and not interested in showing off his poetry. He then both compliments and teases Charles about Bacchus and poetry, exploring their connection at such sympathetic length as to give incidental reassurance that he could perhaps match the conviviality of his friend. Then he offers himself again as the spare-living virtuous poet intent on the highest kinds of composition, far above these elegiac sports. He is the Pythagorean, drinking water, the purified priest before the rituals, the blind Tiresias, Orpheus turned old, Homer, and so on. In a sense this is confessional, acknowledging deep ambition to a friend; but the self is presented with civilised irony and good humour. Finally, just to prove that not all is posing and to match Charles' jocular offering with something weightier, he tells him that he has been writing a nativity poem for Christ, which he describes in some detail, and then says that there are some other little poems *patriis cicutis*, in his [Charles'?] native language, waiting for his inspection when they meet – the Italian sonnets, perhaps. This is poetry of friendship at a high level.

Periods of creativity in poetry like that around December 1629, and evidence of liberal literary studies way outside the range of prescribed studies at the university, suggest how Milton was determined to give time to a programme of individual self-cultivation during his latter years at Cambridge. And, although the basis of humanistic learning was the ancient languages, it was also a part of humanistic tradition to use and adorn the modern vernaculars, and, as we have seen, Milton had given full notice of this ideal in 'Hail Native language' in the exercise at the end of his studies for the first degree. There is every reason to think that he was exploring English literature, as well as European, in these years.

Milton's first published poem, 'On Shakespeare' (CF 37), written in 1630 and printed in the Shakespeare Second Folio of 1632, testifies to his sympathetic reading in English literature and his strong interest in drama. Later he was to pronounce that in his view Shakespeare and Jonson had actually improved on the Ancients in their comedies. It is to the comic genius of Shakespeare that the young Milton seems particularly to have warmed, to judge by his allusions, and like others he was to marvel at Shakespeare's facility with the language:

> Thou in our wonder and astonishment
> Hast built thyself a live-long monument.
> For whilst to the shame of slow-endeavouring art,
> Thy easy numbers flow...

Built on the conventional idea of an author's monument lying in his works, and showing touches of 'literary' language, like the false Spenserian archaism 'star-ypointing pyramid', Milton's epitaph nevertheless contrives a well-controlled mixture of celebratory weight and affectionate familiarity.

But in some ways the best tribute to the genial comic spirit of Shakespeare in these years, and the best evidence of sensitivity to his native language, is the inimitable pair 'L'Allegro' and 'Il Penseroso' (CF 41–2). If the 'Nativity Ode' represents an early milestone in these years in terms of English verse, these two poems represent a matching achievement, probably later and certainly an advance in technique. Here, as in the 'Nativity Ode', the authority of ancient verse is mediated in triumphantly English ways, with attractive playfulness. Chief amongst English spirits gathered into these poems is 'my Shakespeare'.

The poems are actually dramatic monologues or, perhaps, something like odes characterising their speakers. The second, 'Il Penseroso', spoken by the reclusive contemplative man, answers the first, spoken by a man of youthful gregariousness and mirth, 'L'Allegro'. One might speculate why Milton gave his personae Italian names. The sister arts of poetry and music are recalled, as in the final references to Orpheus (145–50), and the Italian sonnets make it plain that some of Milton's associates in the sister arts were connected with his cultivation of Italian. The poems may be a record of that milieu, or phase in his life. Or the titles could even suggest Diodati as audience, the named friend and confidant of the Italian poems as of other poems and letters.

The poems wear their learning easily, but they represent a triumph in flexible assimilation of genre and form. Both offer a description of a fantasy of ideal existence, 'such sights as youthful poets dream'; in both, unreality is suggested by comic provocation. To let a character expose himself by confessing a fantasy is an old trick of comedy and social verse. In terms of ancient poetry, also, some kinds of pipedream had become institutionalised as subjects, like those regarding the joys of country life. In the most imitated of such poems, Horace's Epode II, a city-dwelling speaker, a money-lender, imagines ideal 'retirement' outside the city. Although Milton's 'L'Allegro' has been likened to this genre ('*Beatus ille*...: Blessed the man who ...'), his subject is not the same, nor does his poem compare to an epode metrically or in its extended form. Neither do Milton's poems quite correspond to the 'Come live with me' genre, championed as influence by S. R. Watson:[3] Milton's speakers say they will go to live with Mirth and Melancholy, rather than be invited. But a common idea Milton's poems do share with well-known tradition and that is the imagining of an ideal 'day', the idea of making up a list of pleasures ordered in rough chronology in a kind of aggregate ideal day, letting the imagination shift scene and season as it plays.

Thus, 'L'Allegro' hears from bed the lark announce the dawn, comes to a flowery window to bid good morrow to the sun to the distant sound of cock and hens, sometimes goes walking early, whilst ploughmen whistle and milkmaids sing, and so on. His eyes play on a mountain landscape, not the Chilterns, as one believed,[4] but a place of romantic fantasy, in which castles are placed at secluded heights, perhaps containing their princesses ('the cynosure of neighbouring eyes'). Near the speaker 'betwixt two aged oaks' is imagined a shepherd's cot, where as in literary fiction Corydon and Thyrsis eat a vegetarian meal served neatly by Phyllis, who then hastens to help Thestylis bind the sheaves, if it is in harvest time. If at haymaking, L'Allegro may be drawn to 'upland hamlets' to see the feasting and dancing, young and old together and to hear tales of fairies into the night. Or the city might please in the evening, pictured in high romance with knights, tournaments, and bright-eyed ladies, a city preoccupied with marriages and festivals. And finally to a play, comedies of course, by Jonson and Shakespeare.

Point of view is little problem in 'L'Allegro'. The tone is set by the extravagant staginess of the opening exorcism of Melancholy, as a thing of superstitious gloom fit for some desert cell. In this vein the ending of 'L'Allegro' is also extravagant:

> And ever against eating cares,
> Lap me in soft Lydian airs,
> Married to immortal verse
> Such as the meeting soul may pierce
> In notes with many a winding bout
> In linked sweetness long drawn out,
> With wanton heed, and giddy cunning,
> The melting voice through mazes running;
> Untwisting all the chains that tie
> The hidden soul of harmony.
> That Orpheus self may heave his head
> From golden slumber on a bed
> Of heaped Elysian flowers, and hear
> Such strains as would have won the ear
> Of Pluto, to have quite set free
> His half-regained Eurydice.
> These delights, if thou canst give,
> Mirth with thee, I mean to live.
>
> (135–52)

Music and poetry will magic care away; the lines describing music are indeed 'long drawn out' with 'giddy cunning', and Orpheus himself has been outstripped, as if he had not magic enough. With playful triumphs over the moods of darkness Milton ends his poem.

The determination to defy 'eating cares' is a reminder of Horace (Ode II xi 18: *curas edaces*), but of Horace in a certain vein:

> Why, underneath a pleasing Myrtle shade,
> On flowery banks supinely laid,
> Are we so slow to spend a Day;

And, whilst grey Hairs are crown'd with Rose,
Or odorous Oyl our Heads o'erflows,
Drink all our troubles and our cares away?

Brisk Bacchus soon will sordid cares refine,
And make dull Melancholly shine ...[5]

This is in the mood of Anacreon, nostalgia for the spirit of youth
dispelling 'wrinkled Care'. L'Allegro's Liberty and Mirth take his
imagination also through pastoral and romantic references in the
literary mind, but the touching of Anacreontic mood is part of what
is compassed in the marvellous management of the verse measure,
tetrametre couplets of brisk but changing pace and resourceful
variation, frequently using heptasyllabic lines amongst the octo-
syllables. These seven-syllable lines often occur in groups. Thus
'L'Allegro' evokes festive joy:

> Haste thee nymph, and bring with thee
> Jest and youthful Jollity,
> Quips and cranks, and wanton wiles,
> Nods and becks, and wreathed smiles,
> Such as hang on Hebe's cheek,
> And love to live in dimple sleek;
> Sport that wrinkled Care derides,
> And Laughter holding both his sides.
> Come and trip it as you go
> On the light fantastic toe ...
>
> (25–34)

The initial stresses in all but two of the lines induce a trochaic
scansion, seeming to enact the compulsive invitation to youthful
jollity. The heptasyllabic line is a common English equivalent to
Anacreontics; metrics themselves may be allusive, although both
eight- and seven-syllable lines also have an English pedigree. Poets
often used these measures in pastorals, for example, and in songs in
plays. If the 'light fantastic toe' echoes 'Each one tripping on his toe'
in *The Tempest* (IV i 46), the brisk movement might recall the
speeches of the fairies in *A Midsummer Nights Dream* and the stories
of 'Faery Mab' and Robin Goodfellow also a comic spirit of
mischief. For all the depth of allusion the poem celebrates 'native
woodnotes wild' and genial English comedy.

Milton allows his speaker to reveal himself, without direct authorial comment, although his nature had been announced in the title, seeming to trust his reader to read tone and perspective through the speech. 'L'Allegro' presents a persona recognisably akin to that of some of the elegies and poems about love, and it would not be surprising if Milton's friends read the poem with a knowing amusement, seeing a playful portrait of one poetic self.

And such is the case with 'Il Penseroso' too, although not all have read it that way. The fantasy here is of the ambitious scholar–poet, one who, playing the savant, will deal in high poetic kinds and finally be rated prophet. The versification is the same as in 'L'Allegro', yet with a slight difference: there are only half the number of shorter heptasyllabic lines in the second poem; still playful, it takes on slightly greater weight. An early indication of a parodic relationship to high kinds may come, in its equally extravagant opening, with the claim that the 'fixed mind' has no use for such vain toys as Mirth can offer to delude the childish or unmanly mind. A fixed mind, *animus fixus*, is what Dido claimed for her virtuous self when she nevertheless fell for Aeneas, at the opening of Book IV of the *Aeneid* (iv 15).[6] The reader is asked to see self-deluding joys indulged in a character of moral pretentiousness: the Lady doth protest too much.

This poem, too, presents a teasing mixture of mockery and pleasure. Melancholy is gently mocked as 'nun' and offspring of golden-age incest. Against the gregarious sport of 'L'Allegro' we now have Peace, Quiet, Fast, Leisure, and Contemplation. 'Il Penseroso' does not seek company at dawn but prefers to walk at night with the sad nightingale or sit alone by a dying fire, when others have retired, reading late, perhaps, letting the mind soar in metaphysical speculation. If he goes to a play, it will be to a tragedy, or he will read poetry that moves to tears. He hopes for mornings after rain and seeks woodland out of the sun, or he muses, like Shakespeare's Jacques, by a brookside, to atmospheric music. His golden pleasures are tinged with a pre-Reformation indulgence, for he likes to walk the studious cloisters, loves high ceremony in dimly-lit churches, and anticipates age and the hermitage:

> And may at last my weary age
> Find out the peaceful hermitage,
> The hairy gown and mossy cell,
> Where I may sit and rightly spell

Of every star that heaven doth shew,
And every herb that sips the dew;
Till old experience do attain
To something like prophetic strain.

(167–74)

The affectionate smile at youthful romanticism can be missed by critics, like D. C. Allen, who claimed that 'Il Penseroso' is 'much more solitary' than 'L'Allegro' 'and hence a more personal poem' – the gregarious cannot be truly Miltonic – and that 'Il Penseroso' is therefore 'the poem of a poet who has found his way'.[7]

Most famously Dr Johnson seemed to miss the tone: 'Both Mirth and Melancholy are solitary, silent inhabitants of the breast that neither receive nor transmit communication; no mention is therefore made of a philosophical friend or a pleasant companion.'[8] Milton's twin poems do not need such companions within the text, because the knowing companionship is implicit in the reader. Such a thought might lead to a conjecture about the Italian titles. Did Milton use Italian names to confess affectations to a knowing friend? Both speakers corresponded to familiar posing in the personae of his early verse.

Against the prejudices of these older voices on 'Il Penseroso' one might consider recent ideological and cultural placement of 'L'Allegro'. Subjecting both the pastoral genre and the poems of Milton to ideological interrogation, and discussing (as others have) possible contradictions in attitude in the poems of *1645*, Annabel Patterson claims that the 'social élitism' which Milton will later voice through the lady in the masque

is that of 'L'Allegro', the man who sees country life as a structure of his own pleasure, who is contented that rural labourers enjoy their work as much as he enjoys its contemplation:

While the Plowman neer at hand,
Whistles ore the Furrow'd land,
And the Milkmaid singeth blithe …[9]

So Milton is not now seen as lonely melancholic but as an aspiring radical who had not grown out of élitist social attitudes. We do not know what John Milton actually thought, if he thought much at all, of the labours of ploughmen and milkmaids, because the matter was not on the agenda of his writings, but there is surely a problem here, too, of reading athwart the text, whether deliberately or not: L'Allegro, like Il Penseroso, self-indulges, and the reader is trusted to recognise it. Not all have wished to be that kind of like-spirited reader.

As we have seen, Milton's early writing sometimes announced a wish to engage in large heroic themes of national interest and the four years of graduate study had begun with a large vocational gesture in the 'Nativity Ode'. Nevertheless, Milton the student was willing enough to declare himself as poet on set occasions and the main achievements of the years 1629–32, after the 'Nativity Ode', were to be graceful social poetry within rather close circles of cultivated friends and a good deal of that poetry seems to have been addressed outside the immediate university community. What this reflects about all his activities at this time is not certain – we have very little documentation – but it would seem that after the failure of 'The Passion', the vocational aspirations of his writing were standing somewhat in abeyance. Perhaps that is what Milton was wishing to signal, in his presentation of these materials in 1645. The social poet, however, had achieved a distinctive voice: in 'L'Allegro' and 'Il Penseroso' Milton had written something well beyond youthful experimentation.

Notes

1. F. T. Prince, *The Italian Element in Milton's Verse* (Oxford, 1954), 97–8.
2. BM Add Ms 5016 f. 71; LR i 98.
3. Sara R. Watson, 'Milton's Ideal Day: Its Development as a Pastoral Theme', *PMLA*, 57 (1942), 404–20.
4. A. H. J. Baines in *N & Q* 88 (1945), 68–71; see headnote to CF 41.
5. The translation is the later one of Thomas Creech, *The Works of Horace in Latin and English* (5th edn, London, 1708), i 111.
6. A similar irony may be implicit with Satan's 'fixed mind' in *PL* i 97.
7. D.C. Allen, 'The Search for the Prophetic Strain, "L'Allegro" and "Il Penseroso"', *The Harmonious Vision: Studies in Milton's Poetry* (Baltimore and Oxford, 1954), pp. 3–23.
8. Johnson, *Lives of the English Poets*, ed. G. B. Hill (Oxford, 1905), i pp. 165–7.
9. Annabel Patterson, *Pastoral and Ideology: Virgil to Valéry* (Oxford: Clarendon Press, 1988), pp. 159–60; compare her essay '"Forc'd Fingers": Milton's Early Poems and Ideological Constraint', in *'The Muses Common-weale': Poetry and Politics in the Seventeenth Century*, ed. Claude J. Summers and Ted-Larry Pebworth (Columbia: University of Missouri Press, 1988), pp. 9–22.

3

Occasions, Impulses, and the Sense of Vocation: from 'Arcades' to 'Lycidas'

The period following Cambridge formed a distinctive stage of development in Milton's life. The great majority of his university peers took orders soon after reaching the required age, twenty-four. Although he had been destined for the church, Milton declined to follow the crowd, deciding that the heroic pursuit of education would take him well beyond the conventional boundaries of study and require further uninterrupted time. As a regent he could have resided still at Cambridge. Rather, he chose an environment more domestic and less subject to distraction:

> At my father's house in the country, to which he had retired to pass the rest of his days, I dedicated myself to reading Greek and Latin authors, in complete leisure, though sometimes exchanging the country for the city, either to buy books or to learn something new in mathematics or music, in which I then delighted. Having passed five years in this way, I had the curiosity, after the death of my mother, to see foreign countries   (Y iv 613–14)

This retrospective, apologetic account from the *Second Defence* (*Defensio Secunda*), gives characteristic signals: of familial pieties – both parents are mentioned; of a spirit of discovery in ancient and modern learning, both bookish and cultivated; of an assumption that learning should be practical, eventually rounded off by travel; and of independence, the financial freedom of a gentleman (university graduates were thus deemed); and also independence of spirit, in following his own convictions.

When he wrote that passage in 1654, Milton had achieved the status of a man of learning who had championed his own country on the European stage. Back in the mid-1630s nothing was so clear.

One of the most fascinating features of this last phase of his education, occupying his mid- and late twenties, is the evidence of his debating with himself and others the justification of a course of action which did not make clear how his talents were to be turned to practical use. This debate would remain with him: acknowledgements of seeming tardiness, on the one hand, and on the other providential clarifications of purpose became twin poles of his thought. Only John Milton would know when he was ready to act, and how; only he would sense the providential moment.

Although this debate bore on the large issue of his vocation, it also gave a distinctive character to the two longer poems he wrote in the 1630s, the Ludlow masque ('Comus') and 'Lycidas'. Both pieces were occasional; in both the poet seized the occasions as providential gifts, by which his idealism of purpose could be shown. But that is to anticipate. We might look first at a short poem, Sonnet VII (CF 43), written near the beginning of this period, in which he sought to resolve his conscience to himself:

> How soon hath time the subtle thief of youth,
>   Stol'n on his wing my three and twentieth year!
>   My hasting days fly on with full career,
>   But my late spring no bud or blossom sheweth.
> Perhaps my semblance might deceive the truth,
>   That I to manhood am arrived so near,
>   And inward ripeness doth much less appear,
>   That some more timely-happy spirits endueth.
> Yet be it less or more, or soon or slow,
>   It shall be still in strictest measure even,
>   To that same lot, however mean or high,
> Toward which time leads me, and the will of heaven;
>   All is, if I have grace to use it so,
>   As ever in my great task-master's eye.

How much less clear this is than the blazing vocational purpose of the 'Nativity Ode' a few years before. The poem sets patterns of uncertainty against the fixed point of Providential design: his 'inward ripeness' may come 'soon or slow'; when it comes, it may or may not prove to have been a great endeavour – 'be it less or more'; his eventual employment may or may not be in some great office – his lot may be 'mean or high'; but the point fixed by its revelation at the end of the third quatrain, in this cunning poem, is that 'Toward which time leads me, and the will of heaven.' With disclaimers about false motives – he is not just indulging vanity or ambition, for his lot may be 'mean' (still the humble priesthood?), neither will he waste time but 'use' it – he begs an unspecifiable period until he feels ready to use his education vocationally. Such a plea, joining eloquence to godliness, linking the 'strictest measure' of verse and destiny, is indeed hard to answer. Milton probably showed the poem to friends, perhaps to his father. That he sent it with a letter to an unknown, presumably older, solicitous friend, as proof that he was 'something suspicious of my self', we know, because both poem and drafts of the letter survive in the Trinity manuscript.[1] The letter probably dates from late 1632. It refers to the poem vaguely as written 'some while since' and adds that it represented 'nightward thoughts', a night-time meditation. A poem about awaiting the sense of certainty was itself the prompting of a moment, when the spirit came.

An assurance of quick composition, rather than insincere 'set apology', is also made in the letter. The friend had the day before questioned Milton about his 'tardy moving' towards the church. Milton seeks to explain more fully why he does not as yet feel ready to enter a 'credible employment' not 'unserviceable to mankind'. Is he not hiding his talents, evading responsibilities, by proposing 'studious retirement' and 'affected solitariness'? Is there not too much love of learning for its own sake? Against this Milton urges that his conscience is 'not without God' and that he would hardly avoid settling down to work, making some mark in the world and establishing a house and family of his own, without a strong conviction that the greater consideration is to become 'more fit' for whatever is eventually given him. The letter is too long to study here, but well worth the study, both for what is says of the pressure Milton then felt, and also because, existing in two drafts, it shows how artfully Milton revised what originally came to him at his 'best ease'.

And so to the programme of study which Milton followed in this period. Conflating information from several sources – mainly later autobiographical passages and the evidence of Milton's own surviving Commonplace Book, which she was editing at the time – Ruth Mohl offered this sketch, in 1953:

... he was reading and taking notes on the history of Greece and the Greek church, the history of the Western Empire and the

Roman Catholic Church through the Middle Ages, and the
history of the Italian cities; he was also reading the literature of
Greece, Rome, Italy, and England, and he made a few entries from
some of it; he also turned his attention to mathematics and music.

(Y i 348)

In fact our knowledge of his reading in the period 1632–1638 is
considerable and yet tantalisingly incomplete. We have the
invaluable Commonplace Book (Y i 344–513), brief notes or quotations organised by themes within three large headings (ethical,
economic (that is, domestic), and political) taken from his systematic
reading until well into middle age. We have several partial accounts
written in later years. But the Commonplace Book did not come into
use, apparently, until the latter part of this period, a theological
index has gone missing, and dating of entries by handwriting is not
as yet quite precise.

If scholars' dating is correct, and of this we cannot be quite sure,
only two 'groups' of entries belong to the period before the Italian
journey. These are predominantly from histories concerning the
early church and from the early church fathers, though other
periods are represented (Persian Wars, early Italian states) and there
is some poetry (Prudentius, Ariosto, and much Dante). The evidence shows a really thorough programme of reading about early
Christendom, but scholars usually place the first entries in only 1635
or 1636. Whether coincidentally or not, this corresponds roughly to
the apparent move of the Milton family from their suburban residence at Hammersmith, where John senior seems to have retired
about 1631 or 1632, to the more distant country residence at Horton,
Buckinghamshire, whither they removed at some time before March
1637, perhaps in connection with the bad plague of the summer of
1636. (It may or may not be coincidence, again, that one of the 'early'
entries in the Commonplace Book concerns the great plague in
Constantinople in 542.) It is tempting to believe as Parker (145) conjectured that the really rigorous historical reading then began:
'Milton's Horton period was one of relentless study' are the opening
words of his Chapter V. But Milton's studies were always systematic, and we do not know quite enough about them in the early
1630s.

There is wonderfully concrete evidence, however, of the state of
his historical studies in 1637. With some of the old jocular role-
playing, Milton wrote to Diodati on 2 November, in excuse for not

corresponding sooner: '... your habit of studying permits you to pause frequently, visit friends, write much, and sometimes make a journey. But my temperament allows no delay, no rest ... until I attain my object and complete some great period, as it were, of my studies' (Y i 323). Three weeks later, supplying further details, he reported that

> By continued reading I have brought the affairs of the Greeks to the time when they ceased to be Greeks. I have been occupied for a long time by the obscure history of the Italians under the Longobards, Franks, and Germans, to the time when liberty was granted to them by Rudolph, King of Germany. From there it will be better to read separately about what each state did by its own effort.

This letter, of 23 November, also shows excitement about poetry:

> You ask me what I am thinking of? So help me God, an immortality of fame. What am I doing? Growing my wings and practising flight. But my Pegasus still raises himself on very tender wings. ... I shall now tell you seriously what I am planning: to move in some one of the Inns of Court, wherever there is a pleasant and shady walk; for that dwelling will be more satisfactory, both for companionship, if I wish to remain at home, and as a more suitable headquarters, if I choose to venture forth. Where I am now, as you know, I live in obscurity and cramped quarters.   (Y i 327; LR i 347–50)

The poem he refers to in excited mock humility is 'Lycidas', to be published in the Cambridge memorial volume for Edward King. About the same time, also, he prepared the text of the Ludlow masque for publication. He was showing signs of wishing to break out of obscurity and rustication. The wonder is that he stayed in the family house so long.

The wealth of historical and literary reading he had done since university suggests a keeping of options open with regard to vocation. By the study of analogies in past history he now better understood the church for which he had been intended. As he read more and more of the corruptions of the early church, exploding facile mythologies, he came to analyse more critically the role of a wealthy hierarchy of bishops and the unwisdom of the interference of the state in ecclesiastical affairs. His more general reading in history also fitted him for other responsibilities, more in the line of statecraft, and the decision to go to Italy in 1638 suggests secular as well as ecclesiastical interests. He probably thought of great plans for poetry. Not that poetry excluded other vocations, but it would, if taken into the most ambitious kinds, like study itself require much time.

Of the poetry of this period we have the most marvellous record in the autograph Trinity Manuscript, in which he copied his chief compositions, sometimes correcting drafts, so that some of the process of composition is shown. Although the date of the first entry, the entertainment 'Arcades', is not known for certain, it seems to me likely from a variety of considerations that the use of this manuscript book began pretty much at the time that Milton finally came down from Cambridge. It might be taken as a sign that Milton left Cambridge knowing that he wished to take poetry seriously, his father by now aware that he wished to be known as poet as well as scholar. It was on the theme of poetry that Milton mounted his third large apologetic statement of his period, the delicate and carefully considered *Ad Patrem* ('To my Father': CF 44). Not many poets have achieved such monuments of affectionate familial piety.

Ad Patrem is a poem of thanks and a defence of poetry. It is deeply serious and respectful, yet flexible in social tone, as to a friend. High ambitions are confessed in a way which suggests the possibility of self-mockery: even to a benevolent father Milton may now be a little shy of showing his heroic, idealistic self-image as a potential poet of the highest kind, but *Ad Patrem* finally affirms poetry as amongst the highest of vocations, remembering epic poets in heroic times or the singing saints in heaven and it defends true learning as beyond suspicion: *'securaque tutus / Pectora, vipereo gradiar sublimis ab ictu* – with a quiet mind I shall stride on, raised high above the sting of the viper [Calumny].'

In fact the poem sets out to justify to the man who had made it possible the tenor of John Milton's life at Hammersmith. It is written to smooth away whatever misgivings Milton senior may have had about his son's refusal to settle to an employment. Milton points out that it is his father who has taken him into the country. This and the context of a debate about intentions seem likely of the early days at Hammersmith, when, as in the Letter to a Friend, a course of life was under active discussion. Whatever its date, *Ad Patrem* is apt persuasion: the father's gifts are returned in kind – it is you who made me what I am; you protected me from a money-making occupation like the law. Can a musician despise poetry, the sister art? If this youthful poem survives, it will immortalise your name as well as mine. Against the odds, history proved the poet right.

The first poem Milton recorded in the Trinity manuscript, 'Arcades', like the sixth, the Ludlow masque, shows him writing an entertainment text for a great house. To some, knowing the lines in *Paradise Lost* about wanton masque in degenerate courts (*PL* iv 765–77), this association has seemed surprising; to others it has been a sign that Milton was seeking patronage. Whatever it was that effected the connection between Milton and the Dowager Countess of Derby's household at Harefield, Middlesex, where 'Arcades' was performed, probably in late summer 1632, it is not altogether a surprise to find him furnishing an entertainment text, since he had already graduated in such things in the Vacation Exercise. Yet when Milton wrote for Harefield and Ludlow, he did so with an integrity of spirit, taking the office of poet instructionally as well as meeting the festive spirit of the occasions. Renaissance humanists often saw themselves as counsellors of the great; Milton is that humanist and more, a poet–priest moving amongst the aristocracy.

In the verses for Harefield (CF 46; only entitled 'Arcades' for first publication in *1645*) the poet serves members of the countess' family by dedicating an entertainment to her honour. The countess was seventy-three; the Arcadians who bring song and dance to her are younger relatives, probably grandchildren. We shall see that it is possible to guess their motives. As far as Milton was concerned, the dedication of these verses to the countess evidently meant a good deal to him, for in the new edition of his shorter poems issued at the end of his life, in 1673, he kept the headnote identifying the subject of these verses, whereas mention of the Earl of Bridgewater's family, for whom the Ludlow masque was written, was dropped.

For young Milton to write in praise of the dowager was to connect himself with Spenser, amongst other poets and, therefore, with old patronage of keen Protestants. Born Alice Spencer, daughter of a very wealthy Midlands family, she had married as her first husband Ferdinando Stanley, Lord Strange, who became Earl of Derby in 1593, a title which included the ancient right of King of Man. Alice had indeed become, as in Milton's text, a kind of queen. The Stanley house was the famous 'Northern Court' at Knowsley, Lancashire, where the style was cultivated and lavish. Ferdinando died early, leaving his widow with three daughters, and the earldom passed to William Stanley, his younger brother, with whom Alice was in dispute about the inheritance until the matter was settled by Parliament in 1609. Nevertheless, she never allowed anyone to forget that she had moved in the highest circles, and she had herself participated in court festivities and masques. Although her second marriage, to Lord Keeper Egerton in 1600, was in personal terms a disaster, she still moved for a time at least in court circles, and she and Egerton entertained the queen at Harefield on the last progress in 1602. To present an entertainment to her in old age was to remind her of her courtly past. Egerton, however, had been dead since 1617 and by 1632 the dowager rarely stirred far from Harefield.

'Arcades' brings courtly Arcadianism to Harefield for her delight.[2] That is to say, 'nymphs' and 'shepherds' in the pastoral disguise then fashionable about Queen Henrietta Maria, bring theatricals, song, and dance to a new 'court' in the country. Milton's 'part of an entertainment' seems to be the first, dedicatory section of 'this night's glad solemnity'. All is in 'honour and devotion' to the lady of the house; she it is who finally defines the spirit of the place. Arcadianism finds at Harefield its truest home.

Milton's 'part' is based on the fiction of a quest ending at the chair of state in which the countess sits. Although the pretence is that the arriving Arcadians come through the park, they almost certainly appeared at one end of the great hall, gesturing towards the other end of the room where the countess sat, whilst singing:

> Look nymphs, and shepherds look,
> What sudden blaze of majesty
> Is that which we from hence descry
> Too divine to be mistook:
>   This this is she
> To whom our vows and wishes bend,
> Here out solemn search hath end.
>
> (1–7)

Playfully they hazard guesses as to the identity of this goddess of whom Fame has spoken. Each guess – Latona, Cybele, Juno – reinforces the idea of a mother-figure to a great family. As they begin to 'come forward' towards the state, a Genius of the Wood appears and halts them. Genius was evidently played by a musical employee of the house. His speech welcomes the Arcadians and gives definition to place and its mistress. He then offers to conduct them across the floor to the state, singing as he goes: 'O'er the smooth enamelled green / Where no print of step hath been, / Follow me as I sing ...' When they arrive at the state, the aristocrats in the group ('all that are of noble stem') kiss the hem of the countess' garment. Finally, in a new song, Genius invites the Arcadians to leave their own 'stony' country for 'a better soil': 'Here ye shall have greater grace, / To serve the Lady of this place.' 'Such a rural queen / All Arcadia hath not seen.'

The movement towards the state imitates masquing and, rudimentary though the spectacle probably was, the general disposition in the hall probably imitated arrangements for a masque, with dramatic discoveries at one end of the room, the state of the chief beholder at the other, and a space of floor between on which dancing could take place. (There is no evidence of dance during Milton's 'part', only mention of it; if they danced, they danced later.) The manuscript text, like that of the Ludlow masque, predates performance whilst also showing post-performance changes, and it indicates that Milton originally imagined a more masque-like spectacle: it first read 'the Genius of the Wood rises', as if with machinery, rather than simply 'appears'. 'Arcades' recaptured the *idea* of courtly masquing.

Of relevance to that idea might be the fact that some of the grandchildren had recently participated in court masques. The family of her second daughter, Frances, wife of Egerton's son, John, Earl of Bridgewater, had attended and participated in court masques since the 1620s, most recently in the queen's Shrovetide masque of 1631/2, *Tempe Restored*. Milton may well have studied this text and other dramatic entertainments given at court, and it is not impossible that young Egerton children brought to Harefield some sample of their court performance, as far as was possible. More locally, the two girls of the dowager's third daughter, Elizabeth, Countess of Huntingdon, were being brought up at Harefield; one, perhaps both, were instructed in singing. The two boys of her first daughter, Anne, Countess of Castlehaven (by her first husband, Grey Brydges, Lord Chandos), were also being housed at Harefield, and the older boy was soon to be introduced to court and court masquing. The dowager took interest in those now engaging with court festivity, a symbol of family pride, and Arcadian arts belonged to the place itself.

Milton was deft in the arts of aristocratic festive pretence. Yet there is rather more to 'Arcades' than the gentle pleasures of pastoral play. The idea of Arcadianism finding a truer home, though a piece of conventional celebration, may have carried special significance for the occasion. To begin with, with regard to the family itself, the action imitates both a happy visit to the house and also a happy residence: a visit might in fact turn into residence in the better Arcadia. This may allude to the situation of younger members of the family. Some of the nymphs and shepherds, like the Egerton children, whose country residence was some sixteen miles away at Ashridge in Hertfordshire, may have been visiting, but some were actually resident at Harefield. The dowager managed the lives of members of her family who had run into difficulty. Her third daughter's husband, Henry Hastings, Earl of Huntingdon, had inherited estates so badly entailed that he often hid away ignominiously at his Leicestershire home, accumulating new debts, unable to pay subsidies, even having furniture in London pawned. For some years the dowager had taken into her home the two Hastings girls, Alice and Elizabeth, assuming responsibility for their upbringing. Alice became her companion; Elizabeth was to be married from the house in 1634.

Further obligations of thanks were due from Anne's two sons, George Brydges, Lord Chandos, and William. The Brydges children had come under their grandmother's care in 1631 after their stepfather, the notorious Earl of Castlehaven, had been tried and executed for unnatural practices. In the last years of her life the dowager's great task was to champion the reputation and financial security of this branch of her family; Lord Chandos would be her heir. Milton's verses, especially the intricate speech of Genius, establish Harefield as a place of unusual favour, a godly establishment depending on the example of its 'rural queen'. A servant of Jove as well as of the countess, Genius protects the plants of the estate against the harms of the night; providence blesses the godly. Knowing the protection the countess gave to stricken kin, we may appreciate a fiction which drew visitors and residents together in thankful recognition of the special blessings of this Arcadian 'home'.

With the idea of establishing a true aristocratic example in a better Arcadia Milton defined his own role also as a religiously instructive poet. This was to be one of the themes of the Ludlow masque, applied there in a vision of a whole land. At Harefield there was a scrupulousness in the complimentary figures: the goddess of the place is to be reverenced, but Jove it is who adds the providential healing. If the device of the questing Arcadians was meant partly to convey the bringing of court masquing arts to Harefield, then an implication of finding it a better Arcadia may have been to establish moral superiority over the court. Retrospectively, at least, when he titled it 'Arcades' for the 1645 volume, Milton seemed to challenge the recognition that true nobility was founded on piety. Back in 1632, was his connection with Harefield made on the assumption that he would be seeking patronage for employment in the church?

The Ludlow masque (CF 50), performed in the castle on the evening of 29 September 1634, also shows itself concerned with godly education and fit example. It was performed before the Earl and Countess of Bridgewater, the dowager's son-in-law and second daughter and featured as the three masquers their youngest children. Lady Alice Egerton, fifteen, played the Lady and the two brothers were John, Lord Brackley, the heir, eleven and Thomas, nine. These ages should be remembered; not only is this an educational masque, it was also written with a nice calculation of tone for the parts of the children. Of marriageable years, the Lady gives mature judgements though with the fierce fervour of youth; the boys display precociousness and good learning whilst permitting the audience a smile at their naiveté. Meanwhile Henry Lawes, the court musician who had taught singing to two of the Egerton girls, plays tutor and presenter in the role of Attendant Spirit. (The identities of the other participants are not known.) But this is no mere family entertainment: the subject of the masque bears upon the presidential occasion in Wales and the nature of the occasion needs some explanation.

Like his father, Bridgewater had served many years on the Council of Wales and in 1631 was nominated to be the next president of the council. At the same time he was to become Lord Lieutenant of the Welsh and border counties. The Council of Wales was the prerogative court designed to keep law and order in the principality and Welsh marches. The administrative centre was Ludlow Castle, in which the Great Hall, where the masque probably took place, was the room for the court itself. Bridgewater was a conscientious overseer of the council. However, he was also a busy man at court, a privy councillor and it was not until the summer of 1634 that he made his first visitation as president. There had been delays, after expectation that he would come in an earlier summer. Milton's Ludlow masque was performed near the end of this first visitation.

The presidential party arrived in Ludlow on 4 July.[3] They stayed about a month, the president being very busy at that time. At the beginning of August they set off on a tour, up the border, staying at big houses like Eyton Hall and Chirk Castle (where an entertainment was presented at supper), paused a while in Denbighshire, and finally turned east again at the north Welsh coast, passing from Mostyn to Bretton Hall, by Dunham Massey Hall to Lyme Park, at the foot of the Pennines, where they stayed three weeks in the house of Bridgewater's kinsman Sir Peter Legh. They returned to Ludlow in three days, via Market Drayton, arriving this second time on 17 September. The masque was performed on 29 September; by early October they had gone back to London.

In other words, the new president was showing himself and the region was honouring him. Though Milton could hardly have known the details of the itinerary, he would have understood the kind of occasion for which he was writing: something was to be made of the coming together of the president's family and the Welsh region, in the context of good governance. For the president's children the masque may have been a vacation project, prepared partly at Lyme no doubt (where Lawes stayed with them), but in actuality, as in the text, the final goal was Ludlow Castle, the seat of the Welsh court. Court officers, with families, and a few representatives of the town would have crowded into the masque hall.

As at Harefield the masquers progress towards a presentation at the state, but at Ludlow that movement has been allegorised as a journey comprising trial. In a romance-like fiction suiting their ages, the three young aristocrats traverse a dark wood in which they meet an enchanter, whose magic figures the dangerous, deceptive powers of habitual intemperate living. Topically, the fiction also suggests that the children are coming to Ludlow 'to attend their father's state, / And new-entrusted sceptre' (35–6). Kinds of governance are on view. As in all masques, what is finally to be achieved is the symbolic harmony of the dance, into which the action leads. Before 'victorious dance' can be achieved, then, the children must shake off the influence of the false enchanter, come out of the dark wood of temptation and be presented to their own parents as scions of the ruling class who have shown their exemplary education. So the Attendant Spirit sings

Noble Lord, and Lady bright,
I have brought ye new delight,
Here behold so goodly grown
Three fair branches of your own,
Heaven hath timely tried their youth,
Their faith, their patience, and their truth,
And sent them here through hard assays
With a crown of deathless praise,
To triumph in victorious dance
O'er sensual folly, and intemperance.

(965–74)

This progression in the masque is also marked by the three 'scenes'. The first is of the dark wood; for the temptation this changes to the feast at the Circean palace within the wood, the dangers of high living now apparent within the pastoral setting. Only after Sabrina has freed the Lady does the scene change to a representation of the present place, Ludlow town and castle. The dance proceeds when the occasion has been redefined in the best terms, or has enacted its own reformation.

Masquers at court were usually 'discovered' in a splendid set on stage and constituted a group large enough – twelve or so – to be able to form intricate dance figures when they descended to the floor between stage and state. They did not usually act; acting was for social inferiors. At Ludlow there are only three children as masquers and they act considerable roles, so that they are drawn into the ritual dramatisation of trial and experience in a way unlike court masque. What is more, Milton does not trade freely in the compliments of heroism or divinity for his aristocratic exemplars; the action interests itself as much in the limitations of virtue and in the need to refer to godly training and providential aid. In other words, although Milton's text is celebratory like all masques, it is embued also with a moral realism akin to that of *The Faerie Queene*.

Like Spenser also, Milton offers analysis of prevalent social ills: what is revealed in the dark wood and what must be banished from the stage is a spirit which might pervert the celebratory, festive occasion. Comus, the enchanter, takes his name from *Kōmos*, revelry, or in the negative sort feared by the Lady, 'riot, and ill-managed merriment' (171). The discipline of a great house, or of a society, can be read in the way it conducts its festivities. As son of Bacchus, Comus deals in drunken excess and transformation; as son of Circe he stands for intemperance, purveys magic deceptions of the truth and, again, brings about transformations. He traps his victims by flattery, offers the inebriating glass, with a rich feast and sexual enticements to follow – 'And she shall be my queen' (264). The Lady, separated from her brothers, is his target: should she accede to his propositions, she would inaugurate a corrupt example at Ludlow and yet one gathers no worse than the customary, for men are 'easy-hearted' (163) and 'most do taste' (67). The young aristocrats are up against a laxness of thought so ingrained in social attitude as not easily to be avoided. It is not sufficient to assume that virtuous young nobility from court can conquer provincial disorder: what Comus stands for is common as much in court as in the regions and, indeed, may begin there. To put it another way, the programme of the Ludlow masque interrogates the pastoral pretences of courts as much as pastoral disorders in the principality.

The slippery slope to degeneracy is beautifully illustrated in Comus' opening speech, cast in the same jaunty measure as 'L'Allegro'. Beguilingly its evening invitations begin: 'Meanwhile, welcome joy, and feast, / Midnight shout, and revelry, / Tipsy dance, and jollity' (102–4). There is humour in the claim that 'Strict Age, and sour Severity' (109) have gone to bed, when they are sitting in the hall, and also in the absurd boast that his heavy-footed rout imitates 'the starry quire' (112). But the speech leads inexorably, through nocturnal love, to the 'sport' of Cotytto, licence and obscenity, in a guilty 'concealed solemnity' (142).

The progression into depravity is also shown by the two interviews with the Lady. In the first Comus deceives her in the guise of a villager offering help; though she notices faults in his speech, she trusts him and is thus trapped. This is a fictional world of moral realism in which innocence will be deceived by hypocrisy. No great blame attaches to the Lady, any more than sharp-eyed Uriel is to blame in *Paradise Lost* for being deceived at first by Satan's hypocrisy (*PL* iii 645–742). In the temptation scene proper, when she sees the true nature of the courtly deceiver beyond the pastoral disguise, the Lady counters all his arguments point by point, in fact reads a kind of sermon about conspicuous expenditure in big houses. Her mind is free of him. But she is nevertheless compromised, stuck in a chair from which she must witness depravity, however unwillingly. So perhaps, a righteous soul sitting in high places will find no easy escape from pollution.

The Lady's godly education is evident from the moment she steps on stage. Her opening soliloquy shows an exemplary turning to virtuous thoughts for strength in a situation of fear and she expects providential aid. She enlivens her spirits, so that she may sing her famous Echo song, a Lawes party-piece. The display of education through the boys is somewhat different. The Elder Brother talks of the power of chastity, but they are not subject to all the temptations of Comus. Put into the role of knights trying to save the lady in distress, they rehearse fortitude, each in somewhat different measure: the elder summoning all the courage he has and more, to impress the younger; the younger's greater fears being somewhat borne out in fact by the revelations of the Attendant Spirit. The Elder Brother is precocious in his language and booklearning.

There is, however, another issue at stake, which has often been misread. The Elder Brother propounds the theory that virtue, in the form of chastity, is self-sufficient – 'She that has that, is clad in complete steel' (420). He then silences his little brother with an exposition of Platonic idealism. But dramatic context demonstrates that such fetching high-minded idealism is not quite commensurate with experience in the fallen world and when the boys offer to rush off to tackle the enchanter it is something else which the Attendant Spirit offers them as protection: the magic herb Haemony, which they must keep with them against enchantments. As I have written elsewhere,[4] the basis of this notorious allegory is religious. Haemony figures the Word of God, often downtrodden, bearing tribulations, but leading to immortal bliss. It protects from 'surprisal' because falsehood is detected on the basis of biblical truth. The young brothers and the audience are reminded that the foundation of all virtue is in the gift of godly instruction. Even so the boys fail to finish the job of freeing their sister and are mildly rebuked: the enchanter is banished, but his wand was not seized – all heroism, even in masque, is fraught with mortal forgetfulness.

The last saving resource identified in the masque, the purifying waters of Sabrina, the River Severn, is presented in what is the climax of the masque in terms of theatrical spectacle: invoked magically by song, she rises, with chariot and attendants, also sings, moves across stage, and performs lustral rites. She serves the occasion, in that she derives from the presidential region, and as a goddess she honours the presidential feast. Yet in another sense she is beyond the family, and Milton clearly intended that the boys, like everyone else, should simply watch and listen as the Attendant

Spirit shows what Orphic powers of verse and song can produce. In this final phase of the action the presidential family encounters resources to be drawn by poetry from the region itself.

Just what kind of power is represented in Sabrina takes some understanding. She is actually drawn from the past, from poetic history; she is an idea, a potentiality. As daughter of Locrine she is related to myths of Trojan British ancestry, therefore to images of national greatness. The kind of heroic greatness Milton wished to invoke is made plain by the way the river and the region are described. A land of happy prosperity, free of misfortune, blessed with plenty and content to return pious thanksgiving (841–50), is formed about a river which takes chaste discipline to its centre. Though it is expressed in picturesque pastoral terms, this is a formula for regeneracy in nations, and it is the language of poetry itself which can thus 'unlock / The clasping charm, and thaw the numbing spell' (851–2), in other words, it can provide that final inspiration which may raise minds beyond the customary debilitating influences. Masquing arts and historical fable have come together to exemplify the persuasive functions of poetry itself; verse and song unite with that power which the Renaissance attributed to Greek drama. Rivers may be associated with regions and also the poet's muse. Thus, through the Attendant Spirit, Milton validated his own offices within the Welsh gubernatorial occasion.

In this connection we should note the sources of authority named by the Spirit, who is the medium of instruction. There are two notable moments in which he cites them, as he unfolds resources of moral strength. The first is when he tells the two boys that they should keep Haemony about them; here the source of information, in the playful pastoral tale, is 'a certain shepherd lad', that is, a true humble pastor, 'of small regard to see to'. The reforming clergy take their place in the education of the youth of the ruling classes. This from a poet who had himself been intended for the ministry. The source of information about the second power, of Sabrina, is 'Meliboeus old', the type of the true poet. Milton's vocational interests are on show, in the most high-minded fashion: the persuasive power of poetry has joined the ministry of the Word in the instruction of the ruling class; ministers and poets both are shepherds to the people.

When one puts it like that, the parallel with 'Lycidas', to which we must now turn, is all too obvious. 'Lycidas' is addressed to, or perhaps through, the institution of the university. Expressed in this remarkable poem is an idea of the true university, producing shepherds to guide the nation. Both poems are hortatory, in that they define the role of educational leadership in the reform of the spirit of the whole nation, both assuming that discipline is lacking in many of those who lead: as Comus reigns in courts, so most ministers, trained in the two universities, fail to feed their sheep.

One of the marked differences between Milton's 'Lycidas' and other poems in the Cambridge memorial volume for Edward King[5] is the way in which Milton's poem used its elegiac occasion to speak out on the matters of ecclesiastical discipline and Catholic menace, 'by occasion' foretelling 'the ruin of our corrupted clergy then in their height', as he put it retrospectively in 1645. 'Lycidas' is political in its use of the pastoral – ecclesiastical satire within pastoral eclogue is not uncommon, but within pastoral elegy uncommon and challenging. Both the masque and 'Lycidas' discriminate between 'true' and 'false' pastoralism; both to different degrees encompass church and court culture. In ways we might expect the explicit polemics of the poem about the church, in Peter's speech, are set in the context of reminders of British Protestant destiny, for the drowning of King at sea, with the vision of his bones hurled down western shores, with the guardianship of St Michael in his mount in the south-west looking towards 'Namancos and Bayona's hold', are tokens of providential deliverance from the Armada and the threat of Catholicism from without in 1588. Coming at the end of the English poems in the *Justa* volume, 'Lycidas' challenged its audience prophetically to rouse its spirits to the cause of continuing reformation, to resist now the infection of the nation from within.

The accusations of the church are expressed as backsliding, false discipline, and betrayal of the Word of God, even to the point of encouraging Romish incursions. Church authority has become enmeshed with temporal concerns and affairs of state; not just lucre in the church but the imposition of tyranny of conscience through the highest courts, and, what is worse, a false example from the court itself: the grim wolf with privy paw registers the growing practice of open Catholic worship in court circles, encouraged by the influence of the queen. Many issues had accumulated by November 1637. Much of the invective is against the policy of the imposition of uniformity under Archbishop Laud, the false use of the keys of discipline registering the growing dismay in more radically reforming circles at such as the punishments of Bastwick, Prynne, and Leighton. The year 1637 itself renewed fears about censorship, saw the worrying arrest of Bishop Williams, and some wondered what the imposition of the English prayer book on Presbyterian Scotland portended. The universities themselves were under pressure to conform, Laud recognising how crucial they were in the formation of future attitudes in the English church.[6]

A more specific issue is also signalled in the celebrated textual crux of line 129, where Milton first wrote, in manuscript 'And nothing said', later modified in the manuscript and in the university volume to 'And little said', only to revert to 'nothing' in 1645. The point was worship at the Catholic chapel of the queen at Somerset House and the notable converts to Catholicism being made through the queen's circle. The crisis came with the conversion of the Countess of Newport in October 1637, following which the earl complained loudly to Laud, who put pressure on the king.[7] It was a test case. Ardent Protestants hoped to force some anti-Catholic measures out of the king, to stop the 'daily devouring'. Everyone expected *something* to be said. By November, when Milton was composing 'Lycidas', nothing had been said. By the end of December something had been said, but the royal proclamation on the matter of conversions was so anodyne that it is was as good as nothing. Hence, Milton's 'little'. Church and court seemed to be betraying the Protestant destiny of the nation; false discipline spoke tyranny, and tyranny, Milton learned from history, was the sign of weakness and irrationality. The scholar speaks, in the pastoral, the student's genre, through the university, of the heroic free-spirited educational search for reform with which the country should be concerned.

How did this cry of protest arise from the specific occasion? The volume to which Milton was invited to contribute was a memorial tribute to a young fellow of Milton's old college, Edward King, who had been drowned when the ship on which he was travelling home in the long vacation of 1637 sank on the voyage from Chester to Dublin, on 10 August. King's father was a Privy Councillor for Ireland and Secretary to the Irish Council, his uncle a bishop, and the young man had been granted a fellowship at Christ's in 1630 at an unusually young age and by royal mandate. In other words, he had been a rather lucky young man of good family connections. He may well have featured in Milton's Vacation Exercise of 1628, but, although all residents of similar age would have known one another in a college community, we have insufficient evidence to establish whether King and Milton were particular friends. Nothing of King's character is revealed intimately in the elegy: Lycidas is portrayed by the 'uncouth swain' as an ideal product of the university, a liberal scholar who took his ministerial vocation seriously, one neither university or church could afford to lose in these times. The 'swain' shares those ideals with his lost fellow scholar.

The loss of King therefore becomes a signal to the nation, an occasion of warning, even perhaps a kind of prophecy for the times, when, as in Isaiah, the righteous man is taken from the evil to come.[8] In this sense the occasion of lament has been broadened. All elegies for the dead lament, and Christian elegies come to consolation in their closes, but through the dramatic use of the singer's voice and by the taking of other voices into the poem Milton's elegy accumulates a peculiar range of questionings of Providence about the meaning of the death, touching the meditations of shepherds of true vocation in those times. So urgent is the question of vocation for the speaker, that it is impossible to separate thoughts of the destiny of private lives from thoughts of the destiny of the nation. This questioning of the meaning of the death of a true shepherd before his work was done is expressed, formally, in a remarkable way, for the audience is engaged by something imitating the emotive experience of high tragedy. By calling his poem a 'monody', the song of lament of a single voice, Milton seems to have signalled a relationship to Greek tragedy, and by crafting that famous calm ending he advertised that passions such as those raised by tragedy had just been spent in the questioning and final understanding of Providence.

Hence, also, perhaps, the bold dramatic strategy. Milton's elegy features a singer whose dominant presence must be accommodated by the reader, and he also presents that singer in such a way that the reader only comes to understand him by hearing the process of his discovery of the significance of the occasion and of his own reactions to it. This speaker is not introduced by a narrator at the beginning, only briefly described at the end as 'uncouth swain', a spokesman for the flock, perhaps; at the disturbing opening of the poem the reader is dropped into the middle of unreconciled utterance, and such are the turns of thought and mood, that critics have sometimes sought relief from the demands of following that cathartic train of thought by explaining their suddenness away. So, for example, there has been a recent attempt to claim that the sudden consolation – 'Weep no more, woeful shepherds weep no more' (165) – is actually spoken by another voice than that of the singer (by Lycidas himself; there have also been claims for St

Michael).[9] But that sudden realisation must be attributed to the singer himself and it is symptomatic of Milton's dramatic method and of his analysis of the workings of Providence. The poem plays out in its assembled voices the full bewildering experience of anxiety and resolution, in which the very function of godly, liberal education seems to be at stake. In his struggle to come to terms with the death, the swain displays the immaturity of his own conception, hitting out at the way things are, being corrected, correcting himself, apportioning blame, constantly rethinking until understanding is finally given. The reader is forced to learn in the process of the poem. The effect might be said to be both educational, for those who have not shared the thoughts of true shepherds at this time, and therapeutic, for those who have. Thus the university itself, which should be made up of true shepherds, is galvanised and comforted by its son.

Modern readers tend to come to the poem with more knowledge of John Milton than of the institutions of the 1630s, and 'Lycidas' expresses such familiar personal themes of Milton that many have read the poem as more private than public in function. In particular critics have seized on the fear so vividly expressed in the Orpheus reference:

> What could the muse herself that Orpheus bore,
> The muse herself for her enchanting son
> Whom universal nature did lament,
> When by the rout that made the hideous roar,
> His gory visage down the stream was sent ...
> (58–62)

The university publishers allowed the voice of a *poet* in the meditations on the death of a scholar-minister. In the anxieties about Fame and being cut off by death before having done one's work the mind of the swain seems to have been imbued with a Miltonic sense of vocation. Perhaps Edward King may thought less heroically of his own vocation then this singer:

> Alas! What boots it with uncessant care
> To tend the homely slighted shepherd's trade,
> And strictly meditate the thankless muse,
> Were it not better done as others use,
> To sport with Amaryllis in the shade,

Or with the tangles of Neaera's hair?
Fame is the spur that the clear spirit doth raise
(That last infirmity of noble mind)
To scorn delight, and live laborious days;
But the fair guerdon when we hope to find,
And think to burst out into sudden blaze,
Comes the blind Fury with th'abhorred shears,
And slits the thin-spun life.

(64–76)

Milton challenges recognition of common purpose and, as I have said, those organising the university memorial volume evidently allowed the personal interests of a poet to be advertised within the high-minded meditations of the poem

For all the use of a *persona*, the self-presentational aspects of the poem are remarkable, its technique prefiguring some of the peculiarities of the presentation of the narrator in *Paradise Lost*. There is no epic which presents such a distinctive range of presences of the narrator as *Paradise Lost*, where the guiding voice is sometimes distant and objective, sometimes intrusive in emotive reaction or judgemental comment and, sometimes, as in the invocations, appears to speak more privately to its audience. Back in the Vacation Exercise, Milton had also dealt in artful candour and sought a spirit of understanding in his hearers; these rhetorical transactions are a recurrent feature of his writing.

More generally, the whole crisis and meditation of 1637 is defined – personal, communal, ecclesiastical, and political – and a sense of vocation is defined. The hortatory effects of this discourse can be related to the developments of the text of the Ludlow masque after its performance for general publication in 1637. There had already been various tensions between what Milton seems to have written before the performance in 1634, to judge from the witness of the early stages of the Trinity Manuscript text[10] and what was actually allowed by the organisers at Ludlow. In some ways, Milton had had his earnest instruction softened. For example, there had been a large deletion from the Haemony–shepherd lad allegory, toning down its preacherly effect.[11] There had also been an amusing compromise in the last episode of the action, concerning the dignity of the President's two sons. Milton had intended them merely to watch the actions of the Attendant Spirit and Sabrina, like the rest of the audience, after they had failed to complete the release of their sister from the chair, but the organisers at Ludlow, perhaps fearing offence at the powerlessness of the noble boys in the last action of the masque, made them share in the summoning of the river goddess.[12] For the published text Milton stuck to something like his original intentions and also reinforced his text in further instructional ways, to make it more hortatory. So, he extended the debate between the Lady and Comus (778–805), to allow the Lady a new passage of pious challenge concerning the mystery of godliness. He also extended the epilogue (999–1011), adding a new allegory about the differences between having one's mind on mere earthly festivals (like court masques) and their heavenly equivalents.[13] Thus both the Lady and the Attendant Spirit had been given more strident voices in a text which spoke in rather more hortatory fashion to the nation at large than it had to the assembled company at Ludlow. It was as if, once he had taken the decision to publish his masque text, Milton availed himself of the opportunity to speak out, with more of a prophetic licence, just as he had in 'Lycidas' at about the same time. The time 1637–8 begins to look like a time to speak out.

In his two major poems of the 1630s, then, Milton realised the occasions given to him as if Providence had furnished them as opportunities on which his full vocational purpose could be proved. Yet the earnestness of his inspirational office was elaborately hedged about with disclaimers that he had not sought print of his own volition, that his preferred mode of discourse was private, and that his preferred sphere at present was still studious retirement. There can be little doubt, though, that in all these years of tardy moving, he came to trust in a sense of his own convictions that he and only he would know when to speak. One cultivated readiness; an inner certainty prompted action. It was a formula calculated to build up tense doubts about the course of life, and the overmeasure of earnestness in the masque and 'Lycidas' makes it abundantly clear that one result of this regime was a bursting out of ambition in writing, when an occasion was accepted. There is a sense in which both texts are very distinctively larger than their occasions, revealing the depth of ambition in Milton's idea of the poet's office, as he wrote from the meditations of scholarly seclusion.

Milton himself may not have been unaware of the uncomfortable paradoxes of his position. There is an amusing instance in his correspondence with his old friend Alexander Gil, in early December 1634. Gil had sent him some Latin verses, as we now know, thanks to Leo Miller, a bawdy, witty epithalamium.[14] Milton repaid the compliment by sending a Greek offering of his own, together with a jocular explanatory letter, also in Latin (Y i 322–3), thanking his friend, explaining his own poem, and expressing the wish that they will bump into one another on Monday in the bookshops. The letter deals in a kind of candid, humourous self-presentation. Gil's hendacasyllabics were polished and charming or facetious (*lepidum*). Milton's Greek might be a bit rusty, therefore inferior in manner, but his subject is higher: he sends in return a version in heroic measure of Psalm 114 (CF 51) – David surpasses Gil in subject, as Gil surpasses Milton in art. Apart from the amusing balance or imbalance of the exchange, reflecting the characters of the senders, what is of interest also in Milton's gesture is his description of how he came to do the version of the Psalm. He did it last week '*nulla certe animi proposito, sed subito nescio quo impetu ante lucis exortum* (before daybreak, with no set purpose in mind for sure, but suddenly, upon some impulse or other)'. Through the casual manner we read characteristic advertisement of trust in the given impulse and of the meditation of high matters amidst studious retirement. The psalm, one of the same he had rendered in English at the age of fifteen, celebrates the unity of Israel in Egyptian bondage and remembers the miraculous power of God then evidenced for his chosen people. One does not translate without thinking of the import; neither does one expect Gil of all people, who had been punished by the government for his out-spoken political comment, to miss the resonance of the psalmist's words for the continuing cause of Reformation in England. Suburban peace and scholarly pleasure do not erase great causes from the mind in 1634; all the more, by the crisis of 1637, will the pastoral scholar–poet of 'Lycidas' show recognition of national themes demanding utterance. Reading in history gave ever sharper definition to the present, and the times, as 'Lycidas' also seems to say, were breaking in on pastoral calm.

Notes

1. Y i 318–21; see the manuscript drafts reproduced in *John Milton: Poems, reproduced in facsimile from the manuscript of Trinity College, Cambridge, with a transcript* (Scolar Press, 1972), ff. 6 and 7. Second draft only at LR i 262–5.
2. Evidence and argument concerning 'Arcades' bear a relationship to those in 'Milton's *Arcades*: Context, Form, and Function', *Renaissance Drama*, VIII (1977), pp. 245–74; *Milton's Aristocratic Entertainments*,

pp. 41–56; '*Arcades* in the Trinity Manuscript', *RES*, xxxvii (1986), 542–9.

3. The evidence concerning the presidential occasion for the Ludlow masque bears a relationship to that in 'The Chirk Castle Entertainment of 1634,' *MQ*, xi (1977), 76–84; *Aristocratic Entertainments* pp. 12–39; 'Presidential Travels and Instructive Augury in Milton's Ludlow Masque', in *Comus: Contexts* (*MQ*, xxi, 1987), 1–12.

4. 'The Shepherd, the Musician, and the Word', *JEGP*, lxxvii (1979), 522–44; *Aristocratic Entertainments*, pp. 104–31.

5. It was a two-part volume, the first of poems in Latin and Greek – *Justa Edouardo King naufrago* ... – and the second in English – *Obsequies to the memorie of Mr Edward King* ... (Cambridge, 1638). Milton's poem came last in the second part and in some ways formed a conclusion.

6. Something of the political and ecclesiastic context can be found in David Norbrook, *Poetry and Politics in the English Renaissance* (London: Routledge and Kegan Paul, 1985), pp. 275–85.

7. See 'Milton and the Idolatrous Consort', *Criticism*, 35 (1993), 429–30.

8. See 'The Death of Righteous Men: Prophetic Gesture in Vaughan's "Daphnis" and Milton's "Lycidas"', *George Herbert Journal*, 7 (1983–4), 1–24.

9. This particular idea is that of William G. Madsen, *From Shadowy Types to Truth: Studies in Milton's Symbolism* (New Haven: Yale University Press, 1968), p. 13.

10. The fullest comparison of the versions is in *John Milton: A Maske, the Earlier Versions*, ed. S. E. Sprott (Toronto, 1973).

11. The Bridgewater manuscript (a presentation copy probably of the performance version) omits lines 631–6. The offence was probably in the 'dull swain' of 633. On this and the following matters, see *Aristocratic Entertainments*, pp. 132–52.

12. In the Bridgewater Manuscript the summoning verses (866–87) are shared between the Spirit and the two boys.

13. In the published version the last part of the Lady's final speech (778, from 'Shall I go on?' to 798 is an addition; the extension to the epilogue is 996–1010).

14. Leo Miller, 'On some of the Verses by Alexander Gil which John Milton Read', *MQ*, 24 (1990), 22–5.

4

Italy, Politics, and the Voice of Authority

It was not uncommon for well-born young Englishmen of the time to have a spell abroad, usually in France, perhaps in Paris or at the Protestant college at Saumur, sometimes further afield, but not many scriveners' sons went on a tour to Italy. In early 1638 John Milton, gentleman–scholar, now twenty-nine, was preparing to go to Italy and Greece, seats of ancient learning. Henry Lawes helped procure a passport; experienced travellers, like old Sir Henry Wotton, at Eton College, were consulted; and contacts were made. With a manservant, presumably, Milton set off across the Channel at the beginning of May. In Paris, where he stayed for a short time in mid-May, and where he took further advice over his travel plans, Milton met one of the joint ambassadors to France, John Scudamore, Lord Dromore, and through him the famous Dutch scholar Hugo Grotius. His exhilerating contact with continental men of learning had begun.

From Paris he went south to Nice, took a boat to Genoa, and thence to Leghorn. In June in Diodati's Tuscany he travelled by Pisa to arrive in Florence probably in late July and found in the city of Dante and Petrarch a cultured society he would never forget. He was to spend two months there, August and September, in 1638, and two further months, March and April, in 1639. Why did England have no such societies of polite learning as the academies of Florence? And how graciously he was received there. But with these gratifying memories Florence also gave him another instance, to which he would revert in later writings, of something to be deplored: outside the city lived the aged Galileo, now blind, but a symbol of liberated learning and a victim of Counter-Reformation censorship. To the serious young Englishmen, championing the liberation of minds in the cultivated Reformation state, Italy presented a severe paradox of enlightenment and bondage.

In his references to his Italian experience Milton was careful to indicate that he travelled to observe and widen his experience rather than to learn new principles. 'I change my sky but not my mind, when I cross the seas', he wrote, modifying a tag from Horace, in the autograph book of a Genevan nobleman, as he emerged into Protestant parts.[1] This was still John Milton Englishman. But there was no denying that the arts flourished better in the southern climes.

We know that he listened to and collected music whilst in Italy, and as an outsider he observed societies. Our chief documentary records, however, concern his relationships with scholars or cultivated men, from whom, or to whom, letters or poems survive. Milton preserved these documents as an index of the way in which he was welcomed by educated men in the Italian cities. As far as Florence is concerned, most of his contacts seem to have revolved around two academies, the Svogliati and the Apatisti.

There was Agostino Coltellini, lawyer, linguist, and founder of the Apatisti, a champion of Dante and the Tuscan language; Carlo Dati, a personable, sociable young man of eighteen who had wide interests including science (he had studied with Galileo), acted as secretary to the Apatisti, and who wrote a poem and subsequent letters to Milton; Valerio Chimentelli, a priest, and Benedetto Bonmatthei, an older scholar–priest, soon to complete his great dictionary of the Tuscan dialect (Milton asked him to include a guide to pronunciation for foreigners}; Benedetto Fioretti, president of the Apatisti, critic, and grammarian; Antonio Francini, who wrote a poem to Milton; the wealthy and influential Jacopo Gaddi, head of the Svogliati, collector of art treasures and plants and student of philosophy, theology, and poetry, who hosted his academy in his rich houses; Vincenzo Galileo, son of the astronomer; Antonio Maletesti, a witty, humourous poet who also presented verses to Milton. In these academies men read papers and poetry, often as frequently as each week. These were humanists who celebrated reason; they were often also pious men, and they showed a pride in the culture and language of Tuscany. From such a learned social group Milton must have hoped that educated elites were possible. The national dimension was important. Writing to Bonmatthei, Milton suggested that the greatness of a nation went together with a proud discipline in its language; the observation also pointed to the English to which he must dedicate himself (Y i 328–32; LR i 419).

Those admitted to the academies were expected to give proof of their abilities. We know that Milton recited from memory to the Svogliati an old composition in Latin hexameters. In their tributes to him Francini and Dati comment on his linguistic skill, his learning, and his memory. In this company, in fact, he had promise of what he wished to be, an English man of letters on the European stage.[2]

After Florence came Siena, but Rome was Milton's next major stay in October and November of 1638 and again in January and February of 1639. His account, in the *Second Defence*, does not mention St Peter's but says he viewed the famous antiquities and had, as before, the company of 'learned and ingenious men' (Y iv 618). Here he befriended the young scholar Alessandro Cherubini, here (probably) someone called Selvaggi wrote him a complimentary couplet;[3] and here a Giovanni Salzilli wrote him an epigram, in which Milton of England ranked above Homer, Virgil, and Tasso. When Salzilli was ill, Milton repaid the compliment by wishing him health in 'limping' Latin verses, scazontics (CF 58).

Another subject of verses written in Rome, probably in the second stay, was the famous singer Leonora Baroni. It was the fashion in Rome to write verses in praise of her. Milton's three Latin epigrams (CF 55–7) employ the expected playful extravagances: in the first she is literally divine, in the second she would have cured Tasso of his madness, and in the third Parthenope is still alive. These poems have a further self-presentational aspect: in the second and the third Milton studiously displays a knowledge of things Italian.

On his second stay, also, Milton visited the famous librarian of the Vatican, Lucas Holstenius, and was shown the treasures there. Holstenius presented him with two books, Greek texts he had edited, and even asked him to copy a manuscript for him when he returned to Florence. Through Holstenius, Milton was introduced to Cardinal Barberini, prime minister of Rome and chief counsellor to the Pope. Barberini treated Milton with great courtesy, both at a musical entertainment in the Casa Barberini, to which Milton had been invited, and then in a private audience the next day. In such circles Milton saw princely patronage of the arts far beyond that known in Protestant England. Memories of Rome may well have contributed to the paradoxical picture of the arts charming the senses of fallen angels in the first two books of *Paradise Lost* (i 710–98; ii 506–67).

In December 1638 Milton was staying in Naples, in the south, then in Spanish control. Here too he met with notable patronage, for he was befriended by the celebrated, rich nobleman, Giovanni

Battista Manso, founder of the Humoristi academy, erstwhile patron of the poet Marino, and earlier, of the great Tasso. Tasso had addressed *De Amicitia* to him; Manso had written Tasso's biography, and, according to Milton, Marino's. Thus, the young Englishman tracked great figures of the Italian literary world.

Manso furnished Milton not only with gifts (probably of two books) but also with a revealing distich (perhaps written in one of the books) paying tribute to his graces and to his proud principle of being frank, when asked, about religion: '*Ut mens, forma, decor, facies, mos, si pietas sic, / Non Anglus, verum hercle Angelus ipse fores*: If to your mind, form, elegance, features and manners your religion were matched, I swear you would be not an Angle but a very angel.'[4] When Milton had this with other tributes from his Italian acquaintance printed at the head of his Italian and Latin verses in 1645, he may have been as proud of the friendly rebuke as the compliment: one could be a knight for one's country's religion. And in the long poem of thanks he gave Manso, the earliest confession we have of his ambition to write an epic on an Arthurian theme, there is patriotism fully fledged in literary plans. In *Mansus* (CF 59) Milton casts himself in the line of the great epic poets and, like the social Virgil of the eclogues, he has friendship and patronage for a theme: Manso is friend, like Gallus, and patron, like Maecenas, to poets. This fluent, easy Latin poem, is the most important literary monument of the Italian tour.

The opening of the poem celebrates Manso's record of support to Italian poets. Though an Englishman 'poorly nourished' in poetry under northern skies, Milton writes in thanks on behalf of Poetry and History, Apollo and Clio, and claims that right, because Britain, too, has its traditions of poetry, back to the Druids. For his support of Tasso and Marino, poets in trouble, the marquis will share in their fame. Only those specially favoured of the gods are permitted to befriend great poets; perhaps that is why he remains so sprightly in old age. Then, as to a friend, Milton confesses his desire to find such a friend in England, if he should succeed in his great plans for an English epic about the fabulous times of King Arthur. Known for his courage in war as well as devotion to literature, Manso would appreciate that poem, for it would be about a great-hearted fellowship of knights fighting the tyranny of invasion. Nevertheless, even as he candidly expresses his ambition, Milton gracefully acknowledges that, with him, not as with Manso, all is yet to do: the final vision (78–100) is fraught with ifs and whens – when, having written his British epic, he achieves old age, then perhaps some friend would do as Manso did for Marino, give him due rites, even have an effigy made, like the bronze of the Italian poet in Manso's house; then perhaps John Milton too will lie in peace of spirit; then perhaps even – 'if one can be sure of these things and if rewards do really lie in store for the righteous in heaven' – the spirit of John Milton will go to some corner of that distant world and look down upon the doings of men, *'tota mente serenum / Ridens* – with my whole mind serenely smiling', *'Et simul aethereo plaudam mihi laetus Olympo* – and with pleasure I shall applaud myself on ethereal Olympus.' In this mixture of candour and humorous self-puncturing Horatian irony has crept into the singing of the Virgilian heavens. The self-gratulation, as has been suggested (VC i 281), echoes the Athenian speaker of Horace's first satire (I i 66), who can never have riches enough – *at mihi plaudo.* Critics have sometimes thought the vision of the poet's death and immortality intrusive or indicative that he had recently heard of the death of his bosom friend Charles Diodati, but these thoughts seem intrusive to a reading of the poem, which has an internal logic. What might be recognised is the candid cultivated manner. When would Milton ever be able to write such to an *English* nobleman?

We do not know why Milton abandoned earlier plans to continue to Sicily and Greece. Later he was to speak of his conscience about affairs in England and concern about the political situation. After his second stays in Rome and Florence (from which he evidently made a pilgrimage to Diodati's Lucca), he set out north again in April 1639 and took in Bologna and Ferrara, briefly, then Venice, for about a month. Here he shipped home books he had collected, especially much of the best contemporary Italian music. Then he went through Verona and Milan, and over the Alps and to Protestant Geneva, before the end of May. There he would have seen the famous theologian, Giovanni Diodati, uncle to his friend Charles. Perhaps it was here that he learned of Charles' death the previous August. Then he travelled home through France. It is usually assumed that he was back some time in July, possibly August. Though he spoke of his tour as for his pleasure, Milton had approached it with characteristic thoroughness of purpose. He could hardly have made more of his chances, especially with regard to learning and the arts. For his pleasure he had received, beyond the usual benefits of travel, a wealth of congenial, learned company such as he would never encounter in such a short space again. Beyond that, he seems to have come home with a new sense of confidence, a greater sense of his own purposes, and with his sense of Protestant Englishness confirmed.

And he had decided to try to write a British epic. Setting up in London, at first in rented accommodation in St Bride's churchyard near Fleet Street, he began making notes in his Commonplace Book on early British history. It was to be in *Epitaphium Damonis* (CF 60), his elegy for Charles Diodati written no earlier than the Autumn of 1639, that he explicitly mentioned having tried to make a start on an Arthurian epic, some eleven days before. Like 'Lycidas', his other pastoral elegy, the *epitaphium* confides ambitions, but whereas the memorial volume for King provided an institutional occasion, sharing matters of vocation with the university, this Latin poem for Diodati purports to be private in mode, confiding aspirations to the dead friend as he had often done in life. The abortive beginning, like verse tributes he had brought back from Italy, would have been shown to Charles had he been there. There would have been much to tell.

Epitaphium Damonis has a further self-presentational purpose. Milton had copies printed privately to give to friends and suitable parties, and we know that he sent at least one to Italy (P 187). The memorial for his friend of Tuscan family would report back to the Tuscan academicians, keeping hold of that literary world. It might interest the Florentines, to hear that he had acted on the matter of making a vernacular epic.

The poem is thus private and confessional and also maintains an interest in presenting a learnedly sociable front, to fellow 'shepherds' (*pastores*). Shepherds are not as in 'Lycidas' those marked out by Christian vocations of teaching so much as the society of friends and literati. Pictures of friendship afforded by the conventions of pastoral eclogue are well suited to subject and audience. In a poem of wide allusion, for which Theocritus i (with Theocritus xiii and the EPITAPHIOS BIONOS) is mentioned as ultimate model, seventy echoes of Virgilian eclogue have been noted. English Milton puts himself beside Roman Virgil in imitation.

The singer's sense of 'Damon' is fully given in a progression coming ever closer to the realisation of pain. From line 19 onwards there is a catalogue of virtues to commemorate: fidelity to Protestant religion, 'just' life, cultivation of learning, finally, friend to a poet. Who will now be the companion of the singer in work and at play? Then:

Pectora cui credam? quis me lenire docebit
Mordaces curas, quis longam fallere noctem
Dulcibus alloquiis ...

(45–8)

To whom shall I open my heart? Who will teach me to soften /
eating cares, who will beguile the long night / with pleasant
chatter – ?

Laughter, 'Attic wit', and 'cultured jokes' are remembered and set
against the present melancholy of the grieving singer. Other
companions try to charm his sadness away, but none compensates
for Damon. Man alone amongst the creatures seems to suffer this
agony of soul companionship: 'it is hard for a man to find one
kindred spirit amongst thousands of his fellows' (108), harder still to
have that one removed by Fate.

Accordingly, the refrain shows the singer neglecting his duties, at
odds with Providence: *'Ite domum impasti, domino iam non vacat, agni*
– Go home unfed, lambs, your master has no time for you now.' Yet
there are reassurances that the melancholic singer is at base a
sociable being, a balanced and even popular man: not only do
young friends come to comfort him, but he has enough poise to give
wry characterisations of them – there is Mopsus, for example, who
knows about the stars and the language of birds, who therefore
diagnoses malign heavenly influence, or Aegle, Baucis' daughter,
who in a reminiscence of Horace is *'Docta modus, citharaeque sciens,*
sed perdita fastu – Instructed in music, expert with the lute, but
ruined by scorn' (89). The poet presents himself as civilising and
seeking his cultivated constituency.

It used to be complained that despite its binding refrain *Epitaphium*
Damonis seems to 'ramble', whereas 'Lycidas' has an evident progression, to do with the questioning of Providence (VC i 284–97). It is
true that the Latin poem does not question Providence so directly, but it
shares with the English poem the depiction of a singer being
unreconciled, then suddenly, as if providentially, coming to recon-
cilation at the end. Its refrain represents both a desolate cry and a state
of mind which must be removed. Shepherds must look after their
sheep, having continuing responsibilities. The recalling of Damon, in
the first half of the poem, has led to an indictment of Providence, that
man alone has been created unsatisfactorily, with regard to companionship and as the singer complains, he casts about, rather as in 'Lycidas',

for things to blame. Most of all, he wishes to blame himself, for enjoying himself abroad when Damon died. Yet how can he regret coming to know Diodati's own countrymen? He portrays the Tuscan academicians, as he would have done to his friend in life, and in fact that literary companionship in Italy had often brought Diodati's earlier companionship to mind. It is in the context of this unresolved conflict, between whether to celebrate and recount the Italian journey, or whether to regret it in the circumstances of Diodati's death, that the rehearsal of his recent literary experiences and plans is made. He wishes to tell Damon of his Arthurian project, yet feels he is being *turgidulus*, big-headed, in doing so, yet the recounting of these plans is given with such candour as to suggest that friendship has not died, and with such excitement, that there is a prospect of his pastoral pipe being given over, as he matures like Virgil to the epic task of his career. He is proud of his desire to serve an English audience.

All this makes the refrain, given for the last time in line 179, sound out of tune with the surrounding verse. There is to be some breaking of the melancholy spell, but it is not clear how this reconcilication will be achieved. The ultimate 'turn' in the poem occurs, fittingly, in a description of literary gifts, as the singer runs on to tell of the wonderful friendship of Manso in Naples and of the gift of the two 'cups' (books of poetry), which he then begins to describe. Amongst the subjects treated in these poems are religious themes, and it is when the celestial Cupid is being described, the love that fills the minds of the spiritual elect that the complaint is finally lifted and consolation suddenly comes: '*Tu quoque in his* (198) – You too are among the gods.' It seems to mean both that reconciliation with Providence has been imitated within the span of the poem, as in 'Lycidas', and also that the way forward is to be found in literature itself. Where literature seemed at first a distraction from the occasion, it now seems an answer. That is apt in commemoration of a literary friendship. Providence can instruct through literature itself, even in moments of sudden realisation; future literary projects will also form a memorial to his dearest literary friend. This other friends will understand. Publication is more than a memorial: it is an act of faith that such other friends exist.

If by now Milton had a conviction that his future might be bound up with writing – 'I might perhaps leave something so written to after-times, as they should not willingly let it die' – then the means to that end, the preparation for the conviction of what and when to write, would be study itself – 'by labour and intent study (which I take to be my portion in this life)' – as he was to put it in *The Reason of Church Government* in 1641 (Y i 810). Thoughts of the priesthood had probably receded by the time of 'Lycidas', before he left for Italy; if there were any vestiges of hope for an ecclesiastical career, they would have been dispelled by what he found when he returned to England, Laud's stiff-necked attempt to turn highchurchmanship from a policy into a principle' in the Canons of May 1640 and the fact that the endeavour to impose episcopal conformity on Scotland had resulted in actual war within the Protestant union. With the king's calling of the Long Parliament in November, to pay for the Scottish war, 1640 was to match 1637 as a time of popular outcry especially in London against tyranny in the church. What he would perceive as Protestant Britain's need for guidance from writings supported by proper historical research would draw Milton, by 1641, into the publication of political prose.

Such occasions were to be met as Providence provided them, and other kinds of use could immediately be made of study. He could teach, for he had strong views about education, and private pupils in his own house could perhaps share in the discipline of his studious life without destroying his own objectives. Accumulating several pupils – his young nephews John and Edward Phillips (his sister's children), and one gathers several other young gentlemen – during the early 1640s, and needing quiet for reading and room for books, he moved, probably in 1640, to a good-sized house of his own in Aldersgate. A glimpse of study in this house can be had from Edward Phillips' life of his uncle (1694). This account has apologetic colouring and runs together the experience of some years, but is vivid in its outlines. First, for the pupils:

> the many Authors both of Latin and Greek, which through his excellent judgment and way of Teaching, far above the Pedantry of common publick Schools (where such Authors are scarce heard of) were run over within no greater compass of time, then from Ten to Fifteen or Sixteen Years of Age, Of the Latin the four Grand Authors, De Re Rustica, Cato, Varro, Columella, and Palladius; Cornelius Celsus, an Ancient Physician of the Romans; a great part of Pliny's Natural History, Vitruvius his Architecture, Frontinus his Stratagems, with the two Egregious Poets, Lucretius, and Manilius. Of the Greek; Hesiod, a Poet equal with

[contemporary with] Homer; Aratus his Phænomena, and Diosemeia, Dionysius Afer de situ Orbis, Oppian's Cynegeticks & Halieuticks. Quintus Calaber his Poem of the Trojan War, continued from Homer; Apollonius Rhodius his Argonuticks, and in Prose, Plutarch's Placita Philosophorum & PERI PAIDON AGOGIAS, Geminus' Astronomy; Xenophon's Cyri Institutio & Anabasis; Aelians Tackticks and Polyænus his Warlike Stratagems; thus by teaching he in some measure increased his own knowledge, having the reading of all these Authors as it were by Proxy. ... Nor did the time thus Studiously imployed in conquering the Greek and Latin Tongues, hinder the attaining to the chief Oriental Languages, viz. The Hebrew, Caldee and Syriac, so far as to go through the Pentateuch, or Five Books of Moses in Hebrew, to make a good entrance into the Targum or Chaldee Paraphrase, and to understand several Chapters of St. Matthew in the Syriac Testament, besides an Introduction into several Arts and Sciences, by Reading Urstisius his Arithmetick, Riffs Geometry, Petiscus his Trigonometry, Joannes de Sacro Bosco de Sphæra; and into the Italian and French Tongues, by reading in Italian, Giovan Villani's History of the Transactions between several petty States of Italy; and in French a great part of Pierre Davity, the famous Geographer of France in his time. The Sunday's work was for the most part the Reading each day a Chapter of the Greek Testament, and hearing his Learned Exposition upon the same, (and how this savoured of Atheism in him, I leave to the courteous Backbiter to judge). The next work after this, was the writing from his own dictation, some part, from time to time, of a Tractate which he thought fit to collect from the ablest of Divines, who had written of that Subject; Amesius, Wollebius, &c. viz. A perfect System of Divinity, of which more hereafter. Now persons so far Manuducted into the highest paths of Literature both Divine and Human, had they received his documents [instructions] with the same Acuteness of Wit and Apprehension, the same Industry, Alacrity, and Thirst after Knowledge, as the Instructor was indued with, what Prodigies of Wit and Learning might they have proved! the Scholars might in some degree have come near to the equalling of the Master   (D 60–1)

The breadth of reading prescribed for his young pupils signals not just the thoroughness of Milton's ideas of education but also a determination to use the languages as tools with which to cultivate the mind with useful knowledge, not to deploy in abstract scholastic exercises. His ideas of a practical, liberal method were later to be published, in 1644, in the tractate *Of Education* (below, p. 94). A demythologiser, a sifter of authorities, he was to work out his own answers in the matter of education, as Phillips reports him doing with a system of divinity (presumably related to the work which was continued in the 1650s; see below, p. 139), and he revised but left unpublished at his death, *De Doctrina Christiana*. Phillips' account also expresses awe at the single-minded order of his uncle's life not just as a teacher but also in his own work, 'perpetually busied in his own Laborious Undertakings of the Book or Pen'. Parker (194) tries to give an idea of the disciplined rhythm of life in that house, conjecturing from evidence in *Of Education* and *An Apology* (1642): reading from five or six in the morning, until the mind was saturated; some exercise or perhaps music around lunchtime, to set the mind back in receptive frame; more bookwork in the afternoons; a plain supper; and expounding scripture until bedtime. When Milton himself talks of such a regime, he insists upon its discipline not just as heroic but also as the foundation of rational liberty: so he says, of mornings

> in winter often ere the sound of any bell awake men to labour... in Summer as oft with the Bird that first rouses ... to read good Authors, or cause them to be read, till the attention bee weary, or memory have his full fraught. Then with usefull and generous labours preserving the bodies health, and hardinesse; to render lightsome, cleare, and not lumpish obedience to the minde, to the cause of religion, and our Countries liberty, when it shall require firme hearts in sound bodies to stand and cover their stations   (Y i 885)

As far as Milton's own reading in this period is concerned, the Commonplace Book gives evidence of a very large programme during the 1640s and, as far as one can tell from handwriting and circumstantial evidence, the great bulk of his systematic reading during the first two years or so after the return from Italy was in English history, gathered under headings which suggest more than searching suitable subjects for an epic. History was being scanned for its lessons and to establish reference points in political discourse. This reading in early English history up to the time of the Norman Conquest would also eventually find use in Milton's *History of Britain*, a work begun in the 1640s, though apparently picked up again in the 1650s and finally revised in the Restoration and published in 1670. Part of Milton's purpose in this work seems to have been to test out facile interpretations of the early stages of British history; another part to furnish warning examples of calamities befalling nations in degenerate, ill-disciplined times.

The Trinity Manuscript furnishes evidence that he was trying other literary plans. In seven fascinating, closely written pages hard to date exactly but of the early 1640s Milton recorded notes for possible tragic dramas, listing many subjects from the Old Testament and early British history, with a few from New Testament or Scottish subjects. Some of these are drafted as plans, with indications of *dramatis personae* or even five acts: 'Paradise Lost'; 'Abram from Morea, or Isack redeemed'; 'Baptistes' (about John the Baptist); 'Sodom' (with the title suggested of 'Cupid's funeral pile'), and 'Adam unparadiz'd'. Others from the Old Testament stand as promising titles only: 'Dinah'; 'Elias in the mount'; 'Gideon Idoloclastes', and so on. British subjects and Scottish subjects more often stand as indications of a subject without a title, though occasionally there is a longer note:

> A Heroicall Poem may be founded somewhere in Alfreds reigne. especially at his issuing out of Edelingsey on the Danes, whose actions are wel like those of Ulysses

The last suggestion is for 'Christus patiens', Christ suffering, beginning in the garden of Gethsemane and 'the rest by message & chorus. his agony may receav noble expressions'.[5]

It is evident that the majority of these projects were conceived in the mode of Greek tragedy though mediated through the example of the great symbolic dramas of seventeenth-century Europe. As with the Arthurian epic, the aim would be to give English literature tragedies to match the best abroad, especially perhaps the Counter-Reformation. Some of the stories chosen would, like the *History*, teach the nation warning lessons. Both Jewish and British history furnished ample examples of the falling away of the national spirit into self-inflicted bondage. Here are the beginnings of plans for a drama such as *Samson Agonistes*; for a large work on the subject of fall, though that would develop from a tragedy to an epic around a tragic subject, and for a large poem on the life of Christ, though the scene of that would shift from the garden to the wilderness. These large projects would be finished only in old age.

Some of Milton's new-won knowledge of early British history found immediate practical use in 1641 in the developing pamphlet war about the church, precipitated by the Long Parliament. Under-estimating the strength of opposition, Bishop Joseph Hall had tried to counter the anti-episcopal feeling in Parliament by issuing in January his relatively moderate tract, *A Humble Remonstrance to the High Court of Parliament*. A notable riposte came from a group of Presbyterian divines using the pseudonym SMECTYMNUUS, from the initials of the participants: Stephen Marshall, Edmund Calamy, Thomas Young, Matthew Newcomen, and William Spurstow. Of these the most senior was Milton's old mentor Young, although the most vigorous organiser may have been Marshall. This book, finished in late March, carried an unsigned postscript, giving instances from English chroniclers of how bishops had hindered the crown and tyrannised liberty of conscience. It is often assumed, though with no certain proof, that Milton supplied this historical support, so similar is the evidence to what he would use in *Of Reformation* and had already collected in his Commonplace Book.

Of Reformation (Y i 517–617) is Milton's first authenticated contribution to the pamphlet war about prelacy. This tract, far more artful and less chaotic than was once thought, is designed both to reason and to move. It seeks to reinforce radical determination, whilst distinguishing true evidence from false in the great argument for Reformation. The tract was probably published in May 1641 at a time of excitement but uncertainty as to how far Parliament would prosecute its grievances. At this stage Milton favoured a Presbyterian church.

Beginning on the keynote of liberty, Parliament had seen Prynne, Burton and Bastwick released and returned in triumph to London, before Christmas; on 11 December received the Root and Branch petition, signed by 15,000 Londoners, for the abolition of episcopacy; declared Laud's Canons as void, by 16 December; moved to convict Strafford of high treason, in November, and seen him executed by 12 May; moved to impeach Laud in December and had him in prison awaiting his trial by the end of February 1641; and had set up a committee to consider the London Petition together with the more moderate *Minister's Petition* on 23 January. On 27 May Dering was to introduce a bill for Root and Branch.

Presumably Milton's tract comes soon before, as an encouragement to Parliament to continue its work of Reformation.

Milton's opening rouses the spirit of Reformation, galvanising his reader to see a subject of tragedy and consolation:

> I do not know of any thing more worthy to take up the whole passion of pitty, on the one side, and joy on the other: then to consider first, the foule and sudden corruption, and then after many a tedious age, the long-deferr'd, but much more wonderfull and happy reformation of the Church in these latter times.   (519)

England, which once led the way, now betrays the cause of Reformation:

> The pleasing pursuit of these thoughts hath oft-times led mee into a serious question and debatement with my selfe, how it should come to passe that England (having had this grace and honour from GOD to bee the first that should set up a Standard for the recovery of lost Truth, and blow the first Evangelick Trumpet to the Nations ... should now be last   (525)

Beginning with Wycliffe, can it be that England should end with the idolatrous formalism and secular richness of Laudianism?

The ending of the tract is equally emotive. It consists of a great prayer and call for judgement, delivered prophet-like, or as in the denunciations of the pulpit; or, to put it another way, a renewal of the voice of St Peter in 'Lycidas'. This peroration is also stuffed with reminders of England's providential past: the nation's deliverances from the Armada and from the Gunpowder plot, after the five invasions of its impetuous earlier history. England contemplates the possibility of being able to offer thanksgiving for final deliverance from tyranny and, if it is not lukewarm, should wish hellish judgement, of becoming 'most underfoot and downe-trodden Vassals of Perdition' (617), on the lordly prelates who stand in the way. So much for Laud and those under him.

The emotive aspects of the tracts are important. Milton brought to his polemical prose all the resources taught in the ancient rhetorics of how to move minds by variety of performance, including the making of lively images, the inclusion of invective to relieve dullness, even the adoption of the bearing of an actor or the tragedian's voice. Such practice, preserved in Renaissance teaching and related to biblical example, had also been assimilated to the kind of Christian rhetoric used by puritan writers in tract or sermon. The affective design of these tracts should no more be underestimated than that of *Paradise Lost*. But *Of Reformation* also depends on an 'orderly', rational exposition of 'the causes that hitherto have hindered' true Reformation in Britain because of false discipline in the church. Like others before him, though with greater scholarly research, Milton divides his analyses of these hindering causes into those affecting 'our Fore-Fathers dayes' and those 'into our Times' (528). The first are divided between the reigns of Henry VII, Edward VI, and Elizabeth; the latter being divided into the false teachings of three groups: antiquarians, libertines, and politicians. Each of these divisions is further subdivided and there are sections of refutation. The method is of logical disposition within a framework laid down in rhetorical practice.

In the historical evidence he adduces Milton repeats some familiar radical ideas, but he is not content to use historical evidence uncritically. He sees political conditions in the reigns of Henry, Edward, and Elizabeth as inimical to proper reformation in the church and dispels easy notions of ideal conditions in the primitive church. Many including his Smectymnuan colleagues characterised the reign of Constantine as a golden age for the true church. On the contrary, Milton had learned from his research, it might be more accurate to trace to that emperor many of the most fundamental problems of the church, for Constantine it was who had invested it with the secular riches which had plagued it ever since. He knew also from his careful study of the early Fathers, that primitive doctrine had not been pure. As for the English church, he would not allow the popular kind of martyrology encouraged by Foxe to go unsifted either; writing against bishops, he challenged Cranmer, Latimer, and Ridley as true pastoral examples.

This is the tract of the scholar, one who searched whatever the current opinions to 'vindicate the spotlesse Truth from an igno-minious bondage' (Y i 535). In a sense it is like 'Lycidas' a university work, though seeking to move a Parliament, showing how learning can come to serve the state at a crucial time. We should perhaps not be so sure as older scholars seem to have been, when they blamed *Of Reformation* for bad structure, that Milton first wrote it in the first months of 1641 and then added passages near the end of Book II, to react against *The Humble Petition of the University of Oxford, in Behalf of Episcopacy and Cathedrals*, a tract of 24 April. Milton allows this tract to precipitate something like a crisis in the whole rhetorical shaping of the work: 'Sir would you know what the remonstrance of these men would have, what their Petition imply's? ... Can this bee granted them unlesse GOD have smitten us with frensie from above, and with a dazling giddinesse at noon day? ...' Thereafter comes a turning to Grace, for clarification:

> O Sir, I doe now feele my self in wrapt on the sodaine into those mazes and Labyrinths of dreadfull and hideous thoughts that which way to get out ... I know not, unlesse I turne mine eyes, and with your help lift up my hands to that Eternall and Propitious Throne.   (613)

As well as showing how Milton used the address to a friend rhetorically, like a preacher, to promote kinship of feeling through creating a kind of intimacy, this suggests that he had saved up to last the adversary closest to himself. Antiquarians and politicians of the present age had long been obscuring the truth for their own ends; now one of the universities used its learning for the wrong side. No wonder that the son of Cambridge, intended for a pastor, should respond, with the help of Providence itself.

In June 1641 Milton allowed himself to be drawn further into contention against the bishops. Towards the end of May, about the time that a bill was being introduced in parliament to abolish episcopacy, the establishment wheeled out in something of a hurry the venerable, much-respected, rather puritan James Ussher, Archbishop of Armagh (1581–1656), to defend the ecclesiastical order of which he was a noted part. In this sixteen-page pamphlet, *The Judgement of Doctor Rainoldes touching the originall of Episcopacy, more largely confirmed out of Antiquity by James, Archbishop of Armagh.*, Ussher reprinted a celebrated Elizabethan tract by the influential John Reynolds (or Rainolds; 1549–1607) and added a section of new materials supporting episcopacy out of the Fathers of the church. To this 'antiquarian' John Milton rose to reply: close reading of early church history showed only a decline from apostolic purity, certainly little in the way of a reliable witness of an episcopal hierarchy in apostolic times. To all intents and purposes the words presbyter and bishop meant the same.

Milton's *Of Prelatical Episcopacy* (Y i 624–52) sets out to establish 'first the insufficiency, next the inconvenience, and lastly the impiety of these gay [specious] testimonies [i.e. of the Fathers], that their great Doctors would bring them to dote on' (627). In fact the great bulk of his tract is about 'insufficiency' – the unreliability of the evidence and the dubious nature of the witnesses. Accordingly the piece is mainly one of mocking of false authority, of the 'undigested heap, and frie of Authors, which they call Antiquity' (626) and his style has all the colloquial, satirical edge allowed by authorities on rhetoric. He sometimes writes as if he were facing the spectres of the Fathers in live debate: 'Tertullian accosts us next (for Polycrates hath had his answer) ...' (644) Milton gave himself the same kind of freedom that he had enjoyed in college debate.

Such freedom, however, pales before the zealous mockery of his next attempt to influence Parliament in the matter of the bishops, his *Animadversions upon the Remonstrants Defence against Smectymnuus* (Y i 661–735) of the dogdays of July. This was written to support his Presbyterian allies in their pamphlet war with Hall. Specifically it was a blow-by-blow riposte to Hall's *Defence of the Humble Remonstrance against the frivolous and false exceptions of Smectymnuus*, first published in April.

Milton's *Animadversions* takes the form of a dialogue. He prints with page references about one hundred and fifty of Hall's statements, then seeks to ridicule them and their author by every means. It is intended as formalised personal humiliation. In his preface he justifies his 'rougher accent' by scriptural example: Christian rhetoric recognised a zealous laughter, to shake the proudly foolish or to free the minds of men from 'subtile dissimulations'. In *Paradise Lost* scornful corrective laughter will also be allowed, where levity will not.

Milton took his celebrated opponent back to grammar school, questioning the standard of his language and the quality of his thought and argument. He also convicted him, beyond stupidity, of being a bad man, or at least a bad priest, concerned with 'superiority, pride, ease and the belly' (665). Though there are precedents for this kind of method in the Elizabethan and Jacobean periods, critics have tended either to lament it as a descent into unproductive unpleasantness, as if Milton had been drawn unwisely to these means, or to explain it away as consonant with puritan theories about the functions of zealous denunciation. However, the distinctively different form of *Animadversions* may also be explained as deriving from the specifics of the occasion.

Milton squared up to Hall as a notable opponent and chose his means, having taken careful measure of his man. The bishop had himself been a satirist. What is more, as has been pointed out, he had used a similar (and already familiar) method of refutation, on a similar subject, writing against Separatists in Amsterdam in 1608. What finer ironic way of seeking to silence the chief establishment voice than by turning the tables on him and using a method which Hall himself had used to try to silence anti-espiscopal dissent? This was 'to send home his haughtinesse well bespurted with his owne holy-water' (Preface: 662).

But *Animadversions* is also varied in texture. The speeches of the answering voice include long passages written in a rousing style, especially towards the end of the work. These passages descant on blind regard for the Fathers (698–70); the idea of a 'true bishop' (702–3); previous reformations in Britain (703–7); the word presby-ter (707–9); ordination and the concept of 'true Evangelicall jurisdic-tion or discipline' (713–17); and the difference between true and false pastors (717–24), ending with a quotation from Spenser's 'May' eclogue from *The Shepheardes Calendar*. It seems to have been an element of design to include amongst quick-fire mocking answers, especially towards the end, a number of passages which draw minds to remembrance of key reforming ideas and ideals, allowing an exhorting mode more and more to compete with the satirical, and these passages give as impassioned expression to their familiar themes as any amongst the prose tracts. The mind is dis-abused of false impressions, then supplied with truer matter. Both modes are functions of zealous instruction. The end of the passage about ordination and jurisdiction makes plain where he is looking for appropriate action, to Parliament, where the fight against church hierarchy is currently in hand.

Parliament was the ultimate audience for his next tract, *The Reason of Church Government* (Y i 746–861), written probably in the autumn and early winter of 1642, finished by the beginning of January and published in January or February. The Commons and Lords are addressed in the rousing peroration, where Milton details the mischief done to the state by 'prelaty', appealing to an already established sense of liberty and freedom, using illustrative stories and touching national rallying calls once more. What is new about this tract is a changed mode of address, having considerable impli-cations for Milton's later methods in prose in consideration of his actual audiences. To compare it with *Of Reformation* is to see a decision to abandon the scholarly bandying of historical evidence with the 'antiquarians' of the episcopal party. Sensing that the appeal is more effective to a wider audience than the scholarly ('every meaner capacity' is his elitist phrase; 749), Milton adopts a more accessible mode of persuasion, speaking amiably in the prologue of the need to 'charm' his hearers in Platonic fashion. He also appeals for the first time in his own name, as Mr. John Milton, and progressively reveals himself as one of cultivation and spiritual self-discipline. Everything about *Reason* is calculated for persuasive effect – the gentle prologue, the reminders of national destiny in the peroration, the famous long digression at the beginning of Book II depicting the *ethos* or character of the writer and giving testimony to personal calling; and most of all the fact that his method is to discredit the prelates by drawing on the Bible itself, the source most familiar to all readers. In places his method approaches biblical paraphrase, letting the Word speak for itself.

Critics have noted the difference between the abusive satire of *Animadversions* and the relative gentleness of *Reason*. Rather than try to give a psychological reason for this difference, as for example that Milton was weary of satirical mockery (P 214–15), we might seek answers in function, occasion, and appropriate genre. (If satirical mockery had become tedious, why did he revert to sustained vituperation in his fifth tract, *An Apology against a Pamphlet*?) If we assume that the chief context of *Reason* was parliamentary, Milton's decision about manner of address reveals some intelligent solutions.

Reason seeks to discredit prelatical episcopacy, persuading its audience not to be overawed by authority and tradition. Thirteen bishops had been impeached on 4 August. Milton refers to the impeachment near the beginning of his tract. On 30 December the bishops were arrested and imprisoned on charges of treason. In the latter parts Milton refers to their 'haughty looks' having been 'justly immur'd' 'within strong walls' (860). A sense of crisis had been increased by the outbreak of Catholic rebellion in Ireland in the autumn, causing many to demand the reimposition of traditional authority, but Milton on the contrary wished Parliament to complete the humiliation of the bishops, to rid England finally of a temporal church hierarchy, not to take fear. (They were in fact to be excluded from the Lords on 7 February.) If the obstacle is timid respect for authority, the means of persuasion is an encouragement to radicalism in the guise of civility. That was an intelligent approach.

Yet the situation was fraught with paradoxes. For one thing, despite the seeming candour, there was an element of deception in presenting himself as a new writer on these themes. Nor is the manner of address uniform. He defends the necessity of 'sharp, but saving words' in such times (804), not scrupling to use them in this tract also, where conviction requires. When he writes in defence of the need for ardent rebuke, he speaks in general terms of those who have had to do so, not clearly admitting his own part. For all its self-revelation, *Reason* is in fact selectively candid.

There are also uncertainties about its reception. The famous auto-biographical digression in the opening section of the second book, aiming to win hearers by giving personal testimony, is largely about Milton's conviction that he had been called by God to be a true poet to his country, and here a fear is allowed expression: only the 'learned and elegant reader' (807), 'the gentler sort' (808), 'any knowing reader' (820), may credit what he has to say about high poetic calling. The author therefore shows himself conscious of reasons for speaking to deaf ears.

One could say that these thoughts are shown for persuasive purpose. If those who have been 'admitted mourners' (806) for the lack of true leadership and have spoken out with vehemence for the true cause of reformation are feared and reviled by men whose minds cannot see beyond custom, he will blame such fear on the prelates themselves. The prelatical party has been *encouraging* the people to fear and persecute the truth. So John Milton and other wit-nesses to the truth are cast in the role of Jeremiah, rejected in their own lands, their special spiritual knowledge becoming a burden to them. This produces both lament and self-aggrandisement, and a claiming of a special office and a special hearing. If true poets may speak too fine a language to be understood by the generality or are even suspected, he can find cause here too to blame the leaders of the nation, who had given the wrong example in that notorious Book of Sports. If only England gave proper attention to the dis-cipline of *minds*, as the academies had been doing in Italy. In a truly educated state, free minds, confident of their powers would not be deaf to the high expressions of poetry. Of course, some of his readers may wish to be enlisted in the elegant and learned few; the educated may also be galvanised.

As we see from many examples through Milton's writing career, the problems of fit audience cannot simply be explained away, and there remains a discrepancy between the audience of the body of the tract and that truer audience who might understand the digression and the poetry he wishes to write. Was the candour of the digression wise within the context of his general method, aiming at 'every meaner capacity'? On the other hand, spiritual self-witness, for this is what the digression develops into, including dramatised debates of conscience, could mean nothing if it was not sincere.

The nature of Christian witness also goes a long way to explaining the persuasive method of *Reason*. The tract does not actually 'reason' so much as remind its audience of those things it ought to remember. It exhorts and encourages; parliament needs to remember the great work it has begun. What begins by promising Platonic charm actually develops the hortatory tone of a Pauline epistle. The pastoral epistles of Timothy and Titus are especially important models:

> S. Paul after his preface to the first of Timothy which hee concludes in the 17 Verse with Amen, enters upon the subject of his Epistle which is to establish the Church-government with a command. This charge I commit to thee son Timothy: according to the promises which went before on thee, that thou by them might'st warre a good warfare   (758)

Nor is Milton averse to echoing the rhythms of Pauline rhetoric, here Phillipians 4.8, as he describes the offices of poetry:

> Lastly, whatsoever in religion is holy and sublime, in vertue amiable, or grave, whatsoever hath passion or admiration in all the changes of that which is call'd fortune from without, or the wily suttleties and refluxes of mans thoughts from within, all these things with a solid and treatable smoothnesse to paint out and describe.   (Y i 817)

This is to encourage a faith already implanted in the audience.

Specifically, the 'argument' of *Reason* covers the following ground in the first book: to begin with, that church government is clearly prescribed in the Bible, which stresses discipline; next, that the pattern for church government ought not to be taken from Old Testament prescriptions, as some episcopalian apologists have done, Aaron especially not being a fit model; and, lastly, that the prevention of schism is not an adequate argument for episcopal government, notwithstanding the capital that traditionalists are making out of the Irish rebellion. In the second book, after the digression, Milton argues that prelaty is against the 'reason and end' of the Gospel: bishops abrogate the humble service enjoined on ministers, following the pattern of Christ; prelatical ceremony obscures the purity and simplicity of doctrine; and the jurisdiction and censorship of the prelates impede the growth of free conscience and the self-esteem which should be nurtured in the reformed nation. The latter point leads into the reminders in the peroration of the liberty and freedom which are assumed to be Britain's true destiny. With some semblance of hope, Milton exhorts the spirit of the reformed nation at a signal moment.

At a time which Parker (219) conjectures to be soon after 25 March an anonymous answer to *Animadversions* was published, called *A Modest Confutation of a Slanderous and Scurrilous Libel*. This found the author of *Animadversions* dangerous to the state and convicted him, on the evidence of the text, of being a down-at-heel, unprincipled young university man full of egotism. Milton replied anonymously but personally, with equal satirical energy and as a matter of principle and honour, in *An Apology Against a Pamphlet call'd A Modest Confutation...* (Y i 867–953), published probably in April 1642.

In general, *An Apology* follows the method of *Animadversions*, passing comments on his opponent's text, offering to read the whole style of the man, ridiculing his manners, convicting him in schoolmasterly fashion of ignorance, submitting him to plain insult as a bad student ('lozel Bachelour of Art', 920), and generally keeping up a sort of virility in satirical invective. Humiliation of the confutant is mixed with humiliation of Bishop Hall in his earlier writings: the whole episcopal opposition is defamed by contamination. But *An Apology* like *Animadversions* is also a work of widely various style and tone. There are interspersed passages of zealous idealism, including two long digressions: one the celebrated statement near the beginning about his own education and self-discipline, in which he champions the importance of poetry and uses chastity as a sign of personal integrity and the other an impassioned praise of the men of the Long Parliament, portrayed as truly educated Englishmen working against tyranny, even of minds. Between these digressions there is a long defence of pious vehemence, which is said to copy the example of Christ, the prophets, and men like Luther. Towards the close of the tract there is a defence of his zealous closing prayer in *Animadversions*; a fresh diatribe against bad ministers, occasioned by the question as to whether the people have the right to judge the clergy; a set-piece exposition on 'set forms' of worship; and, finally, another exposure of the corruption of the church of Constantine, followed by a closing tirade against corrupted churchmen of the day. Once again, it is as though loud mocking laughter is being used to divest minds of merely habitual reverence, whilst zeal is meant progressively to move minds to re-establish themselves to the cause of Truth. Even within a tract of satirical attack, then, there is considerable rhetorical strategy and the resources of the rhetoric for each occasion in this series of tracts should not be underestimated.

An art of self-presentation is also clearly an important part of the design of these last two tracts in particular, as it is in so many of Milton's major works. Modern audiences have grown familiar with the notable autobiographical passages in *Reason* and *An Apology*, often in isolation from their immediate contexts. In the opening section of Book II of *Reason*, where the context is one of civilised explanation of his part in polemics, as to a friend, Milton protests that true learning is more burdensome than any physical exercise. The endeavour is heroic, a God-given task. He recalls his careful education in the languages, the early promise of his verse, the encouragements of the learned world in Italy. These are signs of God's intended purpose with him. He must write a great epic or tragedy, something 'doctrinal and exemplary to a Nation' (815). The educative office of poet stands beside that of the ministry for which he was once intended. The functions of poetry, as he idealistically defines them, deserve to be borne in mind as measures of the great poems of his later life. 'These abilities', he says (of being a true poet),

wheresoever they be found, are the inspired guift of God rarely bestow'd, but yet to some (though most abuse) in every Nation: and are of power beside the office of a pulpit, to imbreed and cherish in a great people the seeds of vertu, and publick civility, to allay the perturbations of the mind, and set the affections in right tune, to celebrate in glorious and lofty Hymns the throne and equipage of Gods Almightinesse, and what he works, and what he suffers to be wrought with high providence in his Church, to sing the victorious agonies of Martyrs and Saints, the deeds and triumphs of just and pious Nations doing valiantly through faith against the enemies of Christ, to deplore the general relapses of Kingdoms and States from justice and Gods true worship. Lastly, whatsoever in religion is holy and sublime, in vertue amiable, or grave, whatsoever hath passion or admiration in all the changes of that which is call'd fortune from without, or the wily suttleties and refluxes of mans thoughts from within, all these things with a solid and treatable smoothnesse to paint out and describe. Teaching over the whole book of sanctity and vertu through all the instances of example with such delight to those especially of soft and delicious temper who will not so much as look upon Truth herself, unlesse they see her elegantly drest ... And what a benefit this would be to our youth and gentry   (816–18)

The autobiographical statements in *An Apology* are made in the context of defending reputation, but they too lead to literature. He had not spent a riotous youth at the university, but had found 'more then ordinary favour and respect' (884) and had in fact been invited to stay on. There was nothing wrong with the London suburb in which he now lived, and as for spending mornings loitering the city, far from it, he was up with the dawn to study. His contempt for 'gallant' drama would answer the charge that he spent the afternoons in playhouses. But it is in response to the charge of visiting whorehouses that he begs leave to tell the reader of the connections between his programme of reading and having the highest standards of personal morality. From a youthful affection for Ovid, he had graduated to works in which he respected the ethical authority of the writers. Dante and Petrarch, celebrators of chaste love, he especially admired and then he mentions a fondness for romances, in which knights perform heroic deeds in defence of virtue. Then there were his favourites Plato and Xenophon, moral writers who taught him of 'chastity and love' (891), not to mention the New Testament teaching, which he took to heart in his later years, about not being defiled with women. That he should defend his reputation is not so surprising; that he should connect his moral education so much with literature is more remarkable, as if some indifferent reader would warm to his youthful identification with virtuous heroes of romance.

There is something idealistic and even knightly about Milton's self-presentation in these works. It is not just the very high idealism about the role of poetry in the nation expressed in *Reason*. The apologetic opening sections of *An Apology* are especially full of touches of heroic self-projection: a whole youth given to 'wearisome labours and studious watchings' (869); saying that he answers the *Confutation* for the sake of his friends, the Smectymnuans; and the naming of the cause for which he fights as 'the truth' (871). The taking on of a satirical exchange seems like a challenge to personal combat, a quest for glory within the realm of learned authorship, and, despite the disclaimers about time being wasted on 'tedious antiquities and disputes' (953), he seems to believe that these tasks, too, are God-given, something for which his long years of preparation had fitted him. He claims to serve the interests of others and the will of God. He seeks to cover purely personal motives by claiming the causes of honour and truth.

Milton's whole demeanour in these prose tracts suggests a new access of certainty of direction, after Italy. He often draws attention to the unusual length of his self-education, capped by the Italian experience: 'my life hath not bin unexpensive in learning, and voyaging about ...' (929). There is a show of authority in much of the writing, even an arrogance of self-presentational style, part of the strategy of impressive entertainment in *An Apology*. He talk witheringly of those who have not 'so much learning as to reade what in Greek APEIROKALIA is' (888); they are ignorant, with no taste for the beautiful. There is a mission for freedom in England and instructive writing has a role in that mission.

Yet such a mission breeds a corresponding set of doubts. What if England is so largely composed of inelegant and unlearned men, that there is no ear for poetry or they will not listen to the results of learned enquiry? The fears are not so extreme as those of the 'barbarous rout' in *Paradise Lost* (vii 32–4), but the repeated acts of apology, self-justification, claims of providential cause, and thoughts of audience in these later anti-prelatical tracts seem to be symptoms of constant need of confirmation of purpose.

Such a debate is wonderfully expressed in Sonnet VIII (CF 64), one of the great civil war poems of the language. The occasion needs to be outlined. According to the usual dating it was written in November 1642, at a time when London, protected by Parliamentary forces, was expecting an assault from the king's army. A lot had happened in the few months since *An Apology* was written. Through the early summer King and Parliament were moving inexorably towards a trial of strength. By 13 August Charles had ordered Oxford to be put into a state of defence; on 22 August the king's standard was raised at Nottingham; and on 23 October there was the major engagement at Edgehill, after which the king quartered in Oxford, then in Reading, until London expected an assault from the west in the second week of November. The Earl of Essex and trained bands drew up in readiness at Turnham Green. The great confrontation did not actually occur, but Londoners lived in suspense, wondering whether the monarch would attempt to attack his own capital city.

The poem pretends to be inscriptional, as if it were posted on the door of his house just outside the city walls. Will his house be spared from the ravages of the Royalist troops, because he is a poet? Pindar, the poet of Thebes, had his house saved, when all else, 'temple and tower', was destroyed about him by Alexander ('the great Emathian conqueror'). Even more, would the presence of a poet save the whole city? Lysander, about to sack Athens, had relented on hearing a poet from within the city sing some verses from Euripides' *Electra* at his feast.

> Captain or colonel, or knight in arms,
>> Whose chance on these defenceless doors may seize,
>> If deed of honour did thee ever please,
>> Guard them, and him within protect from harms,
> He can requite thee, for he knows the charms
>> That call fame on such gentle acts as these,
>> And he can spread thy name o'er lands and seas,
>> Whatever clime the sun's bright circle warms.
> Lift not thy spear against the muses' bower,
>> The great Emathian conqueror bid spare
>> The house of Pindarus, when temple and tower
> Went to the ground: and the repeated air
>> Of sad Electra's poet had the power
>> To save the Athenian walls from ruin bare.

Wordsworth was right to admire Milton's political sonnets. Sonnet form has been given heroic weight; there is weighty diction and sustained sentence structures, and the sestet is run together into one poised sentence adopting the Horatian method of ending a poem by naming examples. The poise and stoically controlled tone are also Horatian. Irony permeates the poem. Present dangers in barbarous war are held up against images from the past. There are signals to magnanimity and chivalry as well as violence. The party addressed is called, mundanely, captain or colonel, but also mocked as a knight in arms, echoing royalist pretensions. Should not knights behave in civilised manner, if even that war-machine Alexander could? If the captain has a mind to a 'deed of honour', perhaps he will be flattered by the offer of a poet to give him immortality for an act of grace. There is a contest in civility with the Royalist side, which only John Milton can win.

In a new situation of danger here is a voice of authority, but the cool control of the utterance is set against a recognition of inevitable barbarism. Not without heroic self-projection or excitement at danger, though careful not to claim too much fame, Milton speculates on the 'power' of poets in the uncertainties of civil strife. Authoritative cultural utterance faces those who are APEIROKALIOI, without knowledge of the beautiful. Here is, learned in history and poetry, teacher to his nation, the self-appointed, dignified voice of free England's city. After Italy, Providence had given him that role.

Notes

1   LR i 419; C xviii 271; on some of the significances of this Horatian tag, see 'Horatian Signatures: Milton and Civilized Community', in *Milton and Italy: Contexts, Images, Contradictions*, ed. Mario di Cesare (MRTS: Binghamton, 1991), pp. 329–44. The treatment of several Latin poems in this chapter relates to this essay.

2.   Commendatory verses before Milton's *Poemata* (1645), pp. 5–10; also LR ii 207–9.

3.   On the identity of the mysterious Selvaggi and others Milton met at the English College in Rome, see Edward Chaney, *The Grand Tour and the Great Rebellion: Richard Lassels and the 'Voyage to Italy' in the Seventeenth Century* (Geneva and Turin: Slatkine, 1985), pp. 282–3.

4.   *Poemata*, p. 4; LR i 399–401.

5.   TMS ff. 35–41; C xviii 20–6; Y viii, Appendix A, 539–85.

5

Cultural Renewal in a Time of Free Speaking

Milton's English sonnets, the chief poetic output of his middle years, pronounce the civilising writer, staking out matters of public notice and displaying private style. We ended the last chapter with the ironic 'Captain or Colonel'; we begin this with two sonnets to women, both found in fair copy on the same page of the Trinity Manuscript and printed adjacently in the edition of 1645, both bearing the marks of social exchange, each establishing with moral seriousness a different type of woman. Neither is precisely datable; one might guess at about 1642. Since the early 1640s also saw Milton's first marriage and his divorce tracts, images of women seem a good place to begin.

We should however acknowledge two further sonnets, because in fact four of Milton's English sonnets of middle age construct types of women. In 1646 he wrote piously on the death of Mrs Katherine Thomason, wife of the celebrated book-collector George Thomason (CF 73: 'When faith and love which parted from thee never'). The sonnet may have been given to Thomason originally. Mrs Thomason was like her husband a person of intellectual curiosity, with a library of her own. Then there is the remarkable if enigmatic sonnet-elegy for one of his wives (CF 9I: 'Methought I saw my late espoused saint'), to which we must return (below, p. 138). There seems to be an interest in women who were spiritual and intellectual companions to men. When such poems were originally published, with no titles identifying the subjects, they functioned as celebrations of model types. To some extent they must have functioned in that way even as social transactions.

Noting that Milton seems to like to celebrate cultivated companionship, male or female, we may turn to the first of the pair. In 'Daughter to that good Earl' (CF 65) Milton addressed Lady Margaret Ley, a near neighbour in Aldersgate Street. Although married to Captain John Hobson (later of the Parliamentary army) in December 1641, she retains in the heading to the poem in the manuscript her aristocratic family name, as daughter of the late James Ley, Earl of Marlborough, the lawyer whose court career is rehearsed in the first half of the poem:

> Daughter to that good Earl, once President
>   Of England's Council, and her Treasury,
>   Who liv'd in both, unstained with gold or fee,
>   And left them both, more in himself content,
> Till the sad breaking of that Parliament
>   Broke him, as that dishonest victory
>   Chaeronea, fatal to liberty
>   Killed with report that old man eloquent,
> Though later born, than to have known the days
>   Wherein your father flourished, yet by you,
>   Madam, methinks I see him living yet;
> So well your words his noble virtues praise,
>   That all both judge you to relate them true,
>   And to possess them, honoured Margaret.

This is not a straightforward celebration. The context is made to seem the poet's belated rediscovery, in the 1640s, of honest nobility. This was a result of her reports to him of her eminent father. In this account, Marlborough was a true servant of the crown who put the highest respect upon Parliament, the voice of liberty. Just as the orator Isocrates died four days after the battle of Chaeronea, which signalled the end of Athenian freedom, so Marlborough, who retired from the Privy Council in December 1628, died of a broken spirit four days after Parliament had been forcibly dissolved, on 10 March 1629. His integrity is seen in her loyal portrayal; she has imaged him and to the poet has become an image of him. Since the poet was too young to judge Marlborough's spirit himself, he takes her word for it, saying that 'all' believe her – the lady was persuasive – and that she herself has the virtue she generously and faithfully claims for another.

   This has political edge and a teasing social grace, and the oblique definition of the poem matches the technique of a Ben Jonson: as a reader she might note (for the poem mentions the question of verification) the circularity of the evidence, that as it is presented all credit turns on her word. In the end the poet matches one generosity (of her report) with the generosity of another report (of what people witness of her). It is a world of noble trust. As well as deference in the poet we have a claim of power, for he has commanded the terms of celebration, called the tune. Poetry is arbiter and teacher of moral qualities. Margaret found herself enlisted as one of the true nobility who had the parliamentary liberty of the nation to heart, in about 1642.

Milton has also registered the type of woman who has, in the pre-judicial phrase, a 'masculine' apprehension, unusual intelligence and culture. (All we know is from Edward Phillip's vague report many years later, that she was 'a Woman of great Wit and Ingenuity' who 'took much delight in his Company': D 64.) The other sonnet, which has not been the favourite of twentieth-century readers, because of its 'puritan' imaging, seeks to establish another type of woman, one bound by private contemplative virtues within the home. Yet this type is presented as of equal importance:

> Lady, that in the prime of earliest youth,
>   Wisely hath shunned the broad way and the green,
>   And with those few art eminently seen,
>   That labour up the hill of heavenly truth,
> The better part with Mary, and with Ruth,
>   Chosen thou hast, and they that overween,
>   And at thy growing virtues fret their spleen,
>   No anger find in thee, but pity and ruth.
> Thy care is fixed and zealously attends
>   To fill thy odorous lamp with deeds of light,
>   And hope that reaps not shame. Therefore be sure
> Thou, when the bridegroom with his feastful friends
>   Passes to bliss at the mid-hour of night,
>   Hast gained thy entrance, virgin wise and pure.
>
> (CF 66)

This is to a young woman (her virtues are still 'growing') who promises a devout course of life .

The language is biblical, of conventional piety. That may be functional, used as appropriate to the young person involved: like verse epistles, these sonnets have decorum in suiting the addressee. It is also possible, if hard to prove, that the poem has more social art than many have assumed. Is this virtuous girl, like one of the wise virgins, to prepare only for *another's* wedding, to have 'hope' only for the other world? There is no doubting the seriousness of the commendation of piety, but it is possible that the final reference to marital consumption is also an oblique way of indicating that she might one day have a marriage of her own.

No one has ever been able to identify the addressee, but there is again no doubt that Milton regarded godliness as pre-eminent amongst female virtues, and it may be that what he praised in this girl of modest, retiring, contemplative demeanour was something like what he thought he saw in the sixteen-year-old Mary Powell in the summer of 1642. So much fiction has accumulated about Milton and his marriages that it is difficult to approach the subject in an objective way. Honigman's speculation is no less plausible than most that have been put forward about the girl of the sonnet:

> After the event, apparently, [Mary] found 'a Philosophical Life' not to her taste, but before marrying her Milton no doubt supposed her sympathetic to his stricter ways. In *The Doctrine and Discipline of Divorce* he complains 'that the bashfull muteness of a virgin may oft-times hide' her real feelings, and that inexperienced ... men are 'not so quick-sighted' as to guess them.... If Mary Powell, in the weeks before her marriage, was the 'virtuous young lady' of the sonnet, she would fit the facts in other respects.... Milton was thirty-three and his bride sixteen. Comparison 'with Mary and with Ruth' ... would be peculiarly appropriate. And the oblique allusions to marriage would have special point if the poet and 'Lady' were themselves to marry.[1]

According to the usual assumptions, Milton went to Oxfordshire in June 1642, to chase up a defaulted payment on one of the loans upon which his income depended, to Richard Powell JP, of Forest Hill, just east of Oxford and, it should be noted, the next village to Stanton St John, from which his own father had come. Whilst there, according to Phillips (D 63), he met, courted, and married within about a month young Mary. Some of her family are said to have come back to London, for a period of festivity. Thereafter she spent a month or so with Milton in Aldersgate Street, and then went back to Oxfordshire, supposedly for a visit. She was not to return until 1645.

There is little secure knowledge. Mary was very young; that is clearly important. It is likely that Milton would have entered into marriage with high expectation of the supporting role of a wife. Most have liked to speculate that there was too large a difference in life-style between Forest Hill and Aldersgate Street, and we know that Milton did not find his in-laws kindred spirits. Difficult to assess is the interference of the Civil War. Oxford was put into a state of defence on 13 August; by autumn there was conflict; after the battle of Edgehill (28 October) the king's forces quartered in Oxford, then came to Reading, where Milton's brother Christopher, who had in recent years given a home to his father, was busy in the royalist cause. By January 1643 Parliament ordered communications between London and Oxford to cease. In the spring Reading was beseiged by Parliament and fell; Milton's father and sister-in-law sought refuge in London, eighty-year-old Milton senior coming to Aldersgate Street. Mary was at home near Oxford, in a royalist family; Milton was in London, the loyalities of his family divided, but he himself with Parliament through and through.

Though trained in fencing and a supporter of military training for young gentleman, Milton was no soldier, but he presented himself as a champion of freedom and truth, and this period is marked by many projects of the pen. A range of tracts, not all completed, sought to demonstrate the importance of various reforms connected with liberty of minds in a newly invigorated state. Four tracts which earned him notoriety concerned a freedom at the heart of each family: the right to use divorce to promote the true spirit of marriage as Milton saw it. In July 1643 there was the first meeting of the newly constituted, mainly Presbyterian, Westminster Assembly of Divines, the advisory body set up by Parliament to settle matters of public worship. To this body, with a show of fervour and dispatch, Milton presented around the beginning of August *The Doctrine and Discipline of Divorce* (Y ii 217–356), a work which was to see four editions before the end of 1645.

Milton expended great energy in the controversy which followed, as if indeed spoiling for a fight. The second edition of *Doctrine and Discipline* (February 1644), addressed to Parliament itself, thus offering to bypass the Assembly, whose commitment to true liberty Milton had begun to suspect, was about twice as long as the first. It showed a greater structural method, the addition of many supporting authorities which Milton had been seeking in the months following first publication, and a new rousing opening. In the way of support, in what was a proving a lonely witness, Abdiel-like, for what he perceived as the truth, he also issued about 6 August 1644, *The Judgement of Martin Bucer concerning Divorce ... Wherein a late book restoring the doctrine and discipline of divorce, is here confirmed and iustified by the authority of Martin Bucer* (Y ii 421–79). This was translated from Latin passages in the second book of *De Regno Christi* by the celebrated sixteenth-century German reformer, who had fled to England to escape persecution and he wrote it in the last part of his life whilst Professor of Divinity at Cambridge. Bucer's reputation Milton reinforces with testimonies printed at the beginning. The translated passages themselves, chosen to parallel the arguments of *Doctrine and Discipline* and further selected and quickened in translation, are framed by an eight-page introductory address to Parliament and a highly rhetorical two-page postscript, a prophetic, admonitory tailpiece challenging Parliament to prove new champions of England in its moment of fresh renewal and taking note of what Bucer had offered against the bondage of custom to Edward VI and the nation in 'those more knowing times' (436).

Seven months later, about the beginning of March 1644/5, after a deal of bookish research, Milton tried to support his position in a double unlicensed publication of *Colasterion* and *Tetrachordon*. *Colasterion* (Y ii 721–58) is a contemptuous refutation of an anonymous pamphlet of November 1644, *An Answer to a Book, Intituled, The Doctrine and Discipline of Divorce* .... *Tetrachordon* (Y ii 577–718) is an exercise in biblical exegesis, an attempt to reconcile the sense of 'The four chief places in Scripture, which treat of Marriage, or nullities in Marriage' (586) in a way which supports his case. This volume took some time to work up: it cites more authorities than any other prose work and includes a list of them at the end from the Fathers, Roman law, canon law, and modern theologians and lawyers. It also has a substantial address to Parliament, largely a defence of his name and frank practice against the attacks of the two divines who had railed against *Doctrine and Discipline*, Herbert Palmer and Daniel Featley. Milton heaps praise on Parliament, for persuasive purposes, one takes it, and out of gratitude. Palmer had preached before them, and they had not done as he suggested, burn the book. True magistrates were still in the land.

The symbolic importance of Milton's writing for a rational liberalisation of divorce can hardly be overestimated: as he saw it, it concerned the discipline and spirit of the nation, and the campaign revealed to him the conventional restraints of the new church authorities, whose conception of the educative role of rational debate in the state was clearly far short of his own. By the end of this period the self-styled church-outed priest had signed his own divorce from the Westminster Assembly of Divines. An amusing instance of the way in which all the divorce tracts after the first

edition of *Doctrine and Discipline* tried to drive a wedge between
Parliament and elements of the clergy can be seen on the title page
of *Bucer*. The motto, 'John 3.10. / Art thou a teacher of Israel, and
knows't not these things?', can only refer to the custom-ridden
ignorance of some of these clergy.

As Milton developed his arguments about divorce in succeeding
publications, and worked through all the detail of comparing
authorities and interpreting biblical texts, he shifted his ground on
some issues, but the essential nature of his argument never changed.
It is based on a very high expectation of marriage as support to the
free contributions of individuals to the work of a reformed society.
There is no doubt shown about the hierarchy of the sexes: 'Who can
be ignorant that woman was created for man, and not man for
woman; and that a husband may be injur'd as insufferably in
mariage as a wife' (324). (Looking forward to *Paradise Lost* and *Samson Agonistes*, we might note that it was chiefly 'female pride' which
Milton had in mind.) He recognised that divorce might be needed to
protect abused women, but the essence of his case is that the man
should find the right support from the woman in the pursuit of his
work for the reformed state: the man must be able 'to redeem
himself from unsupportable disturbances to honest peace, and just
contentment' (229). The man should therefore be able to divorce 'a
mute and spiritles mate' and seek 'an intimate and speaking help, a
ready and reviving associate in marriage' (251). Whereas even
reformed divines defined the bond of matrimony as concerned with
physical union, Milton put spiritual companionship above all
considerations of physical union (and its failure, frigidity), even of
actual adultery. No Adam and Eve speak to each other as much as
Milton's. To think mainly in terms of the physical is tantamount to a
superstition about the law: 'The greatest burden in the world is
superstition; not onely of Ceremonies in the Church, but of
imaginary and scarcrow sins at home' (228). The final appeal is to a
transcendent sense of charity:

> No place in Heav'n or Earth, except Hell, where charity may not
> enter: yet mariage the Ordinance of our solace and contentment,
> the remedy of our lonelinesse will not admit either of charity or
> mercy. (229)

The 'lawful liberty' which should be had, Milton sets out to
reconcile with the chief biblical passages in both Testaments.

Predictably he presents his case as a recovery of a lost liberty, a matter in which England might again lead reformation in the world.

How this appeal relates to the expectations and experiences of Milton's own first marriage we cannot securely know. In the tracts the matter is of course generalised throughout. One may be paying scant tribute to his intelligence to assume that the whole persistent, unpopular campaign for a new divorce is founded solely on his own limited experience in the early 1640s. He expected Parliament to acknowledge *general* truths about the state of marriage and the role of women. Was it with a political cunning, for example, that he appealed to the precedents of Ezra and Nehemiah in the address before *Bucer*?[2] Hastening to explain why he had only translated the passages from *De Regno Christi* about divorce, he explained that

> it will be soon manifest to them who know what wise men should know, that the constitution and reformation of a commonwealth, if *Ezra* and *Nehemiah* did not mis-reform, is, like a building, to begin orderly from the foundation thereof, which is mariage and the family.... . How can there els grow up a race of warrantable men   (431)

What those prophets of Israel performed was to rid the Jews returning from the Captivity, a nation needing purification from idolatrous custom, of their foreign wives. If anyone in Parliament read Milton's book, he would surely have been put in mind of one notably troublesome foreign wife, the queen, whose Catholic entourage had been a source of distrust since 1625 and whose recent effort to supply her husband in war from the Continent Parliament had been busy trying to intercept. This was a notable case in England of a wife failing to give the truest spiritual support to a man who, more than any other, needed to serve his Protestant people. (The idolatrous foreign wife spoiling God's servant would surface again in Dalila.) But political subtexts are not the main issue here. There cannot be much doubt that the man who had been accumulating notes in his Commonplace Book on marriage and in some cases on divorce before the time of writing the divorce tracts felt it to be a cause worth fighting: 'And farewell all hope of true Reformation in the state, while such an evill as this lies undiscern'd or unregarded in the house' (230).

In this seeking to persuade the nation through Parliament, which he was approaching as a kind of patron, to recover the brave spirit of the early reformers, Milton offered himself as learned guide or admonitory prophet. He sometimes even suggested he might be thought of as an instrument of Providence. He inculcated heroic endeavour: ' … a high enterprise Lords and Commons', he said about the burden of study, 'a high enterprise and a hard, and such as every seventh Son of a seventh Son does not venture on' (224). If the matter of marriage dominated his scripturient labours in 1644–5, another issue needing reform and also covered in his 'economic' index had its part: the education of children. Along with the little tractate *Of Education* (Y ii 362–415: published June 1644) we might also consider his tract on state censorship, *Areopagitica* (Y ii 486–570) and an educational work probably begun about this time amongst Milton's many continuing projects, *The Brief History of Moscovia* (Y viii 471–538).

True generous education is also a freeing of the spirits, a best use of the talents, so as to furnish good leaders for the nation. For the 'want' of such education, he said in *Of Education*, 'this nation perishes' (363). Milton's suggestions must relate in some way to his own experience of teaching young gentleman in his house, but what he outlines is an ideal academy for gentleman of about one hundred and thirty students and twenty staff, an establishment which could provide his 'fit audience tho' few'. Those who finally attained eloquence together with their practical knowledge in his system would find their places in Parliament, at court, or in the ministry. He saw his academy as replacing grammar school and university: between the ages of about twelve and twenty it would do the job of both up to the standard of the degree of Master of Arts, with a saving of three or four years.

As in his distant humanistic models, the academies of ancient Greece, the aim was holistic, to foster health in mind and body. The spirit of reform was however markedly modern, broadly Baconian, bent towards practical knowledge, and setting itself against the remnants of monkish scholasticism. This was in tune with many reforming schemes of the century. It meant in particular the banishment of metaphysics and the postponement of logic and rhetoric from too early in the programme. Dry speculation and logic chopping in young minds had a bad effect on later professional lives. Language acquisition is at the centre of Milton's scheme, because knowledge of languages affords access to important bodies of knowledge, but, although his ultimate goals were ambitious for many students, demanding a new excellence in Latin, solid Greek, Hebrew (with Aramaic and Syriac), and Italian picked up on the way, the induction is gradual, through play and entertainment, fostering a spirit of heroic endeavour, and largely through reading on practical subjects. This is akin to the liberal instructive spirit of old Damoetas in 'Lycidas', even, in a sense, to the firm but encouraging method of Raphael in *Paradise Lost*.

The long day was to be divided up and it included a period of physical exercise before lunch – swordsmanship or wrestling – followed by music before and during the midday meal, as well as two hours of military exercises with riding before supper. There were also to be field trips on horseback in spring and summer from the middle years onwards, to learn about the countryside, husbandry, town buildings, ports and harbours, and the like. (A continental tour, however, was only to be undertaken after the age of twenty-one.) Study between supper and bedtime was also to be in a more relaxed vein, with readings of stories from the Scriptures for the younger boys, or from the Psalms, Song of Solomon, or New Testament for the older.

As for the main part of the instruction, it was to be gradated from those 'Arts most easie, and those be such as are most obvious to the sence' (374) to those things of greater abstraction or complexity. After early grammar for the twelve-year-olds, education through Latin began encouragingly with an easy 'book of education' and select passages teaching learning and virtue, then moved into prose on 'agricultural' topics, then to elements of geography and natural philosophy, with some medicine. Starting a little later, Greek reading also began with natural history, whilst elementary mathematics were connected with principles of fortification, architecture, navigation, and so on. There were to be visiting speakers on practical skills, such as hunting, fishing, architecture, and engineering. Only near the end of this stage of elementary education were the boys exposed to much poetry, and then in a limited way, in works on natural philosophy and the pastoral and georgic Virgil. They were to begin, then, with more matter and less art.

At the secondary stage students took up moral works and lives of philosophers, then proceeded to a study of domestic duties, through such works as comedies (during the study of which they might pick up Italian), next to the more domestic tragedies, from thence to politics and a beginning in law (where Hebrew studies were to begin, with Moses), then to histories, and not until the latter stages would they be exposed to parts of the arts of rhetoric and logic. Only at the very end of their studies, when minds and languages were mature, would they encounter the highest forms of writing such as heroic poetry, tragedies of state, and political orations.

Milton seems to have been encouraged to publish *Of Education* by the celebrated educational reformer Samuel Hartlib, who was sponsoring such works on a European basis and who must have come to know of Milton's teaching. The tractate takes the form of a letter to him. There were advantages to this form: it allowed the appearance of speaking within the cultural circle, and it justified something brief and pithy, written with seeming informality out of direct conviction, a 'voluntary Idea' as he called it (364), rather than a laboured scholarly disquisition. Despite its small size – it filled only eight pages and had no separate title page – this was the first of Milton's writings to be officially registered and licensed. It has been conjectured that he intended it for private circulation only, but one should be cautious about that, given the importance of the subject and the fact that he had it republished with his 1673 collection of shorter poems.

That subsequent publication of 1673 was prefaced by the explanation 'Written above twenty years since' (an understatement – it was nearer thirty). One reason for the apologetic warning might have been the political asides in the tractate and its evident stress on producing leaders 'equally good both for Peace and warre' (408). The martial awareness may have dated it. There is a comment about the difficulties of recruiting into the Parliamentary army under Essex (412), which Milton attributes to the lack of leadership in the officers. Discourse about the academy was unlikely to neglect the present needs of the nation. Later he would admit the feature but not erase the record.

If *Of Education* imagined better students speaking in Parliament or council, 'honour and attention ... waiting on their lips' (406), then *Areopagitica* shows the kind of communication the master could manage in this kind, through the medium of print. Humanist imitation of the most highly-wrought kind promoted a specific political cause in an address to Parliament. That its rhetoric has been allowed more voice to readers in subsequent centuries, who have championed the text for the sake of their own objectives, is an irony of the situation. Parliament seems to have paid no attention to Milton's recommendation, relatively few contemporary references to the text have been traced, and one visiting German witness of the time thought that it might be ineffective because, although sharp and ingenious, it had a style too high flown and satirical.[3] High art is not always influential; parliament men might not wish to pretend they were ancient Athenians savouring the art of an Isocrates. Nevertheless, as the most rhetorical of all Milton's published addresses, it has been for later audiences the most reprinted of all his prose tracts and has been seen as a classic statement of the freedom of the press. Certainly, it delivers a key Miltonic message about the triumph of Truth through rational trial in a time of radical reformation in domestic and political affairs.

Areopagitica is a plea for voice, to be allowed the power to persuade, as well as a plea for liberty of learning. It needs setting exactly in context. Ernest Sirluck (Y ii 176) has placed its persuasive strategy within the power struggle between the Presbyterian majority and shifting Independent or dissenting groups resisting the tendencies of the Presbyterians to establish through Parliament a new religious orthodoxy. For full details of a complicated and fast-moving situation, the student must refer to the Yale edition. Milton was trying to drive a wedge between the Presbyterian Westminster Assembly, which comes in for rough satire, and Parliament; or, to put it another way, he was offering himself as a guide of more solid learning and pious sense than those narrow, shallow Presbyterian divines. He was seeking the ear of the more Independent and Erastian members. The occasion was the order of 14 June 1643, which reinstated the old royal censorship of the press by the use of a panel of licensers. Milton's impassioned tract, in which he musters all the authority of humanistic art and parades experience in learning, European contact, and various writing for the public good, appeared near the end of November 1644. It is not therefore an instantaneous response. It must have derived from some signal proofs of censorship in action. It does not argue for the complete liberty of the press: for tactical reasons and probably for personal ones, no papistical book is to be allowed nor anything manifestly opposed to 'faith and manners'. It is a plea for freedom of inter-change *within the discourse of a reforming Protestant state*, a plea not to resist the invigorating growth of public debate in print, which many saw as an evil, but which Milton would read as a sign that the nation was busy recovering Truth.

Parliament is addressed as his patron. In encouraging parliament men to side with him and not with the Presbyterian divines as champions of reform, familiar cards are played: the engrossing power of the censuring clique is likened to hated monopolies and patents, tonnage, and poundage, even to Danegeld; he tries the nationalistic call of Britain's Protestant destiny, and encourages pride in the English language and the potential status of English scholarship (as in John Selden) and English literature (as in the national epic poet, Spenser); Imprimaturs are lampooned and modelled in the image of the work of the Inquisition, and he exploits the prestige in Protestant countries of the work of Paolo Sarpi, the exposer of the ways of papal power; and 1643 is offered in the image of 1637, with those infamous popular complaints against Laudian discipline. In this respect, in fact, *Areopagitica*, with its rehearsal of the role of books in the framing of liberal reforming education, stands in a similar space to 'Lycidas', with its censure of false ecclesiastical discipline set against a picture of the liberal idea of a university. Not surprisingly, here too is the image of Peter's keys, applied provocatively by reference to the Spanish Inquistition:

> their last invention was to ordain that no Book, pamphlet, or paper should be Printed (as if S. *Peter* had bequeath'd them the keys of the Presse also out of Paradise) unlesse it were approv'd and licenc't under the hands of 2 or 3 glutton Friers.   (503)

Shaped as a classical oration, *Areopagitica* is usually said to have a four-part argument. Milton seeks first to show through history that licensing had no place in the best societies, ancient or modern, and is only associated with governments which Parliament would wish to revile. Secondly, he treats the difficult subject of the effect of good and bad books, offering to demonstrate that men can only exercise their choice for good by distinguishing it from evil, strenuous reasoning being a part of the created nature of men. Thirdly, he shows that censorship would in any case prove ineffective in its aims. Fourthly, and with a grand apostrophe to Truth, he says that licensing discourages the possibility of all the true discoveries of learning in these exciting times of revaluation: also, a truly reformed nation needs a solid apprehension of the truth, gained through exercise, not a set rehearsal of its supposed tenets. In these 'strong and healthfull commotions to a general reforming' (566), 'let her [Truth] and Falsehood grapple' (561), as they would be depicted doing in Milton's own works, right down to the final affirmations in *Paradise Regained*.

Ultimately, one might recognise not just the role of Milton's conception of learning and education in a state – the 'fall of learning' will be a result of licensing (520) – but also his concern for the effective role of a constituency of learned men like himself. Ignorant men, he says, are not in much danger from bad books, because they merely believe what priests tell them, and we have got rid of papistical priests; as for the learned men, they must find their way by reason. Stanley Fish has somewhat mischievously remarked that *Areopagitica* is not so much about the truth in books, as about the virtue in those who read them.[4] But that also implies, for Milton, a distinguishing between good scholars and good readers, and those less than strenuous in their attitudes. What Parliament must listen for is the voice of 'men of rare abilities' and 'more then common industry' (566), raised by Providence. The proud fight against the Assembly, which is caught sitting splendidly with the ghost of King Harry Vll in the Westminster chapel (567), is for recognition of the true educational elite.

The grand concern is reformed and reforming education, and Milton had other educational projects. In his busy way (and with what accuracy is not quite clear) Hartlib noted in his diary in July 1648, that Milton was at work on two further projects which post-date *Of Education* and *Areopagitica*: '... not only writing a Univ[ersal] History of Engl[and] but also an Epitome of all Purcha's Volumes...'(P 295). We will come back to the *History of Britain* later. The second reference seems to be to what was posthumously published in 1682, in perhaps an unfinished state, as *A Brief History of Moscovia*. Not that Milton's brief geographical account of Russia, as it had been reported by English explorers and diplomatic missions, was an epitome of *all* of Purchas' various volumes of travel literature (itself an early seventeenth-century continuation of Hakluyt's Elizabethan volumes). It was a vigorous distillation of parts that bore upon Russia, as far as China, with little research beyond these sources. It is elementary and rather outdated. The publisher says that it was 'writ ... before his lost his sight' (before 1652); Milton's Preface adds 'many years since ... at a vacant time' (Y viii 474).

Why Russia? There was a diplomatic mission in1649/50, but there seems no convincing connection with Milton's text. We are left assuming that it is an educational model showing how useful distillations might be made to illustrate 'Manners, Religion, Governments and such like' (Y viii 474). It also has some heroic patriotic interest, recording brave adventures of English travellers, such as schoolboys might warm to, as well as some exotic wonders, and more seriously it pictures a land reckoned to be at the fringes of civilisation, with many instances of tyranny, superstition, and civil disorder. The 'vacant time' in Milton's pedagogical period near to the time of the Hartlib entry might perhaps be about 1645–7 and within that period evidence points to the period from autumn 1647, when Milton stopped schoolteaching and moved from his large house in the Barbican to a small one in Holborn. Whether he had merely planned, or actually begun work on the second of the educational projects mentioned by Hartlib, *The History of Britain*, is a matter of dispute. All we know is, as we shall see below, is that he was working on it shortly after the execution of the king, in 1649.

From the burst of prose works published in the mid-1640s, which we have just reviewed, to Milton's rising to the new challenge of the trial of the king, in 1648–9, there was a pause in his prose activity, and a group of very accomplished occasional poems, mainly in sonnet form, fit into this space. Scholars have also wished to fit into it the beginnings of other projects, even the planning and writing of *Samson Agonistes*.[5] (The matter of *Samson* will be reviewed in the last chapter, where it will be placed as a late work.) But what we may see above all is that the poems of this period are distilled expressions of Milton's sense of his public role, often important acts of self-definition and self-presentation, precisely in the context of what he saw as his public responsibilities.

Although all are characterised by claims of cultural authority, advertising the disciplined, discriminating scholar, Milton's sonnets seem designed to display a variety. They show a comprehensiveness of interests in the exemplary cultured life and a flexibility in the supreme rhetorician in verse. This determination may also help to explain a great deal of the presentation of Milton's first collection of poems, the volume of late 1645. Two sonnets, '*Tetrachordon*' (Xl; CF 75) and 'I did but prompt' (XII; CF 71), distil the crisis of authorial function following the adverse reception of his divorce tracts, problems with licensing such books, and the subsequent head-on confrontation with censorship in *Areopagitica*. It will be remembered that some of Milton's tracts appeared without a licence; Parker (263) also speculates that there may have been censorship for a while of the third edition of the fast-selling *Doctrine and Discipline* in 1644–5;

and Milton seems to have been investigated by the Committee for Printing and the House of Lords for his troubling radical views on divorce in the latter half of 1644.

When they were first printed in *1673*, Milton put *'Tetrachordon'* before 'I did but prompt', thus suggesting that his readers could find the general occasion of the latter by the reference to the divorce debate made in the former. But the arrangement of poems in *1673* is not simply chronological, nor is it easy to read simple chronology out of the Trinity Manuscript, for there are several complicating factors concerning the use of pages, the frequent practice of inserting material into spare spaces, and also, as in *1673*, of some grouping of materials by subject. Both poems are entered into the manuscript in two drafts, one autograph and one much later scribal fair copy. If anything, the evidence suggests that 'I did but prompt' was actually written before *'Tetrachordon'* and that Milton originally intended to present them that way round, before the sense of occasion became remote.[6] Neither sonnet is included in the poetry volume of 1645, which was registered on 6 October. We may be looking at a date from late 1645 through most of 1646 for 'I did but prompt' and somewhat later for *'Tetrachordon'*.

The poems effectively encapsulate the whole struggle with hostility and licensing, for all the divorce tracts, and including *Areopagitica*. The manuscript gives Sonnet XII its proper occasional title: 'On the detraction wch follow'd upon my writing certain treatises.' Milton's poem works by issuing to his ignorant judges challenging reversals of standards:

> I did but prompt the age to quit their clogs
>   By the known rules of ancient liberty
>   When straight a barbarous noise environs me
>   Of owls and cuckoos, asses, apes and dogs.
> As when those hinds that were transformed to frogs
>   Railed at Latona's twin-born progeny
>   Which after held the sun and moon in fee.
>   But this is got by casting pearl to hogs;
> That bawl for freedom in their senseless mood,
>   And still revolt when truth would set them free.
>   Licence they mean when they cry liberty;
> For who loves that, must first be wise and good;
>   But from that mark how far they rove we see
>   For all this waste of wealth, and loss of blood.

Trying to raise the age from bestiality, the author has met a bestial reply from his countrymen. The reversals he constructs are defiant. The base-born abusers of the infant Apollo and Diana at the pool in Lycia were punished by being turned into frogs, yet the twins were later to stand for learning and chaste virtue and eventually had great power. It is not I who am licencious, says the poet – Milton's ideas on divorce had been smeared by association with loose livers – but they who lack rationality; and it is their conception of liberty which amounts to mere license, not mine. All this wasting of the country in civil war in the cause of Reformation is to no effect, if men who embrace liberty do not also embrace the good, learned discipline of the poet, whose Truth will eventually prevail.

That Truth is based on biblical teaching, but the distinction between strenuous, rational liberty and irrational license, as many have noted following Smart,[7] is based on the authority of Cicero and other ancient writers. True learning is in the language and the act of the poem. The pitting of knowing art against shallow ignorance is in common between the two sonnets, for 'Tetrachordon' also plays with unlearned incomprehension of Milton's title, which had signalled rhetorical authority in a work 'wov'n close, both matter, form and style'. Against the art encapsulated in that title he pits the barbarity of Scots and Presbyterian names, an unreforming influence spreading south into the England of learned Sir John Cheke:

> A book was writ of late called *Tetrachordon*;
>   And woven close, both matter, form and style;
>   The subject new: it walked the town awhile,
>   Numbering good intellects; now seldom pored on.
> Cries the stall-reader, Bless us! what a word on
>   A title-page is this! And some in file
>   Stand spelling false, while one might walk to Mile-
> End Green. Why is it harder sirs than Gordon,
> Colkitto, or Macdonnel, or Galasp?
>   Those rugged names to our like mouths grow sleek
>   That would have made Quintilian stare and gasp.
> Thy age, like ours, O soul of Sir John Cheke,
>   Hated not learning worse than toad or asp;
>   When thou taught'st Cambridge, and King Edward Greek.

This is really a satirical epigram in sonnet form, and Milton is good at the rough comic manner. Whilst imitating ignorance and playing preposterously with rhyme, the poem speaks authoritatively: matter, form, and style are indeed closely woven.

The other sonnets of this period also present the cultivated man, the bastion against barbarity. They express a superiority. The sonnet to Henry Lawes (CF 70) was written as a commendatory poem to a book of Lawes' music. (Milton dated his poem on February 9 1645–6, perhaps for a book of secular songs, but it did not appear until *Choice Psalms* in 1648.) Lawes was a royal servant, but Milton did not hestitate to include in 1673 a poem to a royalist written in times of civil strife: he owed Lawes some favours, and the community of those of good taste crossed obvious political boundaries. But reforming is in question, in matters of musical style. Milton generously gives to Lawes more influence in the development of seventeenth-century recitative style than was strictly just, but if the musician showed judgement, following the best models, then so too the poet would give tokens of authoritative knowledge in his text. The (slightly laconic?) ending assumes knowledge of Dante, therefore of the fine inheritance of Italian culture, and the formula of praise – 'Thy worth and skill exempts thee from the throng' – sounds that Horatian note which is often the sign of cultural control.

In the Trinity Manuscript a later scribal copy of the Lawes sonnet is on the same page and copied out at the same time as a fair copy of Sonnet XIV ('When faith and love'; see above, p. 86). This is not so much an indication of chronology as a grouping of materials: one poem concerns the exemplary art of a musician friend, the other the death of a bookish friend and both are about private persons and personal accomplishments. There are other such groupings of sonnets in evidence in the manuscript and in the published volumes of verse. Milton was advertising a muse which spoke with equal authority on private and public affairs. Another poem of satirical purpose against the new Presbyterian rigidity is the 'tailed sonnet', 'On the New Forcers of Conscience under the Long Parliament' (CF 72). Whether many readers appreciated the choice of form is open to question: as Smart pointed out (112), the *sonetto caudato* – a sonnet with an extra bit at the end (and Milton's tail is larger than usual) – was developed by Italian poets especially for satirical purposes. Equally nice is the clinching concluding line, which asks etymological understanding: 'New *Presbyter* is but old *Priest* writ large.' The word priest was a contraction of the Latin *presbyter* (elder), so it was of little surprise that the new presbyters behaved with the same proud inflexibility as the old Laudian priests. This is a rough · confrontational poem, challenging the inflexible Presbyterians as 'you' or 'ye' by the use of a 'we' which represents those of true understanding of Christian liberty. In the tail is a warning prophecy of the eventual triumph of Truth: when 'we' can 'find out' and make public 'all your tricks', Parliament will act to 'Clip your phylacteries', put a stop to your pharisee hypocrisy, though the 'wholesome and preventive shears' may 'baulk [stop short of] your ears', presumably because no just government should repeat the barbarous punishment inflicted twice on Prynne. The moment of this poem seems to be in the period in which Parliament, having effectively rid itself of the Laudian hierarchy (though episcopacy was not to be formally abolished until September 1646), was about to take a decision on the advice of the Westminster Assembly about a new Presbyterian form of church government ('classic hierarchy'; 1.7). This step was taken on 28 August 1646.

A later poem addressed to the need of resolve at a key moment, 'at the siege of Colchester', is the sonnet to Fairfax (XV; CF 77) of August 1648. This poem Milton would subsequently group with the sonnets to Cromwell and Vane (both written in 1652), was likewise addressed to great public men. In the Trinity Manuscript those two poems are addressed directly 'to' Cromwell and Vane. By 1652 Milton was a government servant, half within the administration. For the Fairfax sonnet, however, there is indirect address, or apostrophe, 'On the Lord Fairfax'. It is as if the poet was sharing his thoughts with a like-minded third party. Yet the manner of the poem suggests the authoritative confidence of a poet actually addressing the great. It enacts the *voice* of cultured principle, seeking civil reformation after proof of military heroism:

> Fairfax, whose name in arms through Europe rings
> 　Filling each mouth with envy, or with praise,
> 　And all her jealous monarchs with amaze,
> 　And rumours loud, that daunt remotest kings,
> Thy firm unshaken virtue ever brings
> 　Victory home, though new rebellions raise
> 　Their hydra heads, and the false North displays
> 　Her broken league, to imp their serpent wings,
> O yet a nobler task awaits thy hand;
> 　For what can war, but endless war still breed,
> 　Till truth, and right from violence be freed,
> And public faith cleared from the shameful brand

Of public fraud. In vain doth valour bleed
While avarice, and rapine share the land.

The struggle against Presbyterian power has moved on since 'New Forcers of Conscience'. The context for the poem is the near completion of the putting down of rebellion in the 'Second Civil War' of 1648, which followed the power struggle between the Independents, largely backed by the army, and the Presbyterians, in league with Scotland, which had come to an agreement with the king. The army had frightened Presbyterian leaders out of London in 1647, after Parliament had tried to disband it. The Scots ('false North') had signed an agreement with Charles to have Presbyterianism as the new form of church government. The New Model Army, under Fairfax (who nevertheless had Presbyterian affiliations) and with the redoubtable Cromwell as second in command, was setting about the 'Hydra heads', Cromwell repulsing the Scots in the north, Fairfax dealing with the troubles in the south. As victory is in sight, Milton asks Fairfax to use his influence to purge Parliament, where the Presbyterian majority had in his mind been the cause of new strife.

War is not repudiated as an instrument for 'truth' and 'right'; rather, the quality of civil government is questioned which imposes suffering on its people. Presbyterian influence is found to be a new corrupting impediment to the progress of reform. In fact, a good many petitions from army and country at large at this time were also calling for a purging of Parliament and by the Autumn of 1648 the army was again pressurising London, leading to the eviction of Presbyterians and eventually to the execution of the king. (Fairfax would eventually draw back from these events, much to Milton's dismay.) But at this time Milton symbolises the corrupting influence of the Presbyterians in the lack of management of the 'Public Faith', the loans which parliament had raised from private individuals, like himself, only to use them in party interest and to fail to repay the debts. The Public Faith stands as proof in the same way that familiar royal impositions like monopolies had stood in the old regime, or as pluralism had stood in the church.

Although we have moved on to the late summer of 1648, some of the same general issues of self-presentation visible in these sonnets apply to the first published collection of verse in 1645, *Poems of Mr. John Milton, both English and Latin, Compos'd at several times... .* Such a volume makes many self-presentational gestures. Recently critics have been preoccupied with its apparent contradictions: the radical seems to be advertised in the retrospective headnote to 'Lycidas', yet in general the appearance and constitution of the book seem close to 'cavalier' collections. Milton's volume joined others by royalist poets published by Humphrey Moseley which were largely backward-looking, to the pre-Civil War peace, and it advertised his connections with royal musicians and prerogative occasions, even with English and Italian Catholics. Speculations about this mixture of things have included suggestions that it was an attempt to get around censorship, that it was the effect of 'repressed sociopolitical anxiety', and that the publication constituted a corrective to his reputation as a disreputable polemicist in prose – proving oneself a gentleman, after all.[8]

There may be room for speculation about cultural conditioning and the author's self-imaging, but much of what surprises readers is based on too simple an imposition of social and political stereotypes. It is for example an exaggeration to say that the 'Lycidas' headpiece strikes the 'one discordant note' of radicalism in *1645*,[9] for a careful reading of masque and elegy will show that the thrust of those works is to subject magistracy, priesthood, and university to pious, humanistic reformation. Nor will the poet who writes a commendatory poem to his friend Henry Lawes in 1646 be so parochial as to excise all mention of a royal musician, for his loyalism, in *1645*. The cultural world is not to be simply defined by our subsequent ideas of political division.

Specifically, the 1645 volume is made up of two books which could be separated, as they were on occasion by Milton himself. The first part consisted of his English poems, with the masque reprinted with a separate title-page and preliminaries from the 1637 edition at the end. The second, with a separate title-page, was *Poemata*, mainly Latin but including Italian and his bits of Greek. Each book was carefully arranged. Rough chronological development was shown within groupings of similar types of poem, with various opportunities taken for more local positionings.

The by-now infamous frontispiece advertised the poet in a pastoral setting, suggesting that these were mainly works of developing years and that the career development is broadly on the Virgilian pattern (pastoral leading into higher kinds). Both 'Lycidas' and *Epitaphium Damonis*, the two elegies each placed last in its volume, in their own ways advertise the eventual leaving of a pastoral world. The poet has arranged the past, so as to promise for the present and the future. Taken together, what the authorial self-presentation in the prose tracts and in the occasional poems of the 1640s seems to add up to is a picture of a resourceful, many-sided talent, the assurance of moral seriousness yet the possibility of a lighter social tone, the showing of humanistic education and European awareness, the development of precocious talent through school and university compositions (even showing an over-reaching failure, 'The Passion') to the point of engagement with public responsibilities. The realm of action is often poetry itself: the closing poem, *Epitaphium Damonis*, confides to the reader as to his dead friend his plans to make great poetry for his own nation. For all the inevitable multiplicity of cultural determinations on the 'author', one need not see fundamental contradiction between this self-imaging and the self-imaging of the radical prose writer or reforming educationalist. Everything is arranged to present integrity and cultural wholeness in the learned author.

A poem of great self-presentational significance though also a rather special context is the ode to John Rous (CF 74), librarian of the Bodleian in Oxford, a poem which accompanied a replacement copy of the 1645 collection. Rous had asked for copies of all Milton's books in print (the others were the eleven prose pamphlets of 1641–4) but the poetry volume had unaccountably gone astray. Milton plays the old trick of addressing Rous indirectly through the book – thus he speaks to his own self-image, which will carry the message with it. This affords him the appearance of playful intimacy and candid revelation. Rous himself is treated as a patron of liberal learning, one who cares even in a time of barbarous war for the place of poetry.

The ode is based upon the idea of shared experience and shared values. Its free, experimental play with strophic form is in itself a symptom of the recreation of leisured scholarly activity. It also has a shape which expresses the sense of ages past, present, and future, especially the passing of a quieter pre-war age to the desire for another such age in the future. In the first strophe the cirumstances of the composition of his earlier poems are remembered in idealistic pastoral terms; the poet was free, at play, untainted by the crowd. The middle of the poem imagines a barbarous fate for the lost book of poetry in lamentable times. But for the new copy to go into Rous' library is for it to enter the very home of the Muses. In the final epode he tells his book to look forward to a happy rest, strife and envy passed, so that it can wait, a shade in a library, until true hearing may be found in more civilised times. I have used the term Horatian, in a general way, to describe some specific features of the poem and also to indicate something of its general character, depending on goodwill and shared value in the recipient and enacting the hope of continuing civilisation in times of war.[10] Horatian signatures define an elitism both of writer and audience, an ideal world of humanistic communication.

Nevertheless, looking beyond the ode, such a constituency is not securely and presently to be found. Milton's more serious early verse, the masque and 'Lycidas', already distinguished through devices of admonition between those of good and bad ears; the note one hears more insistently through his works of the 1640s, and will continue to hear, through to the famous (Horatian) strictures about audience in *Paradise Lost*, is that of apparent anxiety, that the educated pious constituency is not easily to be found. A similar gesture to that of 'Rous' was made by Milton with the bundle of his works he presented to the Keeper of the Kings Library, Patrick Young, inscribed with the celebrated Horatian formula again, *'paucis ... lectoribus contentus* : content with few readers' (LR ii 125). This anxiety, as we have seen, is not merely in the matter of poetry. The experience of years of prose writing had served to reduce the expectation of understanding audiences: first the Presybterian divines, then Parliament as a whole are found wanting in rationality and resolve. The more he distilled these experiences of disappointment and repudiation in his sonnets, and the more he created in his sonnets and poems like 'Rous' a circle of chosen addressees, the more limited one feels his constituency might have been, despite the suggestions of an urbane, civilising class. This was an art that demanded recognition for its learned endeavour and humanistic modelling, but even as he presented himself as having matured as an effective writer for his nation Milton seems also to have increasingly signalled that the fit audience may indeed be few.

There may have been other projects in 1645–8, some involving poetry. Apart from the Purchas (*Moscovia*) project and the *History* already mentioned, scholars have wondered whether his new Latin Grammar, to replace Lily, and his new Logic (see below, p. 183) might not also have been begun at this period, and Parker (314) further speculates not just about *Samson* but also whether the early stages of his new Christian Doctrine might have begun in the context of teaching. Amongst his projects we should certainly note his translation into common metre (alternating lines of eight and six syllables) of Psalms 80–8 (CF 76). This metre, the established one for metrical psalms in use in popular worship, leaves one poet sounding rather like another, especially when there are elements of stereotyped phraseology. Scholars have associated Milton's set with rivalry in the mid-1640s in finding a new metrical psalter, following the abolition of the old forms of worship.[11] There was a division of opinion between the Lords and Commons about which version to prefer, so that a committee of the Westminster Assembly was charged with revising one of the rival versions (of Francis Rous) in July 1647, then reconstituted in April 1648 to make further recommendations. In *1673* Milton dated his translation April 1648, the time of these deliberations. His set, beginning at Psalm 80, corresponds with one of the divisions the committee was using for purposes of discussion.

Other critics have however seen political expression in Milton's choice of this particular sequence, sensing the Second Civil War and a context shared with 'New Forcers of Conscience'.[12] Psalm 80 pleas for God's help in restoring his nation for present disorders, in the light of old promises. Some images could relate to current violence, and some of the expansions Milton printed in italics, to show where he was not following the literal text (not altogether accurately, incidentally), seem to give political emphasis, as in the election of the 'vine', God's people. Psalm 81 prophecies that God, having freed Israel 'from slavish toil', 'And led thee out of thrall', will eventually show his unchanging love for his people, despite their disobedience. Psalm 82, picturing God as a judge of rulers, seems to stand upon a record of some ill government. Psalm 83 seems written from a point of national emergency, though Psalm 84 promises rest in God's house from earthly tyrannies. Psalm 85, also prophetic, based on the return of remnants from the Babylonian captivity, reviews past mercies and present needs, and hopes that material blessings will accompany spiritual growth. Psalm 86 is a personal lament from a servant in 'sad decay', looking for a personal sign from God, whilst Psalm 88 is often thought of as the saddest psalm in the whole psalter, showing a singer in unrelieved darkness, estranged even from loved ones. Yet Psalm 87 is in praise of Sion, rehearsing God's preference of Israel over tyrannical Egypt, 'where proud kings / Did our forefathers yoke'.

Psalms have such widespread use for spiritual aid and reinforcement of the identity of church and nation that it would be impossible to ascribe to Milton's choice and freedom of expression too narrow a set of functions, and these may in any case have been models for continuing public worship. Yet it is undeniable that the texts carry a political charge, which Milton has fully released. The promises of true Reformation remain, yet the nation still will not 'hear'.

Some have been tempted to give these translations a personal charge.[13] Against the sad isolation of Psalm 88 it is tempting to put passages of his letter to his old Florentine friend Carlo Dati in April 1647. Receiving a letter from Italy has begun to make him feel, he says

> a mood in which I am accustomed often to bewail my lot, to lament that those whom perhaps proximity or some unprofitable tie has bound to me, whether by accident or by law, those, commendable in no other way, daily sit beside me, weary me – even exhaust me, in fact – as often as they please; whereas those whom character, temperament, interests had so finely united are now nearly all grudged me by death or most hostile distance and are for the most part so quickly torn from my sight that I am forced to live in almost perpetual solitude.   (Y ii 762–65)

That was tailored to please a distant friend, yet the sense that a congenial learned society, his true audience, is somehow more real to him than family is difficult to deny.

There were in fact some difficult domestic times in the late 1640s. In 1645 his wife, now a little less of a girl, returned to him, and there was a move into a large house in the Barbican in order to provide house room to her, his aged father, and a more substantial number of pupils. In 1646 his first child (Anne) was born (29 July). She was to be in some way handicapped. Also, following the defeat of the royalists, his wife's family, the Powells – father, mother, and a good number of children – who had had their property sequestered, were dutifully but probably not joyfully given a roof in London. The house was, then, full of family of all ages and, consequently, in the summer of 1646 the number of pupils was reduced. Then Mary's father died at the end of 1646, followed soon after by John's own father in March. There followed considerable legal problems with the Powell estates. When his in-laws finally left, Milton moved to a smaller house in High Holborn, in the summer of 1647. At the same time he seems to have ceased teaching, wanting peace for his studies. At this new house his second daughter (Mary) was to be born, in October 1648. During the whole of this period he had also begun to be seriously troubled with failing sight in the left eye. Neither domestically, therefore, nor in public reception did he feel at ease in the period after his great activity in the mid-1640s. It seems to have been a period of stocktaking, of seeking some more settled peace, making him ready for the next great opportunity to use his pen. That came, as if providentially, with the trial and impending execution of the king.

In the latter part of 1648 political events had moved with amazing speed. Following the defeat of the royalist insurrections in the so-called Second Civil War, many in the army were pressing for the punishment of a king who had caused new strife for his people, but there was widespread reluctance in Parliament, including many of the Presbyterians, actually to bring a king to trial. Parliament voted by a three-fifths majority for reconciliation. The army moved on London and on 6 December, in 'Pride's Purge', forcibly debarred entry of the resistant members to Parliament. By the New Year the purged house had set the proceedings in motion for a trial and, when a few days later the Lords objected, the Commons decided to proceed without the Lords' consent. In truth military force was being used to bring things to a head, but Milton had evidently decided that Cromwell was God's agent for the completion of the Reformation. Some time probably during the trial, perhaps in the latter half of January 1649, he felt that he also could be a providential agent by trying to win over minds to the trial and punishment of a king. *The Tenure of Kings* (Y iii 189–258), seizing an opportunity at a momentous time, was not finished until just after the king had been found guilty and executed. What had begun as galvanising persuasion ended by being a justification. It appeared on or before 13 February 1649.

Though sequence and chronology are not entirely clear, Milton was joining a war of documents, and to some effect. On 20 November the Commons had passed *A Remonstrance of his Excellency Thomas, Lord Fairfax*, defending the army's actions against the king and seeking further reform. There had been a reaction from Presbyterian ministers in London against that declaration, in a document presented to the Commons on 20 January called *A Serious and Faithfull Representation of the Judgements of Ministers of the Gospel,* which inveighed against the acts of the army. Whenever exactly Milton began his pamphlet, he was writing in support of the purged Parliament and against the kind of views represented in the *Representation*, identifying his old adversaries the Presbyterians as the main group standing in the way of the purging not of Parliament but of England. He seeks to show that the group who most of all began the process of resisting royal power are betraying their own cause in resisting the necessary consequences of their actions: they have already put in mortal danger and unkinged a king. The tract is partly of persuasion by reason, setting out the basic roles and responsibilities of kingship and easing minds of the merely customary force of concepts of loyalty and obedience and partly of passionate exposure of the acts of one party. It presents an inimitable mixture of logical force and highly rhetorical structuring; as usual the written performance shows the study of all the multiple effects of ancient oration and there can be little doubt that there is considerable ingenuity and relish in the use of Presbyterian authorities against Presbyterian adversaries.[14]

For all its art, however, and its changes of rhetorical style, *Tenure* is not, by Miltonic standards, too elaborate a work. It has rapidity and selectivity. The concept of kingship is taken back to basics, out of an argument for natural rights, its definitions resting squarely in Aristotle: kings serve their peoples; tyrants serve themselves. The definition of kingship is supported by a broad historical analysis, claiming that kingship first arose in a fallen world simply for the protection of peoples. Not even heredity, let alone Divine Right, can therefore be a part of it. With equal economy (though without the perfect evidence) Milton instances cases of Protestant states bringing their monarchs to book. In the highly rhetorical last section Milton seeks so to shake the merely customary cast of mind as to show, whilst avoiding personal invective against Charles himself, that the king's acts should be interpreted by the simple rational standard of tyranny. Reason, not personal invective, should divest the mind of the fear of this conclusion.

The Presbyterians find instances of Scottish history and authorities such as Knox and Buchanan ranged against them; they find themselves imperiously placed, judged, and marginalised (like deposed monarchy):

> As for the party calld Presbyterian, of whom I beleive very many to be good and faithful Christians, though misled by som of

turbulent spirit, I wish them earnestly and calmly not to fall off from thir first principles.   (238)

Or they find themselves pinned by magisterial sentence construction. 'This I shall doe', he says of tracing the true origin of kingship,

> by autorities and reasons, not learnt in corners among Scismes and Herisies, as our doubling Divines are ready to calumniate but fetch'd out of the midst of choicest and most authentic learning, and no prohibited Authors, nor many Heathen, but Mosaical, Christian, Orthodoxal, and which must needs be more convincing to our Adversaries, Presbyterial.   (198)

Voice now stood with power, not just rhetorical power but political power in the nation. In this cause Milton espoused not a currently inconceivable domestic reform, in divorce, but an action of the party in force. Writing to urgent rather than speculative occasions suited him, and gave his writing point and a sense of excited engagement. In time there were important listeners. Within a few months three separate issues of a second edition of *Tenure* had appeared and John Milton was about to be taken on board, by the party in power, as apologist for the state which had tried and executed a king. *Tenure* led to his subsequent appointment to be a parliamentary government servant.

In the *Second Defence* (Y iv 627–8) Milton says that he worked on the *History of Britain* after finishing *Tenure* and wrote four books, but when the Council of State called on him to work for them, he laid it aside for more immediate duties. A key phrase which has been fastened on occurs at the beginning of Book III (Y v 129), where Milton says that he is writing in a present 'Intereign', that is, in a transitional period, awaiting the formation of a new constitution. If that signifies the period after Charles had actually been executed (on 30 January 1648–9), then one is talking of rapid composition of those four books in about six weeks up to mid-March.

However, such epic projects as Milton's projected history are likely to be picked up at several later periods, as opportunity allowed or the times seemed ripe. One reference in the latter part of Book IV is to a book published in 1652. It is usually assumed that Books V and Vl were being worked on in the mid-1650s and there are also indications that Milton came back to the text much later, when publication was in view. The celebrated Digression to Book III was not printed with the main text in 1670 but survived in a manuscript not published until modern times and also in a version cut and tampered with for political purposes by the Tory pamphleteer Roger L'Estrange in 1681. The existence of this highly polemical Digression has complicated the dating of the first four books of the *History*, for two 'intereigns' have been suggested for it: one the period after the execution of Charles at the beginning of 1649, mentioned above; and the other the eve of Restoration in 1660.[15] (The latter date assumes that the Digression is an interpolation at a later time.) Milton evidently thought of his project as having things to say at different moments. I shall treat only the first four books, without the Digression, here.

The *History of Britain* shares with *Moscovia* virtues of concision and pointedness in narration, its chief model often reckoned to be the succinct Roman historian Sallust. It is part of a large educational project. All we have in the six books published in 1670 is an account of Britain up to the Norman conquest, whereas it may be that the original plan was to come to near present times. It is a pity that Milton never got into the better documented period beyond 1066. His many tart asides about unsatisfactory materials, especially regarding monkish bias, leave one with the feeling that his labour was touched with impatience. However, unlike *Moscovia*, his history gives a demonstration of scholarly research and sceptical comparison of diverse sources. He probably knew most of them pretty well before he began. History is rehearsed for its timeless lessons to the nation, with little of the modern consciousness of relativity and cultural change, but his treatment of chronicles and the like is on the whole efficient and objective. He often points to suspect tradition and cross-checks as many writers as he can.

Schoolteaching during the 1640s can only have reinforced Milton's impressions from earlier reading that no good single history of Britain was available. There was a gap to fill. Although today the *History* is unlikely to find many readers outside specialist study, there can be little doubt that, as far as he went – and what he covered were not the easiest or most attractive periods – Milton did better than anyone had to date in compiling a fast-moving narrative from obscure and unreliable sources. No self-respecting nation should be without an instructive history of its own past. But the project was probably meant to be more broadly instructive and its political significance has been seen to be close to that of *Tenure*, to which it is probably close in the time of composition. Notably, the *History of Britain* offers analyses of the character of Englishmen, and the repeated failings seen in most Englishmen through history chime with his analysis of backsliding by the Presbyterians in 1648 and 1649. England has often fought for its liberties – it does not lack physical courage – but most Englishmen are not good at the mental discipline which will ensure lasting freedom. Backslidings are often to do with lack of rigorous education.

Each Book defines an age. Book I treats the legendary beginnings, before the more documented times of the Roman conquest. For this period he will allow fictions for the sake of instruction or because they are all that exist. Book II treats the Roman occupation, with various observations about such things as native valour but frequent brutishness in the British, and the different degrees of wisdom in Roman military and civil leaders. Agricola emerges with credit as a prudent administrator, whilst the Amazonian Boadicea is rudely dismissed as symptomatic of barbarity. History is not crudely allegorised, however: the evidence is usually sifted, and observations are made in passing.

With Book III something of a more general shaping emerges, for Milton makes the period after the Roman departure into a paradigm of the slack nation still missing its grand opportunity for liberty and renewal. Britain lacked 'the wisdom, the virtue, the labour, to use and maintain true libertie' (131). The application to post-Reformation Britain (in shorter or longer view) is obvious. Milton points in particular to a period of 'long calm' (175), of indulgent ease: kings degenerate into tyrants, the clergy prove to be lacking in learning and true discipline, and Rome proves a dubious influence. As in the common formulation, plenty leads to luxury, and luxury to just disaster.

Book IV, which treats the Saxon period until the ninth century, is full of complaints about having to rehearse the 'bare and reasonless Actions' of so many different kings, yet Milton warns his reader that it would have been much worse if he had also transcribed all the confusing names of ecclesiastical history as well (239). In this period of disunity and civil war he pays special attention to the role of the conversion to Christianity, but reads the Augustinian mission somewhat critically, as a possible example of ecclesiastical tyranny with regard to its intolerance to the pre-existing British church. The final decline of the Saxon kingdoms, rendering them ripe for invasion by the Danes, he attributes not unexpectedly to the decay of learning and neglect of Christian education (255).

Although these lessons about the true disciplines of mind fostered by education were not to be published to Englishmen in 1649, similar lessons would be taught at various moments during the rest of his career. The fate of the nation depended upon the better spirits who *had* developed enough freedom of mind to push all the way towards republican liberty.

Notes

1. *Milton's Sonnets*, ed. E. A. J. Honigmann (London, 1966), p. 107; Leo Miller, 'John Milton's "Lost" Sonnet to Mary Powell', *MQ*, 25 (1991), 102–7.
2. See ' Milton and the Idolatrous Consort', 424–25.
3. Leo Miller, 'A German Critique of Milton's *Areopagitica* in 1647', *N & Q*, 234 (NS 36) (1989), 29–30.
4. Stanley Fish, 'Driving from the Letter: Truth and Indeterminacy in Milton's *Areopagitica*', in *Re-membering Milton: Essays on the Texts and Traditions*, ed. Mary Nyquist and Margaret W. Ferguson (New York and London: Methuen, 1987), pp. 234–54.
5. P 313–22; followed by CF 330–2.
6. On f. 43 there is an autograph fair copy of 'I did but prompt' after a fair copy of the Henry Lawes sonnet (XIII), which dates from 9 February 1645/6 and on the page before Sonnet XIV ('When Faith and Love'), which dates from December 1646. The autograph copy of 'Tetrachordon' appears on the same page as, immediately before and in contemporaneous writing with the Fairfax sonnet (XV), which dates from the summer of 1648. Milton also says in 'Tetrachordon' that his divorce book 'walk'd about the town a while', that is, that the poem was written some time after the publication of the tract itself in March 1645.
7. *The Sonnets of Milton*, ed. John S. Smart (Glasgow, 1921), pp. 59–60; VC ii (2) 396–8.
8. Annabel Patterson, '"Forc'd Fingers": Milton' Early Poems and Ideological Constraint', in *'The Muses Common-Weale': Poetry and Politics in the Seventeenth Century*, ed. Claude J. Summers and Ted-Larry Pebworth (Columbia: University of Missouri Press, 1988), p. 21. Cf. Thomas N. Corns, 'Milton's Quest for Respectability', *Modern Language Review* 77 (1982), 769–79.
9. Patterson, 'Ideological Constraint', 19.
10. See 'Horatian Signatures'.
11. William B. Hunter, 'Milton Translates the Psalms', *Philological Quarterly*, 40 (1961), 485–94.
12. For example, Michael Fixler, *Milton and the Kingdoms of God* (London, 1964), p. 143.
13. See, for example, P 322–35. A recent subtle and detailed account of Milton's use of the psalms is Mary Ann Radzinowicz, *Milton's Epics*

and the Book of Psalms (Princeton, NJ: Princeton University Press, 1989).

14.   The latest edition of *Tenure* (with a new English translation of the first *Defence*), detailing Milton's polemic against the Presbyterians, is Milton, *Political Writings*, ed. Martin Dzelzainis (Cambridge: Cambridge University Press, 1991).

15.   A recent study of the *History* representing the first position is Nicholas von Malzahn, *Milton's 'History of Britain': Republican Historiography in the English Revolution* (Oxford: Clarendon, 1991); the alternative thesis is proposed by Austin Woolrych, 'The Date of the Digression in Milton's *History of Britain*', in *For Veronica Wedgwood These: Studies in Seventeenth-Century History,* ed. R. Ollard and P. Tudor-Craig (London: Collins, 1986), pp. 217–46.

6

Servant and Defender of the Commonwealth

Two sonnets written to prominent men in 1652 show how far Milton had come since 1649 towards occupying a place near the political centre of England and yet how some things had remained the same. His published works of the 1650s show him seeking to command a voice which would be heard in the cause of creating a reformed republican culture, but in some he would speak *for* the government, in others as advice as a citizen *to* the government, and with increasing isolation as the decade wore on.

In March of 1649 the Council of State, the ruling body of forty men, noting Milton's ability with languages and his service to the revolutionary cause in *Tenure*, invited him to become Secretary for Foreign Languages, an official translator and drafter of diplomatic documents (then all in Latin). Now, as a servant of the administration, involved in if not determining its foreign affairs, he moved much closer to the centre of things. Recognising his skill as a writer of political tracts, the Council asked their new Latin Secretary, over and above his other duties, to write for them, first (to select the most important) *Observations on the Articles of Peace* (Y iii 259–334), a defence of the Council's policies in the then-as-now complicated matter of Ireland and, secondly and much more explosively, the work which Milton was to call *Eikonoklastes*, an attempt to counter the propaganda for the cause of Charles the Martyr as represented in the famous 'King's Book', *Eikon Basilike*. *Eikonoklastes* was out by October or November 1649. Three months later he was asked by the Council to take on a larger task of authorship and counter-propaganda to help a government seeking international accreditation after the execution of the king. This was to answer the *Defensio Regia*, an attack upon the outrage of regicide, written by the celebrated French scholar Claudius Salmasius, now domiciled in the Low Countries, but paid by the Catholic French king. By 24 February 1651, Milton's weighty Latin retort to Salmasius of two hundred and twenty-eight pages, the *Pro Populo Anglicano Defensio*, saw the light.

Milton's *Defence* was itself to become a celebrated, almost scandalous, book in Europe and, together with the English *Eikonoklastes*, it achieved for him two things he had always wanted: recognition amongst the scholars of Europe, and literary championship of his own Protestant nation. This was a major scholarly work for England. Besides giving rise to a series of replies, which kept Milton's name in the public eye into the mid-1650s, the *Defence* afforded him an occasion for asserting his voice and, thus, facilitated further publications which he could use to hortatory purpose.

Meanwhile, in May and June of 1652, he wrote in persuasion the two sonnets with which this chapter begins, to Cromwell (CF 81) and to Vane (CF 82). By 1652 Cromwell had become the chief man in the kingdom; and the gifted, cultivated Sir Henry Vane the younger was another member of the Council and its President that summer. A poet seeks audience with chosen men; yet, as we shall see, he was not in all things in tune with the members of the Council.

This movement into negotiations at the centre, and distancing from it, might also be represented by Milton's changes of address during these years. He had been living in High Holborn in 1649. With the call to the Council he needed to be near Whitehall and moved first to temporary accommodation at Charing Cross, a short walk away, and then on 19 November 1649, he was given official lodgings in Scotland Yard. But in December 1651 he was displaced from Whitehall and moved to Petty France in Westminster, next to St James Park. This was not within easy distance for a man without sight. By 1655 he would be allowed a substitute as Latin Secretary, and although he still worked on some translations for most of the decade, he was half back in private life.

During this period of his engagement with government affairs a great deal was also happening in his personal life. Before his state appointment, two daughters, Anne and Mary, had been born to his marriage with Mary Powell. In Whitehall a son was born, John, but after the move to Westminster Mary died, three days after giving birth to his third daughter, Deborah. In the summer of 1652, young John died. Perhaps most important of all, Milton became totally blind in the first months of 1652, after making himself ill in the latter months of 1651 with some desperate and probably irrelevant treatments to try to save the sight in the one 'good' eye (the other having

failed a while before). Petty France, to which he gone as an unwell
man, became the home of a man by now well known in Europe but
handicapped and marginalised in his own country, and in this
house was probably written the meditation about conscience and
duty, and living with the ways of Providence, the sonnet 'When I
consider ...', with which this book began. Although the causes of
blindness were probably clinical, Milton associated it in later
writings with the heroic work he had recently undertaken, against
Salmasius.

Here, finally, are the two sonnets of the recently blind poet to
Cromwell and Vane, of the early summer of 1652. Both move from
praise to petition, and in both the cause is of freedom in religion, the
foundation of a liberal state. The sonnet to Cromwell, under-
standably enough, was not published by Milton himself in the
collection of 1673. This is the text as it appears in the Trinity
Manuscript, in the hand of an amanuensis, including the full title
subsequently deleted in the manuscript but explaining the context:

To the Lord Generall Cromwell May 1652

On the proposalls of certaine ministers at ye Commtee for
Propagation of the Gospell

> Cromwell, our cheif of men, who through a cloud
>   Not of warr onely, but detractions rude,
>   Guided by faith & matchless Fortitude
>   To peace & truth thy glorious way hast plough'd,
> And on the neck of crowned Fortune proud
>   Hast reard Gods Trophies & his work pursu'd,
>   While Darwen stream wth blood of Scotts imbru'd,
>   And Dunbarr feild resounds thy praises loud,
> And Worsters laureat wreath; yet much remaines
>   To conquer still; peace hath her victories
>   No less renownd then warr, new foes aries
> Threatning to bind our soules wth secular chaines:
>   Helpe us to save free Conscience from the paw
>   Of hireling wolves whose Gospell is their maw.

The sonnet to Vane, who was executed as a regicide in 1660, was
also not printed in 1673. The triumphs of Rome recalled in it are
those over Pyrrhus ('Epirot') and Hannibal ('African'). The text here
is based on that in a life of Vane published in 1662:[1]

Vane, young in years, but in sage counsel old,
   Than whom a better senator ne'er held
   The helm of Rome, when gowns not arms repelled
   The fierce Epirot and the African bold,
Whether to settle peace or to unfold
   The drift of hollow states, hard to be spelled,
   Then to advise how war may best, upheld,
   Move by her two main nerves, iron and gold
In all her equipage: besides to know
   Both spiritual power and civil, what each means,
   What severs each, thou hast learned, which few have done.
The bounds of either sword to thee we owe;
   Therefore on thy firm hand Religion leans
   In peace, and reckons thee her eldest son.

The general context is similar for both poems. It concerns a debate in the government about freedom of religion, in which Milton himself was implicated. A group of Independent ministers who wished to see greater conformity and the establishment of their forms brought a petition to Parliament on these matters on 10 February 1652, in which they gave as an example of the evils of lack of control the so-called Racovian Catechism, a manifesto of the Socinian church in Poland and Lithuania recently translated and published in English. A frequent bugbear of orthodox Calvinists, Socinianism renounced the Trinity and compromised the divinity of Christ. As Latin Secretary Milton sometimes acted as licenser. True to his principles of freedom of conscience, as set out in *Areopagitica*, he duly allowed the book, and then found himself cited in the case. Parliament nominated a committee of forty to examine it, and a committee of fourteen, referred to in Milton's title, to discuss the better propagation of the gospel with ministers. On both bodies, Cromwell was known to favour toleration; Vane also favoured toleration and he in any case had some a personal interest in Socianianism. One of many writers of petitions at this time, Milton tries to encourage two key men to keep to the principle of the freedom of conscience in the reformed state. Just as with the Presbyterians in the 1640s, so now with the Independents, old allies were turning into new versions of the prelaty and exercising an enslaving censorship. There was no protecting the Racovian Catechism, publicly burned on 4 April, but the larger principles were to be fought for.

The Cromwell sonnet has been much admired in modern times, the Vane sonnet less so, but we should probably try to see both in the light of their functions and particularly in the context of the men addressed: Milton is using the sonnet as a kind of verse epistle, where a main part of the art is consideration of fitting the named reader.

Of the two, the Cromwell sonnet is the more open and direct. It reaches its eventual petition in the penultimate line – 'Helpe us' – by means of rehearsing Cromwell's triumphs in war in recent years and his moral strength, his refusal to be deflected from his purposes, which are defined so as to serve peace and truth – disciplined order in the commonwealth, and the cause of reformed religion. National feelings are harnessed: the predominant enemy is Scotland, a threatened Presbyterian–royalist hegemony imposed from without, and these references create a persuasive momentum, which helps to give more authority to the statements which then set up the context for the petition itself: 'peace hath her victories ... new foes aries ...' The language of the poem is exact, its persuasive structure easy to follow. Cromwell is praised, but also in a sense put on trial, for his mental resolve. The difficult lessons of the disciplines of peace remained central to Milton's thinking about English reforming throughout his life, and work on his *History of Britain* in these years might be associated with the issue.

The Vane sonnet has a more delayed and a less directly stated plea in its ending, but the general sequence is similar, though suited to the abilities of a many-sided man distinguished both in learning and administration. There is aged wisdom in a relatively young man: Vane seems to have the resolute virtue of the old Roman senators, held up as examples of educated principle. The praise for his astute dealings with the Dutch embassy of De Pauw is mixed with a joke on the name of Holland ('hollow states') and on their language – 'hard to be spelled'. The praise for his distinguished service in supplying the recent naval campaign against the Dutch is delivered not with the directness of expression suitable to a Cromwell but with a more complex construction aimed to please a fellow humanist. All this artfully sets up the authorative tribute which most matters now, that Vane has in the past shown exact knowledge of the 'bounds' of civil and ecclesiastical power, one of the few to see these things straight, from the lessons of history. After that, all that needs to be said to make the plea is to suggest that religion is leaning on Vane's vigorous hand.

We know that the sonnet was presented to Vane[2] and can assume that Cromwell received his, too. But however masterful the rhetoric, whatever authority the poet contrived, the shape of political action was not so easily fashioned. Milton is speaking principles of educated freedom which were finally impossible to share with whole councils or committees, although he would often try.

That this was in fact Milton's attitude to the Council we know, by the fortunate survival of what he told an urbane diplomat from the small German state, Oldenburg, in excuse for the Council's slow and inept dealing with the treaty document he had brought.[3] Hermann Mylius had been sent to London in late 1651 to negotiate a safeguard concerning the right to lucrative tolls on the river Weser. A university man, he knew all about John Milton as author of the *Defense* against Salmasius, visited him and used him as an intermediary in his negotiations. When on 9 February 1652, those present at the Council had made a mess of things, overlooking the main document, Milton, who had not been present, confessed to Mylius that most of those who had been chosen were inexperienced and small-minded, mechanics, soldiers, home-bred people, forceful enough but lacking depth of education or experience of other countries in all but a handful of cases. Amongst such men, says one urbane public servant to another, one sometimes has to keep prudently silent.[4]

There were many issues on which Milton tried to pursue his purer aims and met with a lack of cooperation. It happened even on the level of diplomatic language, where he frequently tried to inject an Augustan correctness into the Latin, only to have the familiar, if barbaric, forms reimposed by others. For example, he tried to avoid the word Parliamentum, which was a medieval barbarism and incorrect in spelling. Parlamentum was somewhat better, but what he really wanted to put, achieving linguistic and republican purity at the same time, was an adaptation of true Roman form: 'Senatus Populusque Anglicanus'.[5] He did not get his way.

Here was an educator, with strong ideological principles concerning the completion of the Reformation and the ridding of the nation of the vestiges of customary thinking, who had little influence in fact. He was not a regular attender at meetings of the Council of State, did not create policy, had regular access only to select people, and was essentially on call, to wait on the Council, when they needed someone to translate a difficult Latin text or to act as translator in the meeting. His carefully phrased drafts were often subjected to revision. When he did attend Council, as we learn from Mylius' report, he stood, whilst the 'senators' sat round the table. With that scenario in mind, we might take yet another meaning from the end of his sonnet of this time, on the powerlessness of an unsighted man –'They also serve, who only stand and wait'.

Yet the rigorous educational principles of the Latin Secretary did fit some of his tasks extremely well, and so did his competitive training in composition and debate. Both *Eikonoklastes* (Y iii 337–601) and the *Defence* are products of rigorous academic training. Neither work is easy for modern audiences, because the form (as with *Animaversions* and *An Apology*) is not that of self-sufficient argument but of a chapter by chapter debunking of the offending book. There are binding principles, but the essence of the genre is that each chapter is treated as a separate bout in a contest. It is clear that people then enjoyed such cut-and-thrust and looked for domination of spirit in each round.

Although Milton protects himself from charges of presumption in satirising the supposed writings of a king, in *Eikonoklastes* – 'I take it on me as a work assign'd rather, then by me chos'n or affected' (64) – there are matters of honour involved, for the Parliament, and the work shows that he thought himself a wholly fit instrument for the task. This is to be a combat in words, where scholars have the advantage of kings, who are 'commonly' 'strong in Legions, but weak in Arguments', and therefore 'weak and puny Adversaries' (63). Milton is keen 'to take up this Gauntlet'. His chief task is, like that of an intellectual sceptic or one well versed in historical analysis, to demystify monarchy, the power of which rests largely in 'custom, simplicitie, or want of better teaching' (338). Uncritical respect for kings is presented as tantamount to religious superstition, and he is keen to associate the culture of Charles' court with the dissemination of false or merely formal religion, which weakens minds. He is aware, too, of the immense power of the pietism of *Eikon Basilike*, summed up in the famous frontispiece of Charles at prayer, a saintly and unworldly figure. If friends of the king have come close to 'adoring' this book, it is largely because of the manipulation of piety in it, and no king has 'putt Tyranny into an Art' (344) as cunningly as Charles. The reality of Charles' qualities as king and of the quality of his court will be revealed 'without circumlocution' in an act of unmasking, of breaking superstitious images, which makes *Eikonoklastes* a true title for the work. The preface is important reading for the serious student of Milton.

Milton clearly knew that his task was extremely difficult, for the hold that 'The King's Book' had taken on the popular imagination was immense. It purported to be a series of private meditations by the king on events of the last phase of his life from the time of calling his last Parliament in late 1640, defending his actions, and showing his good conscience. It was supposed to have been composed in prison before and after his trial. Just how much was actually written by the king, and when has long been in dispute. The book probably began about 1642 and bore some relationship to the 'Divine Meditations' captured with other papers at the battle of Naseby in June 1645. Charles may have worked on it during his confinement at Holmby in the first half of 1647. What is more certain is that it was finally re-authored by others, probably first by Sir John Brattle and his son, then notably by John Gauden, his chaplain and, possibly, by other hands.[6] It was being printed at the very time of the trial. Its title was changed from *Suspiria Regalia, or, The Royal Plea*, to *Eikon Basilike*: it appeared only a few days after the execution, in early February, but too late for any defence or plea.

The publication history was as complicated as the history before publication. There were more than forty editions in England, and more than half as many again in Ireland and abroad. The famous frontispiece exists in forty-seven variations. The prayers, which so offended Milton, were not in the very early editions, but had appeared by mid-March from some other source. It was translated into Latin in 1649, and there were many derivative publications all proving the immense market –versifications, editions of the psalms alone, and settings of the psalms to music, and so on. As he worked on his response from spring to early autumn of 1649, Milton would have known the phenomenal size of his task.

Milton's book was only one in this war in print, and it had a second, slightly enlarged edition in 1650, which ran to two issues, and an official French translation appeared in 1652. This degree of success is some tribute to the trenchancy of *Eikonoklastes*. It subjects the text of *Eikon Basilike* to merciless pressure, reinterpreting every political action of the king to be a facet of his tyranny. Charles' treatment of parliaments, for example, is interpreted as wholly self-serving (Chapter 1); his sadness and contrition at Strafford's death are merely exposed as a case of hypocritical bad conscience, because he himself was reponsible for some of the things of which Strafford was being accused (Chapter 2) and the fear which Milton exploits is that supporters of the dead king are using the book to whip up more civil strife for the people, to start a third civil war.

What is more, *Eikonoklastes* works out a whole critical exposure of the politics of a court culture. It is in this light that one should see Milton's efforts to counter the effect of the famous frontispiece, and the great attention he gave to his discovery (362, etc.) that one of the king's prayers was lifted from a secular book, Sidney's prose romance, *Arcadia*, and his frequent reminders of effeminacy in king and court. Putting tyranny into an art was in Milton's view to exploit religious language for manipulative ends. The frontispiece combines the effects of court theatrical with images of idolatrous religious devotion

> drawn out to the full measure of a Masking Scene, and sett there to catch fools and silly gazers ... what hee could not compass by Warr, he should atchieve by his Meditations ... the Picture sett in Front would Martyr him and Saint him to befool the people.   (342)

Some such critical view of court culture he was already developing by the time of the publication of the masque, and is well recorded in puritan readings of cultural events at Whitehall: court theatricals round the queen masked actual Catholic proselytising[7] and, as in Pandaemonium at the end of the first book of *Paradise Lost*, the bright, temple-like adornments subject foolish observers to awed control. The culture which uses a woman's prayer from a romance with full religious seriousness is in itself an effeminate culture, and the role of the queen in diverting Charles from his duties through an uxorious constancy is often exposed. 'Court ladies', we are told, are 'not the best of Women; who when they grow to that insolence as to appeare active in State affaires, are the certaine sign of a dissolute, degenerat, and pusillanimous Common-wealth' (92).

Salmasius' *Defensio Regia Pro Carolo I*, appearing in England in May 1649, accused the English parliament not just of executing a just and pious king, but also of violating laws which had been recognised from ancient times. Salmasius did not even accord England the status of a true republic. Milton's reply took up the challenge of establishing a legal basis in divine and human law, in order to legitimise the execution and to establish the republic as a true one in the spirit of a free state. The execution of Charles is seen as precisely the heroic act, prompted by God, which enabled the free commonwealth. In terms of the history of political thought, Milton's tract is a culmination of the anti-monarchic writings of sixteenth-century reformers, and also develops the early seventeenth-century concepts of natural law so as to give a self-protective sovereignty to the people, the king being their servant, to be judged and disposed of if necessary according to the success of his service.[8]

It would however be a mistake to measure the first *Defence* solely by the strength or otherwise of its political theory. The performance is that of a supreme rhetorician, showing a great range of techniques. There can be little doubt that Milton bested the laborious and repetitious Salmasius in terms of performance, and that the power of his book was widely recognised on the continent. In Holland, for example, although there was little enthusiasm for his political position, there was recognition of Milton's art, as the letters of the scholar Nicholas Vossius testify: the *Defence* he says, 'is clear, concise, witty, not the least confused throughout, whereas his opponent goes everywhere in opposite directions and makes himself a mere barbarian'. When Milton's book was ordered to be burned in Paris, Vossius commented as would many a modern analyst of the counter-productiveness of censorship, that it

> is generally good books whose fate it is to perish ... in this way ... But those who think they can extirpate the writings of Milton and others in this way are greatly mistaken, for they rather shine out with a wonderful increase of lustre by means of those flames. (P 986)

Part of the success of Milton's rhetorical art in the *Defence* is in establishing the ethos (that is, the moral character) of the writer so as to discredit that of his opponent. It was Milton who said that Salmasius was prolix and repetitious, and a dry grammarian rather than one of solid understanding; it was Milton who delighted in showing solecisms in Salmasius' Latin and displaying correctness in his own language, urbanity in his references, and the range of entertaining effects which Vossius noticed. Most of all, he made capital out of the fact that Salmasius had been paid for the job; no wonder that inconsistencies appeared within the *Regia* and between the *Regia* and his other writings, whereas John Milton was proud to do his country service for honour and out of conviction.

The uncompromising attitude of the *Defence*, which has been felt to stand in the way of appreciation of the work in this century, was probably a main part of its success as a persuasive book in 1652. Its conviction was all the more possible, because Milton had established many of the essential attitudes in earlier work. That Charles was a tyrant he had already said in print. That Parliament itself is the supreme power, and a king its servant, was a position which could all the more easily be maintained after the events of the 1640s. A heroic free birthright for Englishmen he had invoked before; now he had simply to extend that freedom into a justification of a select ruling body which would best represent the interests of the people:

> ... born in freedom, they live in independence, and they can make for themselves what laws they wish; they cherish particularly one law of great antiquity, passed by Nature herself, which makes all laws, all rights, all civil government depend not on the desire of kings but primarily on the well-being of the better citizens.   (Y iv 533)

In 1652 that meant a true republic for a nation which had proved its strength by cutting free from the institution of the monarchy. The Council, derived from the Parliament, is supposed to stand for that body of fitter citizens who preserve the interests of all.

With the confidence of that uncompromising position comes an extraordinary scholarly command. Salmasius' chapters took Milton through the precedents of Old and New Testaments and ancient and modern history. All that systematic reading of the previous years now came to his aid. He gives the appearance of moving with easy familiarity, wherever he is taken by Salmasius' text, and he cultivates a sense of poise, by being able to draw back now and again from illustration to entertain and show the ease of his own cultivated discourse, even embedding some verses. The ease is an achieved effect, and later Milton would wish to testify to the very hard bookwork of the many months of composing the *Defence*. What he signalled also, and what was recognised, was the completeness of the performance, even as his eyesight was deserting him. As often, Providence had given him the opportunity to prove his calling. As usual, he celebrated the realisation in a sonnet, this time, some three years later, addressing one of his young protégés, Cyriack Skinner, who helped him read and write with their eyes after his sight had finally gone:

Cyriack, this three years' day these eyes, though clear
  To outward view, of blemish or of spot;
  Bereft of light their seeing have forgot,
  Nor to their idle orbs doth sight appear
Of sun or moon or star throughout the year,
  Or man or woman. Yet I argue not
  Against heaven's hand or will, nor bate a jot
  Of heart or hope; but still bear up and steer
Right onward. What supports me dost thou ask?
  The conscience, friend, to have lost them overplied
  In liberty's defence, my noble task,
Of which all Europe talks from side to side.
  This thought might lead me through the world's vain mask
  Content though blind, had I no better guide.

(CF 90)

The poem has religious exactitude as well as an urbane manner. In the final lines the speaker admits the thought that he might be liable to forget his divine guide, thus he modifies the stoic self-sufficiency of the main statement. It is a confession of the possibility of pride made intimately to a friend; indeed it is a compliment to Skinner to receive such a confession from a much older man. Nevertheless, the sonnet conveys the sense of identity he had forged for himself in these years: he constructs a career vindicated, a studious talent given providential opportunity, even in the moments of his physical weakness. Milton's favourite way of signing himself in autograph books expressed this paradox, though attributing the power wholly to God: 'My strength is made perfect in weakness' (2 Cor. 12.9).[9]

A similar sense of clarity of purpose is visible in what is usually called the *Second Defence*, the *Defensio Secunda* of the end of May 1654. This was a reply not to a rebuttal from Salmasius, for such was never published before the French scholar's death in 1655, but to a book which took up the gauntlet on Salmasius's behalf, the *Regii Sanguinis Clamor* or *Cry for the Royal Blood*, of August 1652. As often in satirical debate, this book contained scurrilous accusations against Milton as a person of no note, foul, low-born, inhuman, without principles, who had written seditious works. Milton attributed it to Alexander More, a French Calvinist scholar of partly Scottish extraction. Initiating publication on his own behalf, Milton speaks both in self-defence and in prophetic praise and exhortation of his country and the chief men in its republican government. In his method, the heroic purposes of writer and of his nation are made to coincide. The last parts of the tract turn from defences of actions past to encouragements of reforms in the present, needed if the cause of liberty is to be maintained.

In this contest of honour Milton defended his own and that of his republican allies (as well as his country's) whilst dishonouring his opponent, a man who had laid himself open through a reputation for philandering. Indeed he may have been keen to name More exactly because he could exploit that reputation. He wickedly adapted lines from Juvenal's second satire: '... *de virtute loquutus / Clunem agitas: ego te ceventem, More, verebor?*' – 'Having spoken of virtue, you act with your buttocks. Why should I respect you, More, when you use your haunches?' Salmasius had been ridiculed for being hen-pecked by a good-looking wife; More is ridiculed for his appetite for women; one of the women More has compromised is Salmasius' wife: a nice complex, this, showing the effeminacy of Milton's adversaries and their culture, and setting up a discipline which the reformed nation must live up to. In actual fact, More was not the author of *Clamor*, although he owned to writing its preface. Its real author was Peter Du Moulin, an Anglican priest living in England. To Milton, this misascription was an embarrassment which had to be coped with in the third tract, the *Pro Se Defensio* (or *Third Defence*) of 1655, but he made full use of More in the invective of the *Second Defence* itself.

The *Second Defence* has been a work of huge value to Milton scholars, because its passages of defence contain the fullest auto-biographical statements that Milton ever printed, bettering those in *The Reason of Church Government* and *An Apology* . It has been referred to several times in this book. As well as showing the dignity and honour of his life, Milton contructs a rationalisation of his career as a scholar and writer to the climactic point of the *First Defence*. It is also presented as a career validated by the hand of Providence itself. God is thanked for the opportunity of the heroic struggle of England towards liberty, at the outset, and for the writer's part in it, and blindness is seen not as a punishment for impiety but precisely as an occasion for inward illumination, as with seers of old. In form, the *Second Defence* is structured like a ancient oration; but the writer goes beyond a care for the ethos of the speaker towards a claim for prophetic powers, out of which the final exhoration can be delivered. Having been chosen to author the

First Defence, he now had the backing of both country and God as a voice, and could therefore begin to speak out according to the lights of his own reformist thinking. This is a repeated pattern. Even as early as the masque, subsequent publication gave him the opportunity to speak to the nation at large, in ways which also began to adopt prophetic modes. The *Second Defence* renders a freer kind of service to England, the guiding of one who though blind, or even partly because he was blind, could now legitimately claim the role of seer.

Honour and dignity are cultivated in his account of his early career. Learning from an early age is shown as an ardent vocation, and the myth of his expulsion from Cambridge is dismissed. He highlights the Italian tour as an index of authority and of his status amongst men of learning and influence. He defends his sense of integrity, distancing himself from seeking office by means of patronage or for profit. He declares that he wrote nothing against the king until forced into utterance by the attitudes of the Presbyterians in the king's last days. He gives method to his reforming tracts (622–7), by claiming care for liberty in three fields, ecclesiastical (his fight against prelates and their successors); domestic (his prescriptions for marriage and divorce as crucial to domestic discipline, his care for education, and his right of freedom of expression); and civil (dealt with by Parliament to begin with and only joined later by Milton in supporting the arguments about the tyranny of the monarchy). All this leads to the moment in which the Council and God chose him as a fit instrument to defend the English revolution against the Salmasian attack. If one believes in Providence, then one also believes that divine purposes were sometimes, after much labour and doubt, made clear to pious men.

As a man of honour, Milton defends the honour of leaders of the revolution in their services past and present: Bradshaw, for long periods the President of the Council, though now discarded with the Council since the Protectorate of December 1653; Fairfax, for past work and integrity of conscience; and Whitelocke, Pickering, Strickland, Sidney, Montague, and Lawrence. His determination to put fit models of leaders before the public stretches to reformed Europe as well, in his encomium to Christina of Sweden, whom Milton presented (unfortunately in retrospect) as one both learned (which she was) and godly in the Protestant cause (which she proved not to be). The concluding parts of the work, written with impressive display, suggest that he appealed not simply to the international world of scholarly debate but also to the spirits of his fellow Englishmen, encouraging them to renew their efforts for liberty. He had set out his programme for reforms, but he sees a slackening in resolve: he wants more freedom in education, by freeing censorship; he wants clearer separation of church and state and the avoidance of feed ministers. Some have seen here (261–4), a specific criticism of the directions of Cromwell in his Protectorate since the dismissal of Parliament in 1653, a reversion into pseudo-monarchy. As so often in Milton's analysis (as in *The History of Britain* which he mentions) the disciplines of peace were the most important and had always in English history been the hardest to find. As with all his major poems published in times of adversity, the reader leaves the *Second Defence* with a feeling that all is yet to do.

The sequence of Latin 'defences' is completed by the *Pro Se Defensio* (Y iv 697–825), the defence of himself, written after More had responded with his *Fides Republica* (August 1654) and a supplement of testimonials of good character (April 1655). Although the defence of his commonwealth is not lost from sight, Milton had been drawn into an exchange far more to do with personal character. He says that he has the credit of good men, and an unswerving confidence in his cause regarding past and future actions. The *Pro Se Defensio* is brilliant in satirical inventiveness, and it contains a defence of the good uses of personal satire, proved by history, in the ancient world, amongst the Fathers of the Church, and with Christian humanists of the sixteenth century.

Just how formative his defences were to Milton's sense of his vocation as author in the 1650s might finally be demonstrated by the publication of a revised version of the first *Defence* in 1658. To perfect an important Latin work was one thing – Milton was ever the perfectionist – but to parade a full-blown republicanism when the Protectorate had gone sour, when the Commonwealth as Protectorate had lost its momentum, when Cromwell's son was an obviously temporary and unsatisfactory expedient, when most spirits in England yearned for some of the old certainties, was an act of reminding and re-energizing that bordered on the obstinate. That is, however, to anticipate.

Notes

1. George Sikes, *The Life and Death of Sir Henry Vane* (1662), pp. 93–4; P 1015; LR iii 229.
2. On 3 July 1652; see Fletcher i 368.
3. Leo Miller, *John Milton and the Oldenburg Safeguard* (New York: Loewenthal Press, 1985).
4. *Safeguard*, pp. 171–2.
5. Leo Miller, 'Milton's Conversations with Schlezer and His Letters to Brandenburg', *N & Q*, 232 (NS 34), 321–4.
6. Robert Wilcher, 'What was the King's Book for? The Evolution of *Eikon Basilike*', *The Yearbook of English Studies*, 21 (1991), 218–28.
7. See Erica Veevers, *Images of Love and Religion: Queen Henrietta Maria and Court Entertainments* (Cambridge: Cambridge University Press 1989), especially Chapter 3, 'The Queen's Religion'.
8. The latest translation and full analysis of the first *Defence* can be found in *Political Writings* (see Chapter 5, note 15, above).
9. C xviii 271.

7

Prophet to the Commonwealth

The mid-1650s gave contradictory signs to one committed to further reform. Although we do not know exactly when Milton picked up his *History of Britain* again, this may be the point at which to mention that the two further books usually attributed to this period resume the meditation on the nation's tendency to backslide after having created great opportunities.

Book V traces the resistance to Danish marauders, giving glimpses of Saxon glory in that resistance, as with Alfred and some of his better successors. Milton admires Alfred's disciplined life, as exampled in his division of time each day to different activities (291). Book VI tells of the subsequent decline from the time of Ethelred towards 'double conquest' (328) by Danes and then by Normans. His censure of the softened English of this period, too fond of French ways, their 'soft Bones, more us'd to Beds and Couches' (342), is such that he plays the iconoclast with Edward the Confessor, suspecting monkish manipulation of information. He explains once more at the end (not altogether differently from his monkish sources) that learning and religion had gone to pot and men's minds had become effeminate. A familiar lesson from this humanist disciplinarian; doubtless other periods of British history could have been subjected to the same analysis.

It may be possible to relate some of the occasional poetry to what seems to have been, to begin with, a still loyal but not unproblematical support of Cromwell as chief hope for reform, to a later position in which the Protector is exhorted to fulfil the promise of trust, until finally the Protectorate is seen as little more than a pseudo-monarchy which has failed to take the key steps towards liberation from the old structures. If we can see in Milton's impassioned conclusion to the *Second Defence* in 1654 a position in which Cromwell is praised but only with reminders of the fundamental reforms which are yet to achieve, then we may be able to see in the poems of 1653 and 1655 ways in which Cromwell's government is being measured against the expectations of reform.

The reaffirmation of the Protestant cause on a European scale came with Milton's sonnet probably written in May 1655, 'On the late Massacre in Piedmont' (CF 88), commemorating the massacre of the proto-Protestant community of the Vaudois or Waldenses, living in Alpine villages on the French–Italian border, by the troops of the Catholic Duke of Savoy, who 'rolled / Mother with infant down the rocks'. Here was opportunity for pathos roused by the starkest of images – 'bones / ... scattered on the Alpine mountains cold' – and by appeals to apocalyptic language of the broadest kind: the 'marty-red blood and ashes' are to be sown by God, like dragon's teeth or the Word, 'O'er all the Italian fields', to defeat the 'triple Tyrant' and to propagate Truth in God's people so as to 'fly the Babylonian woe'. The poem is a prayer, but it is written for Englishmen to read, and it would be very interesting indeed to know to whom Milton showed or sent it.

Cromwell had taken up the cause of the Waldenses and Milton himself had written, as Secretary, letters of protest to various European leaders and an address to be delivered to the Duke of Savoy. Milton and the government worked together, then, in reaction to religious war on the continent, but the poem, in English, does not fail to remind the reader of how England stood comparatively with the Vaudois back in the thirteenth century, 'When all our fathers worshipped stocks and stones.' 'Forget not' could only have a galvanic effect on English readers who thought themselves part of the cause of godly reformation. As it turned out, this poem, like most of the occasional verse of the 1650s, was only printed in 1673, then also contributing to a retrospective display of self-fashioning and political commitment. When he wrote on ecclesiastical reform in 1659, in *The Likeliest Means to Remove Hirelings*, Milton would repeatedly use the model of the Waldenses for a primitive church of unbeneficed ministers.[1]

An intriguing case of assessing the comparative importance of private meditation and designed effect on readers in a particular political climate is presented by Milton's verse translations of Psalms 1–8 of August 1653 (CF 85), little treated by critics as occasional pieces, in fact little treated at all.[2] The way Milton presented this series in 1673 suggests a mixture of devotional and poetic exercise, but the selection of psalms and one or two wordings admit the possibility of a public context. By dating his translations of Psalms 2–8 on individual days from 8–14 August 1653, Milton seems to want to advertise a poet's version of a commonly prescribed devotional practice, of making daily exercises from the Book of Psalms. Psalm 1 is given only the general date of 1653, as if it did not fit into this daily pattern. Since the first psalm was sometimes treated by seventeenth-century scholars as a kind of preface – a celebration of righteousness as the basis of human happiness – it may be that Milton did that version afterwards, to introduce the series.[3]

The series is also contextualised by the Messianic Psalm 2, a key text for Milton, which may have the same kind of centrality here as in *Paradise Regained*.[4] This prophetic psalm reports the words of God to his people, promising ultimate reward for the righteous, despite the princes of the world, and asserting divine sovereignty. Thereafter, the other psalms in Milton's series record David's voice and may be meant to make a narrative, for which the third, annotated by Milton like his contemporaries as being on the occasion of David's flight from Absalom, seems to set the situation. God's strength is being sought by David in a time of treachery and danger in a divided nation. The series stops with Psalm 8, which by being a praise suggests an optimistic conclusion, so that the effect of the whole is one of reinforcing faith in the mind.

In the past some commentators, seeking to historicise the series in terms of Milton's own life, more personally than politically, have related the laments to the onset of blindness, pointing in particular to Milton's introduction of the word 'dark' in line 14 of Psalm 6.[5] But this particular selection of psalms voices a crisis in the life of David which it is tempting to give a broader reference. Psalm 2 offers a parallel to the nation's reforming contention with tyrannous monarchies. The wording of Psalm 3 conveys the danger of loss of confidence in a leader at the time of the treachery of the Absalom rebellion, and 'distrustfully' is Milton's explicatory word: 'Many are they / That of my life distrustfully thus say, / No help for him in God there lies' (4–6). Psalm 4 could figure the dented reputation of a leader amongst others in authority: 'Great ones how long will ye / My glory have in scorn …' (7–8). But the same psalm, in the repetition of the word 'chose' supplied by Milton, indicates that David will still be adopted by Providence if he is humble: ' [the Lord] hath chose / Chose to himself apart / The good and meek of heart' (13–15). When the singer weeps in Psalm 6 with contrition and grief, there is no need to assume that the 'eye' which 'is waxen old and dark' (13–14) merely refers to John Milton: leaders have their passions, too.

Milton's psalm-narrative is no simple allegory, but it rehearses a story which might make admonitory sense in the political scene of August 1653, seen from a radical viewpoint. Earlier in the year Cromwell, the military hero of the revolution and one who thought himself an instrument of God, had, because of his own impatience and general disillusion, dismissed the Rump Parliament, whose members he finally accused of being sinful, having lost resolve. Parliament, on the other hand, for all that it depended for its existence on Cromwell's army, had kept itself in some jealous independence from Cromwell and his wishes for quicker movement on reform. It had some distrust of his intentions. In a move which he would later see as naive, Cromwell nominated the one hundred and forty 'saints' of the 'Barebones Parliament' in the hope that the completion of the revolution would be forged in the hands of pious and faithful men, and the ageing leader resigned his power to them, telling them they could finally bring about all those things which had been prophesied after the escape from royal power. There was a momentary idealistic hope, for Cromwell and those who supported his move, that dissentions and backslidings would cease. In practice the considerable programme of reforms ran into predictable opposition from conservative elements, and Cromwell felt he had to dismiss this parliament, too, in December, thereafter taking the rule into his own hands, and becoming Protector.

Milton's psalm versions were composed as the new Parliament was about a month into its business, before the renewed dissentions had become apparent. It may well be that as Milton meditated in verse, he was also praying for or urging reunified efforts under a leader who had been a strong militant force, allowing the series of Davidic psalms to meditate the passing of distrust and danger to the cause of the just man, giving Cromwell and Providence a chance, as it were, in the hope of a victory against the residual institutions of tyranny. If such were Milton's hopes in August 1653, he would have been as disillusioned as Cromwell at the eventual outcome: retrospectively, he would see the events of 1653 as disastrous to the Commonwealth.

The exact date of composition was recorded by these psalms in 1673 in a way which obtained of no other psalm series. If this were to signify a national as well as a personal occasion, it was a bold self-advertising move, for it implied a support of militant reform, in relation to a man and to parliaments which no-one could openly celebrate in the post-Restoration world. But whatever their functions, these verse translations also demonstrate a considerable virtuosity, an elaborate poetic service: no two are given the same verse form, and the metrical experiments are in some cases pretty extraordinary, as many have commented, sometimes in disapproval. The key Psalm 2, for example, conveys its Messianic reassurances in a version of Dante's *terza rima* but with such effects of run-on lines as to make the measure seem quite different. The versions are more than technical experimentations: there are signs that Milton wrote in awareness of elements of Hebrew rhetoric, as in the figure rendered in lines 13–15 of the Psalm 3: 'I lay and slept, I waked again, / For my sustain / Was the Lord. ...' , where the figure of sleeping and waking again, neatly contained within a line, registers what contemporary scholars were registering as 'a proverbial speech among the Hebrewes'.[6]

There is, however, the probability that the onset of blindness, with its inevitable limiting of Milton's communications with the outside world, did lead to a new reliance on the cultivation of personal faith during the 1650s. In the sonnet to Cyriack Skinner of 1655, discussed above, the blind man finally acknowledges the paramount importance of his 'better guide'; and at the end of his life Milton would shape the story of Samson to show how blindness, inhibiting the physical, could give new access to spiritual strength. Two documents usually attributed to the hand of a young man who acted as amanuensis from about 1658 to 1660, Jeremie Picard, speak to the compensating importance of religious vision.

One of these is the very moving celebration of Milton's dead wife (CF 91), probably his second wife, Katherine, whom he had married in November 1656 and who died in February 1658, some three and a half months after giving birth to a daughter (who also died soon after). Both the sonnet and the recording of the deaths of mother and daughter in Milton's 1612 Bible are in the 'Picard' hand. The fact that Milton depicts his wife as of extreme saintly purity may also express the meaning of her name in Greek (KATHAROS means pure):

> Methought I saw my late espoused saint
> Brought to me like Alcestis from the grave,
> Whom Jove's great son to her glad husband gave,
> Rescued from death by force though pale and faint.

Mine as whom washed from spot of childbed taint,
   Purification in the old Law did save,
   And such as yet once more I trust to have
Full sight of her in heaven without restraint,
Came vested all in white, pure as her mind:
   Her face was veiled, yet to my fancied sight,
   Love, sweetness, goodness in her person shined
So clear, as in no face with more delight.
   But O as to embrace me she inclined
I waked, she fled, and day brought back my night.

Such uncertainty about physical presence as comes with blindness
as much as with dream helps to define this wish to embrace a figure
not there. The effect is increased by the insistence on his wife's saint-
liness, which leads to the desired view of her only somewhere else,
in heaven. It could not really be like Admetus having the virtuous
Alcestis restored 'by force', nor like the saving of a wife after child-
birth under the Law, but could only appear, in the Christian dispensation, as the reward of a 'saint' in heaven. No imminent sight
after temporary loss can therefore be allowed him, only a delayed
sight. This might be thought preferable as belonging to the sight of
the saints (not as through a mirror, darkly) but also more heart-
rending, as being deferred in time beyond the end of life. The whole
is made more pathetic by the fact that he had never seen the face of
his beloved in the first place; only in faith can the strength and the
consolation come. There is astonishing paradoxical power. In 1673,
where it was first printed, the poem also witnessed to the pattern of
true marriage, just as other sonnets of these years witnessed to the
causes of Reformation or to an exemplary cultivated style of life, a
godly and refined republicanism.

The other 'Picard' document is the notorious *De Doctrina Christiana*
(Y vi), Milton's compendium in Latin of a system of belief, a huge
work (the manuscript is seven hundred and forty-five pages) from
one living in England to try to better the compendia of well-known
Protestant scholars such as Polanus, Wolleb, and Ames. The great
bulk of this long treatise is in the hand of Picard, showing in all
probability that, whenever he had begun it, Milton had taken it near
to the point of preparation for publication in the period 1658–60. It
was not then published, presumably because the Restoration was
not the time to publish strongly individualistic doctrines (some of
which would have been regarded as heretical), but the manuscript

seems to have been worked on from time to time before being passed to his unscrupulous young protégé Daniel Skinner to deal with soon before Milton's death in 1674. Skinner apparently copied out parts anew and made other preparations for publication, which was to be in Amsterdam, but backed off when he learned that the project would do his own reputation no good. The work was not printed from the manuscript until the nineteenth century, and has caused great dispute, both with regard to theological content and to authenticity, ever since. This can only have been a major work destined for a large audience in European Protestantism: hence the use of Latin (rather more refined than in many doctrinal treatises) and the address 'To All the Churches of Christ and to All in any part of the world who profess the Christian faith, Peace, Knowledge of the Truth ...'.

A full description of the content of this work cannot be encompassed here. Perhaps in any case texts which were not published in Milton's lifetime have somewhat less call on space in the present book.[7] I want to make it clear, however, that I am not demoting *De Doctrina* because of a recent theory that the work may not be by Milton at all.[8] Although the jury remains out on many matters concerning the provenence of the manuscript, which is extremely problematic, John Milton's authorship remains still the most likely for the work. There are mentions in Milton's other writing of the existence of earlier theological compilations, and the relationship of these to the extant text is not clear, so we cannot tell how many different ideas Milton may have had at different times about compiling his own notes on theological matters or beginning some sort of systematic theology. In the context of this chapter it remains quite plausible that he would have undertaken the huge task of compilation from biblical study during the mid- to late 1650s, when he had fewer assignments in writing political tracts for the state and when matters of belief may have borne in upon him more urgently. The physical difficulties would have been enormous: despite a well-trained memory, Milton would constantly have needed other people, such as Picard, to look things up, and to take dictation. But difficulty had never been a disincentive.

De Doctrina has a bipartite structure like Wolleb's celebrated *Compendium Theologiae Christianae* which he was seeking to rival: the first part is about faith or knowledge, the second about love or worship; that is, the book is about hearing first, and doing second. This is the same division as used by Milton in *A Treatise of Civil*

Power (1658): 'What evangelic religion is, is told in two words, faith and charitie; or beleef and practice' (Y viii 255). It is chiefly in the opening parts that the bold nature of Milton's rational, humanistic doctrines is apparent and his unorthodoxy was enough to trouble readers who had assumed, or wished to assume, that the poet of *Paradise Lost* was mainly orthodox in his beliefs, when the work was first printed in the nineteenth century. For the modern student of Milton, however, who is unlikely to try to read a translation of the whole work, a perusal of the address to the reader will be found rewarding for all the familiar causes it espouses: it rails against prejudice and unexamined custom in matters of belief, denies the usual understanding of heresy, and, as in *Areopagitica*, there is a relishing of the existence of many voices labouring individually towards the truth:

> God had revealed the way of eternal salvation only to the individual faith of each man, and demands of us that any man who wishes to be saved should work out his own beliefs for himself. (118)

Free discussion and enquiry is, he says, allowed in academic circles, and should be denied to no believer. In this enthusiastic spirit of Protestant individualism, the whole church, filled with 'brightness and light' by such strenuous seeking and debate, becomes in effect like one large, liberal university, for which he writes and in which he will find recognition. His 'dearest and best possession' (121) is being shared with the European Protestant intelligentsia.

The treatise is anti-trinitarian with a rational Christology, is strongly resistant to Calvinistic predestination and shows a humanistic belief in human potentiality and free will, propounds an unusual *ex Deo* creation theory and a kind of mortalism concerning the death and resurrection of both body and soul, and, as one might expect from the reformer in domestic discipline who had written about divorce, he mounts a strong defence of Old Testament polygamy. Scholars have spent much effort reading the particular doctrines into the poetry of the last years. It makes a good deal of sense, for example, to see *Paradise Regained*, with its emphasis on the fully human nature of Jesus, in the light of the similar emphases of *De Doctrina*. But the major effort has to been to reconcile *Paradise Lost* with *De Doctrina*, partly on the basis that Milton may have been working on both at the same time (the usual assumption being that the epic was begun in its present form several years before the Restoration). Such is the emphasis of the presentation of *De Doctrina* in the Yale edition by Maurice Kelley:

> it reveals that our greatest English religious poet – long considered orthodox – was highly heterodox during the period of his last, and major, poems, rejecting among other tenets the trinitarian view of the Godhead, the Reformed dogma of predestination, and the generally accepted belief in the immortality of the soul.   (109)

Kelley is happy to say that for the modern reader the use of the treatise as a gloss on the epic is its main benefit. This very understandable subordination of a great doctrinal work in Latin for a learned European audience to the needs of reading accurately a great epic meant for the English people has its unfortunate side: it has encouraged scholars to treat *De Doctrina* as a work which gives access to Milton's 'real' or 'private' beliefs, in the same way as we might use his Commonplace Book to find out what notes he had been taking on certain topics from the late 1630s through to the 1650s. The only way to appreciate *De Doctrina* for what it was meant to be, in the literary career of John Milton, is to realise its ambitious design, and its bid for recognition on the European stage: potentially, it was a contribution to the cause of Protestantism as ambitious, in the theological sphere, as the *Defence* had been in the political. Yet the author presented his work in the prefatory address, according to expectations of *ethos* in the author, in the light of his personal search for truth.

There may, then, have been a particular concentration on matters of belief and biblical study in the years following the onset of blindness, and all three great poems published in the Restoration period, *Paradise Lost*, *Paradise Regained*, and *Samson Agonistes*, would base their instructive actions on the ground of religious discipline. For all that, a literary career is still being cultivated, on a European scale, and as we have seen the poems ascribed to these years preserve the impression of one who would present to his readers a rounded, cultured style of life. Certainly, when the sonnets of these years were printed in 1673, they included two very accomplished invitation poems from the elderly scholar–writer to younger scholarly men which establish the speaker with urbane authority.

The earlier of these two sonnets (CF 87), probably written in the winter of 1653–4 or 1654–5 and addressed to Edward Lawrence, son of the cosmopolitan Henry Lawrence (member of the Council of State from July 1653 and chairman from January 1654), gives a lesson in style to a man of the educated, governing class in his early twenties. The poet shows his connection with the influential and the cultivated, and figures a friendship in which an authority can be invested in the experience of the older man. The poet offers teasing provocations and trusts the young man to read the tone aright: as if John Milton, Protestant–humanist scholar of national and international repute, *would* merely 'waste' a sullen day. And one should presumably take as teasing exaggeration the enticing mention of the lute or the singing of Italian songs – such are not likely to have happened on each of Lawrence's visits. Such details make a claim for an urbane, Protestant–republican culture, and the Bible (in 'The lily and rose, that neither sowed nor spun') and the example of Horace in his later odes work together in this formulation.

The somewhat later sonnet (CF 89; c1655?) addressed to Cyriack Skinner also plays Horace and teases and like the other poem to Skinner noticed above (p. 128), places a good deal of intimate trust in the judgement of the younger man: the 'deep thoughts' of this young scholar are to be dispersed in drink (but only moderately, it seems). Again, there is an authority in the voice of the poet, as he claims the right to counsel the twenty-eight-year-old (a grandson of the famous Elizabethan lawyer, Sir Edward Coke) in a style befitting a Protestant–republican culture such as Milton would like to see in England.

Large scholarly projects and the celebration of cultivated friendships were however overtaken by a new set of political occasions in 1658 and 1659 to which the blind Milton responded, it seems, with all the spirit of active responsibility, the sense of God-given duty, he had shown earlier in his career. The first occasional publication is a curious one: Milton made available in print some months before Cromwell's death the text of a work apparently in his own possession reputedly by Sir Walter Ralegh: *The Cabinet Council: Containing the Chief Arts of Empire, And Myseries of State; Discasbineted in Political and Polemical Aphorisms* .... It is not in fact by Ralegh – his name had been appropriated for oppositional political purposes many times after his death, building on the idea that he had suffered tyrannically at the hands of James I. One may speculate a good deal about Milton's motives with this publication, but one possible explanation might be that it was a way of suggesting that England was in danger of sliding back to something like the conditions of monarchy: there is much advice in *Cabinet Council* about how to endure tyranny.

However that may be, after the death of the Protector (3 September 1658) and the accession of his son Richard, Milton issued, as is noted above, a revised edition of his renowned *Defence* against Salmasius. This reminder of past heroic services to the English Commonwealth was given with a promise in a postscript that he had 'yet greater things' in hand, of benefit not just to England but to 'men of whatever nation, and to the cause of Christendom above all' (Y iv 1139). The likely reference is to the *De Doctrina Christiana*, a major service to reformed religion, just as the *Defence* had been to political discourse.

Changes of government provided time of opportunity, and there is every sign that Milton wished to have a say in giving advice, pushing the nation towards reform. He would remind and exhort. When it was known that Richard Cromwell's Council of State had decided to call a new Parliament for the end of January 1659, Milton took the opportunity in *A Treatise of Civil Power* (Y vii 238–72) to press the English 'senate', guardian of English liberties, to resist allowing the civil powers to dictate a national confession of religion. As with many of Milton's radical positions on the eve of Restoration, this anti-Erastianism was to be an attempt to make water run uphill: England had been drifting, half thankfully but with no little contention, towards adopting many pre-revolutionary measures. The constitutional outline of 1657, for example, the *Humble Petition and Advice*, had proposed a new Upper House in Parliament, stricter limitation on religious tolerance, some quasi-regal ceremony at Whitehall, and new creations of knights, baronets, and peers. Such developments in opinion probably confirmed Milton's worst fears about the mistake of dismissing the Rump Parliament in 1653. By the late 1650s many of radical persuasion looked back to the old Parliament and its surviving members with rosy-tinted spectacles, thinking that there at least they could identify a body which had some record of progress. The matter of settling the national religion had been debated inconclusively for many years, and many pamphlets had been issued on the subject. The *Humble Petition and Advice* had proposed that the national confession should be agreed by the Protector and Parliament jointly, a conjunction of civil powers. In October 1658, as Cromwell was dying, a group of Independent ministers at Savoy House had put forward an invitation to settle the national faith, but Richard Cromwell was known to be of conservative persuasion. Milton's call on the new Parliament is to re-energize itself, to behave like the Parliament of the 1640s in pressing reform forward. It is invited to see such a settlement as was proposed by the dominant Independent group as tantamount to undoing the work of reform and as working against freedom of conscience.

For all that the radical message of a Secretary for Foreign Tongues, not yet fully retired from his official duties but writing to the new Parliament as a private citizen, fell on deaf ears, *Of Civil Power* has a considerable self-consistent art. It sets out to galvanise reforming spirits by reminding them of something on which all would agree: that the history of the Roman church provided a dominant example of the ills of mixing considerations of state and religion. To allow the state to dictate religion now would be then to institute a new 'civil papacie' (244), to recreate a new 'Roman principality' (254). With this broad appeal to ideas of reformation in history comes a decorum in method in the tract. Supporting the radical position that every true-seeking Christian has his own obligation to settle matters of belief according to his own conscience guided by the clear light of the Bible, Milton himself deploys biblical texts as his main ground of authority.

If *Areopagitica* is well known to students of Milton for its self-displaying humanistic defence of the liberty of the press, *Of Civil Power* should be better known for the clear and uncompromising position of Milton in later life concerning liberty of conscience. The man who had (we assume) brought near to completion a system of divinity which he himself had forged out of his own readings of the Scriptures, but which he would offer to the benefit of the whole of European Protestantism, here defines the authority on which such a project might be made: every man has a 'burden', a duty, 'to search, to try, to judge of these things'. Scripture, the only objective guide, is 'sole interpreter of itself to the conscience' (243), thus relegating church teaching of whatever persuasion. As in *Areopagitica* there is not horror at the contention of individual voices, but pleasure in active debate in a free church: 'nothing more protestantly can be permitted than a free and careful debate at all times by writing, conferences or disputations of what opinions soever ...' (249). The bugwords 'blasphemy' and 'heresy' are neutralised by analysing their root meanings (246–47).

Milton may have written a language too radical for the new Parliament, but one reader we know appreciated its point: in a letter perhaps misdated and only existing in copy, a friend, Moses Wall, registers Milton's complaint 'of the Non-progresency of the nation, and of the retrograde Motion of late, in liberty and spirital Truths' (P 526).

Milton's address to the new Parliament prefigures matters of 'fit' audience and educational and cultural renewal, which will recur in other writings on the eve of Restoration. He is not, like some, seeking government by the Saints, because he values knowledge of statecraft built on international experience and a study of history, but a commitment to reformation in religion stands as a necessary qualification for the republican governors of England. As he reminds the new members of his own close contact with the Council as Secretary, a few of the new parliament men, he says, he has already known in action:

> Some of whome I remember to have heard often for several years, at a councel next in authoritie to your own [the Council of State], so well joined religion with civil prudence, and yet so well distinguishing the different power of either ... that if any there present had bin before of an opinion contrary, he might doubtless have departed thence a convert in that point, and have confessd, that then both commonwealth and religion will at length, if ever, flourish in Christendom, when either they who govern discern between civil and religious, or they only who so discern shall be admitted to govern.   (240)

In this self-advertising yet challenging statement, the desire seems to be to choose only those who qualify as true reformers, and it must mean that Milton's anti-Erastianism presumes a commitment to full reformation in the church in the first place. Such a commitment should be regarded, as it were, as an educational qualification in the men who sat on England's governing senatorial bodies. This was understood by Moses Wall in his letter. He encouraged Milton to pick up his remembrancing pen again in 1659 in the case against 'hirelings', beneficed clergy, which Milton did, producing another radical document which would largely fall on deaf ears, *The Likeliest Means to Remove Hirelings* (Y vii 271–321), possibly in August of that year.

Milton's book was addressed to the new Parliament in the summer of 1659, which was none other than the Rump Parliament which had been dismissed by Cromwell senior in 1653, an act which because it led to the Protectorate Milton was to come to see as symbolising a betrayal of the true commonwealth. (The time between 1653 and 1659 is called, in his famous, contemptuous phrase, a 'short but scandalous night of interruption': 274.) In the Rump, old hands at reform, Milton may have felt that he had a 'supream Senat' (274) which would be both fit readers and fit leaders of the nation, and he inveighed against the evils of feeding priestly bellies and against 'the oppressions of a Simonian decimating clergy' (275) as freely as ever he had in his career. Tithing, one of the central issues of the debate, he denies existed in the primitive apostolic church, seeing it as a 'Judaical' imposition from the end of the fourth century. His target now is of course all bodies of beneficed clergy, including the various 'puritan' sectors. In the long debate of twenty years or so, revived after the restoration of the Rump in May 1659, the Presbyterians had long since emerged as legalistic tithers, and the Independents also had urgent practical matters of organisation to settle, and, for all the pacific, interdominational movements of the late 1650s, they had no wish to relinquish their dominance.

Milton's solution is a return to basic idealism and a denial of the necessity to set up *any* fixed national church. Churches should form freely at the local level; ministers should have a trade, so as to be more self-supporting, otherwise to be voluntarily supported by their flocks, perhaps helped if necessary by local magistrates; and there should be evangelical missions from the better and more prosperous areas to the poorer. As has been remarked (Y vii 94), it all sounds like Wesleyan missions of the next century. Milton often uses the example of the Waldenses for such an organisation as he proposes.

Also of interest are two features which connect with the various proposals for new government Milton would make soon after: an ever-increasing distrust of centralised power and hierarchy; and a determination to set up reformed education at a local level.[10] The regions are not dictated to, but each renews itself. He proposes to set up schools and libraries and hopes to avoid the necessity of sending boys to cities for their education. As in *Of Education*, and rather as in later dissenting academies, the idea is to replace the functions of universities, too, for Milton cannot see the traditional teaching of Oxford and Cambridge as best producing ministers for the churches. Young men educated in these colleges would then *volun-tarily* become ministers in their own areas and each community would be free to find its own way. It is a regionally-based cultural renewal, a devolution to individual consciences, and a Levitical caste has been banished:

> So all the Land would be soone better civiliz'd, and they who are taught freely at a publick cost, might have their education given them on this condition, that therewith content, they should not gadd for preferment out of their own countrey.   (305)

Events were, however, moving fast in matters of state, so as to make Milton's idealistic educational proposals seem out of time. As Richard Cromwell's government was collapsing in 1659, it was clear that the experiment of doing without the certainty of a monarchy was ending. But, for Milton, to revert to monarchy, with its tyran-nicising adjunct, Catholicism, was to betray the Reformation itself. When in *Brief Notes upon a Sermon* (April 1660: Y vii 467–86) he tried to ridicule the royal chaplain Matthew Griffith's calls for a return of Charles II as anointed monarch, he advised that if England were so despairing as to wish a king again, it might at least choose one from home, not France, one 'who hath best aided the people, and best merited against tyrannies' (482). Yet had not God himself favoured something like a senate, as he educated his people in the trials of the wilderness? 'Gather unto me seventy men of the elders of Israel ... and bring them unto the tabernacle of the congregation' (Num 11: 16). Thus, the decree to Moses to institute the Sanhedrin, usually named as the model behind all republican councils, as Israel was nurtured towards a kind of aristocracy of civic and religious virtue before entering the Promised Land. This historical moment in the education of Israel Milton would not fail to mark in Book XII of *Paradise Lost* (214).[9] The selection of fit men from amongst the leaders and magistrates was however no easy matter and it is no wonder that he showed a caution in the stream of texts he wrote about mod-els of government in 1659, as he tried to preserve some form of republicanism against the inevitable tide of feeling for the restora-tion of the monarchy.

The Ready and Easy Way (February 1660: Y vii 351–88) soon dem-onstrates why this historical moment in the wilderness was so formative in the political education of the Israelites and of Adam. Readers are in effect placed at an analogous historical moment, with regard to the progress of England. To have emerged from Egypt and come to the point at which a senate has been adopted by God is to have taken the people to the threshold of liberty; to contemplate monarchy would be to behave like the ignoble waverers in the wilderness, who thought of return to the ease of Egypt with idolatry and alien rule. Moses' asking for help in leading the people was clearly a good thing; whereas the desire of subsequent generations to have a king is seen as a falling off from that standard of government by senate which God had manifestly approved.

In Milton's political writings on the eve of the Restoration a concern is to guarantee the quality and ideological correctness of these senators. By the time his proposals reached their fullest form in the second edition of *Way* (April 1660), it had become clear that he did not wish a council responsive to democratic pressure – 'being well chosen', the senate 'should be perpetual' (433). The broad electorate is the last to be consulted; he dismisses as dangerous 'the noise and shouting of a rude multitude' (442). It is the better and more educated who should choose, and these men, the elders of Milton's times, can save the people from their tendencies to enslave themselves. This is not an argument to please modern democrats and the thoughts of an ageing council of commonwealthsmen have seemed close to absurd.

Faced with the extreme caution of Milton's method of guaranteeing senators, scholars have sometimes tried to explain some of his proposals away as temporising, but the tracts have in them some recurrent characteristics of Milton's thought consistent with writings at other points in his career. His ideas of guaranteeing the quality of senators connect with priorities of religious reform; his proposals for regional government can be linked with the issue; and the unpublished documents, the 'Letter to a Friend' and *The Present Means*, can give us valuable indications to the whole agenda in his developing proposals in 1659.

Milton is most consistent when he enumerates those institutions most to be avoided. He is willing to harness the feelings of crisis: the 'two ... most prevailing usurpers over mankinde' to be avoided in the pursuit of those causes are 'superstition and tyrannie' (421). In 'Christian libertie' (445) is a freedom of rational determination which men must be educated to learn to exercise, and, although the main issue is to do with civil freedom and the avoidance of what he sees as monarchic tyranny, he will say that 'the best part of our libertie' is 'our religion' (420). Those who rule will be tested against the cause of the Reformation. With this broad commitment in mind one may seek consistencies, despite changing details in suggested government, between the 'Letter to a Friend', the manuscript 'Proposals of Certain Expedients', the first edition of *Way*, the *Present Means and Free Delineation of a Commonwealth*, and the second edition of *Way* (to put them in the suggested order of the Yale edition).

In the 'Letter to a Friend' (October 1659: Y vii 322–33) Milton prescribes two levels of government. The first is 'a senate or general council of state', which raises revenue, preserves the public peace, and conducts foreign negotiations. Such a group could consist, he says without much realism, either of the Rump Parliament, or, if the Rump is found wanting in establishing liberty of conscience in matters of religion or in abjuring the rule of a single person, then it could be chosen by the army officers. The senators and army officers should enter into an agreement to support each other in their places, unless either side prove false to those principles of liberty of conscience and abjuration of single rule. As Woolrych (122) noted, there is an indecision here, since Milton first suggests that senators and army officers should be held in place for life, but then he says it is a matter of indifference for the moment as to whether 'the civill government be an annuall democracy or a perpetual Aristocracy' (331). To balance this central council there would be a second tier of government at local level, 'well ordered committies of their faithfullest adherents in every county' (331). The 'Letter to a Friend' (which was not published until 1698) is rough at the edges, but reveals a lot about the priorities in Milton's thought.

In the first edition of *Ready and Easy Way*, after an extended definition of religious and civil liberties, we have the same two tiers of government, but worked out with different detail. The Grand Council of ablest men has its duties defined much as in the 'Letter to Friend', but Milton now declares unequivocally that it should sit 'perpetual', because government is steadiest that way. Here he invokes support from the Sanhedrin, the Areopagus, the Ancients of Sparta and the Roman senate, with conditional support from the constitutions of Venice and the United Provinces (370–1). There is also more detail on the county assemblies. Every county is

> made a little commonwealth, and thir chief town a city ... where the nobilitie and chief gentry may build, houses or palaces, befitting their qualitie, may bear part in the government, make their own judicial lawes, and execute them ... without appeal (383)

I think Woolrych is right to say (183) of this development, that the county governments are 'training grounds for future members of the Grand Council', an idea reinforced by the insistence on education at the local level, in schools and academies, for 'all learning and noble education, not in grammar only, but in all liberal arts and exercises' (384). Training within the local communities, as much as a measure of democracy, is a consideration.

In *The Present Means* (389–95), the letter to Monck of the end of February or beginning of March 1660, the two tiers are adapted to a new situation: Monck had readmitted the secluded members and, thus, ruined Milton's idea of using the Rump as the basis of fit men for his council. In this document, designed to secure a fit council another way, Milton suggests that the chief gentry in each county should be summoned to London, there to be instructed about the dangers of a return to the monarchy, thence to return to their counties to conduct elections of standing councils, and from these councils (thus screened) the representatives for the central council would be chosen. The fitness of the central council is ensured by the *indoctrination* of local gentry into anti-monarchic views. Monck should teach the gentry what they need to know.

Thus, we come to the second edition of *Way*, published when new elections were in process not as Milton wished. The ignorant would choose a king again. New passages reinforce the sense of moral difference between republicanism and kingly rule. The Rump, now gone, is nevertheless defended. Milton is more circumspect in his definition of the powers of the grand council, and, also reacting to public debate, he discusses how far a perpetual assembly should be balanced by a more popular assembly. But essentially he sticks to his perpetual senate of aristocratic virtue, and it emerges that replacements will be elected only by a process of refinement, keeping choice from the popular voice. Selected spirits are to save the people from themselves and compel them to liberty.

These modifications of the two-tier system through the four texts suggest, first, a pragmatic concern: a guarding of the Good Old Cause by first trying to limit influence to those who had proved their loyalty to the cause; and, secondly, a more idealistic concern, the creating of mechanisms by which the councillors coming forward from the counties to the central council would be educated in the right kind of way, or at least would be likely to be freest from corruptive influences at the centre. The elders of Milton's Sanhedrin are, to begin with, those who have shown their allegiance to reforming values in the fight for liberty of conscience, and then a guarantee of right-mindedness is in the old Miltonic insistence on proper education, the liberal instruction of a leading class into rational responsibility, a freeing of guiding minds so as to ensure the liberty of the people.

At the end of his patient account of these texts, Woolrych (217) makes a distinction between Milton's secular prescriptions for government and the rule of the saints optimistically envisaged by more radical parties. There is no denying that Milton's language, schooled in wide reading in the humanities, avoids open millenarian contaminations of the secular and religious, but religious priority is not banished. It is there in the political matter about legislating for liberty of conscience and it is there by implication in that search for remaining true leaders: those whom Milton first wants to trust in the Rump and army are those who have *already shown* commitment to Reformation in the church and state. It is presumably there in the idea of educating gentry in the counties, for if Milton thinks here as he thought in *Likeliest Means*, local colleges would serve free churches as much as free common-wealths. When the great enemies to true liberty are bracketed – superstition in religion and tyranny in secular government – free-dom in secular and religious spheres must be linked. The regions enact their own renewal, free of the corruptive centre.

And can one be quite sure that the passage of hope for such a government until the Second Coming carries no belief? If the Grand Council is maintained, Milton says

> ther can be no cause alleag'd why peace, justice, plentiful trade and all prosperitie should not thereupon ensue throughout the whole land ... shall so continue (if God favour us, and our wilfull sins provoke him not) even to the coming of our true and rightfull and only to be expected King. (374)

One appreciates the *mischief* in that: there is indeed a restoration of a monarch in view, but a greater monarch than vulgar spirits envisage. The pious patterning of the thought is no mere matter of rhetoric. As always, the nation is on trial with God, and if it persists in good government, may God not approve it in a greater way than He did in adopting the Sanhedrin in the wilderness, as the Promised Land is in view? But the nation chose to have a king again, wished to return to Egyptian bondage, and John Milton became, from spokesman of a commonwealth, to admonitory prophet for a commonwealth, one who stood in peril of the new regime.

If Austin Woolrych is correct in his surmise[10] that the infamous Digression of the *History of Britain* dates from about the time of the Restoration, it might perhaps explain why this passage of some two thousand and five hundred words breaks the general method of the *History* in developing an *explicit* parallel, expressed in a tone of bitterness and anger, between a previous age and the present. The Digression compares the state of the British after the withdrawal of the Romans with the state of Englishmen in the seventeenth century. Leaders have failed, in their lack of resolve, after the great opportunity of breaking out of bondage. Blame falls especially on those who ought to have had the Reformation at heart, the shepherds of the church. Those who were initially responsible for the backslidings were the Presbyterians who had failed to press home the creation of a new republican constitution after the execution of the King. We cannot be sure that we have here the long retrospective view, written in anger as the republican revolution was finally failing and a king was being invited back, but we can register that the ultimate causes of failure in the Digression are those of education, just as the ultimate base of the reformed constitutions he was suggesting on the eve of Restoration clearly rested on that of a reformed educational structure.

Notes

1. See p. 162; Y i 379; see the entry in the Commonplace Book at Y i 379. The Waldenses are also mentioned in *Tenure*, *Eikonoklastes*, and the *Second Defence*.
2. An exception is Fixler, *Kingdoms of God*, p. 182.
3. 'This first Psalm ... is by divers of the Ancients rather taken as a Preface or Introduction ... by which ...the happiness of man, what it is, and wherein it consisteth, is declared' (*Annotations upon all the Books of the Old and New Testaments* (London, 1651), vol. 1, under Psalm 1.
4. Radzinowicz, *Psalms*, pp. 29, 60, 145–6, 200, and especially 202–4.
5. VC II pt 2, 1001.
6. *Annotations upon all the Books*, under Psalm 3.
7. The manuscript, now in the Public Record Office, was rediscovered amongst state papers and first published, with translation, in 1825.
8. The argument of William B. Hunter, 'The Provenance of the *Christian Doctrine'*, *SEL*, 32 (1992), 129–42; see also the 'Forum', 143–66; and Hunter's subsequent 'The Provenance of the *Christian Doctrine*: Addenda from the Bishop of Salisbury', *SEL*, 33 (1993), 191–207.

9.   The following section of this chapter shares some common materials with 'Great Senates and Godly Education: politics and cultural renewal in some pre- and post-revolutionary texts of Milton', in *Milton and Republicanism*, ed. David Armitage, Armand Himy, and Quentin Skinner (Cambridge: Cambridge University Press, 1995).
10.   In 'The date': see Chapter 5, note 16 above.

8

Paradise Lost: Spiritual Strengthening for Adverse Times

Facing Milton's greatest and best known work of the Restoration period, *Paradise Lost*, published in the summer of 1667 but worked on for a good number of years before, one might reflect that the very title invites thoughts of great blessings lost for man, as a result of a failure in spiritual discipline. It is not difficult to see some point in that for a revolutionary, as he meditated opportunities lost and the sad consequences, for those of Milton's persuasion, of the failure to reform. But this greatest of English epic poems constructed about the most powerful of archetypal myths will not submit to single readings and purports in any case to be also about recovery from that fall.

This chapter is not a general account of the poem. Two main questions are addressed. First, given Milton's overriding vocational sense of his role as writer, what kind of educational benefits would *Paradise Lost* seem to be designed to have for its audience in 1667? (Whether it has succeeded or not in this aim, for readers, is another matter, on which many different judgements will be given by different readers in different ages.) This enquiry is of course a matter of speculation, as all historical recovery is, even of yesterday, and is not the same thing as trying to find out what meanings the poem may have had for successive readerships. Secondly, given that some influential scholars have recently been tempted to speculate that *Paradise Lost* operates within conditions and codes of censorship,[1] I would like to question, in various ways, to what extent the educative methods of the poet are based on modes of communication which cannot speak bluntly except within tightly limited conventions because of the adverse times.

In the first question another is implicit, to which very different answers have also been returned over the centuries: did this blind

155

radical poet in effect retire from polemic, during the Restoration, into more sublime (and by implication, universal) meditations? To assume so was once the comfortable thought, creating the possibility of giving secondary status to his writings of political functionalism, of elevating the 'timeless' works, and creating a satisfactory if illusory space between the poetic and the political.

In the second case, the question assumes that Milton *is* still in some sense 'political' in his text, but that he could only communicate by adopting oblique and generalised kinds of definition in a method which must be decoded by the modern reader, who may believe that its method was once plainer than it is to us now. Both questions tempt simple answers which I would like to challenge and both issues need to be seen in the context of a broader assessment of kinds of instruction and persuasion attempted in *Paradise Lost*.

No author of a great epic poem communicated in so many obviously instructional ways with his readers through the narratorial voice as did Milton in *Paradise Lost*. His interventions take many forms, some of them direct, like the many judgemental, ironic, or impassioned asides, blatant pieces of didacticism in the narrator-reader relationship; other guiding devices are less direct, like the challenging epic similes, which are often developed to such an extent that a whole judgemental perspective is created in their span of reference, or where Milton has the reader share instructive angelic discourse with Adam, thus feeling the subtle power of a liberal paideia. Had he continued in his erstwhile plan of writing a great exemplary piece for the nation in the form of tragedy, he might not have had access to such comprehensive means of direction. The narrator-reader relationship is sometimes magisterial, sometimes Socratic, sometimes withering, sometimes charming. Readers cannot fail to realise that they are in the hands of a teacher of many directive arts and highly committed views. Nor can that teacher be seen to have retired from polemic, when he comments so often on the political, social, and religious institutions about him. For all its care for spiritual wisdom and the broad universality of its themes, *Paradise Lost* is not a work of disengagement from the business of a fallen world, in fact the author seems to seek to share an apprehension of that fallen world with his readers.

Within the range of such devices no reader is likely to forget the openings to Books I, III, VII, and IX, moments in which the poet speaks, personally but always in the role of poet, in ever-deepening revelation of his endeavours in his great project and of his state of life. Three of these passages are, formally speaking, invocations, such as were traditional in an epic poem, though they are developed far beyond merely formal imitation; all four passages break off from the narrative task at signal moments of transition, in reminder of the almost suprahuman dimensions of the poem. The precise nature of the epic endeavour is thus progressively unfolded with the story, and it turns out to be nothing less than to create for the nation a truer epic than had appeared in English before by exemplifying Christian teaching more rigorously than any modern epic. More than that, since he claims something unattempted yet (in English?) in either verse or *prose*, Milton points to other kinds of instructional work, perhaps to the rationalistic endeavour of what would later be called theodicy (justifying the ways of God to men), through an endeavour which had also been variously embodied in much of the Bible itself. The invocations have some of the nature of prayer, praising and petitioning, and each in different ways reaffirms the poet's service to God. Moreover, they progressively establish a claim to divine presence with the poet. However, the revelations which readers are least likely to forget are those to do with the personal, if typified, circumstances of the poet.

In these aspects, too, each invocation challenges cultural and ideological recognition in the reader. If the opening of Book I takes the reader into alignment only implicitly – by asking for recognition of the supreme value of the 'adventurous song' – the opening of Book III demands a relationship with a poet memorably placed in adversity, trying to compass heavenly light whilst being blind and by God's aid achieving a paradoxical triumph over his condition, seeing all the more clearly in fact by inward illumination. But this mythical self-placement as blind poet or prophet, a Christian Homer or Tiresias, is then deepened again in the opening of Book VII, where the reader must rise to the challenge of a new revelation: not only is the poet blind, but he suffers from earthly persecutions in evil times, with dangers and darkness compassed round, and in solitude, like a true prophet or saint unheard amongst his own people. The terms of the description are both specific – beyond blindness, 'darkness' could imply literal incarceration – and more broadly suggestive – it could, for example, token that his persecutors move in circles of unilluminated superstition. Also, the revelation of this passage gains meaning from its context in the narrative: there is a need for spiritual strengthening before beginning the narration (in the person of Raphael) of the great hexaemeral topic of the Creation of the World. What is more, the whole Raphael episode in which the invocation about isolation and danger is embedded has been presented as a wonderful model of civilised social discourse between courteous angel–teacher and unfallen man–pupil. Thus, the present times of fallen adversity are set in stark, memorable contrast. In general, as the full meaning of Fall is unfolded through the poem, whilst gradually revealing the Providence plan for restoration, so the personal meaning to the poet of living in an ever-falling world is also unfolded, whilst again revealing at each of these 'personal' moments the continuance of divine communication and care. It looks as though Milton has challengingly inscribed his own history into the history of the Fall of the human race.

These are subtle effects of composition. That one critic,[2] seeking to illustrate how Milton might have responded to conditions of censorship, suggested that the revelations about persecution in dark times was put so late in the poem so as to evade the eyes of the cursory censor, makes one want to reiterate the point about artfulness all the more: an explanation based on censorship is a reductive way of seeing the technique of self-presentation. However, the evidence of these great passages may be interpreted in different ways, and, seen from a purely biographical point of view, this gradual revelation of personal circumstance has led some to assumptions about the chronology of composition, which we should examine.

The self-revelations in *Paradise Lost* have been put beside some other sometimes sketchy and not very well corroborated biographical evidence to make a pattern. That Milton felt himself in particular danger whilst approximately in the middle of composing his great poem (whatever the precise meaning of 'Half yet remains unsung') is not too surprising, although of course we cannot securely know how and in what order he wrote and revised the poem. As a leading apologist for a regicide Commonwealth and an officer in its administration Milton was indeed in danger at the Restoration, in the spring, summer, and autumn of 1660.

The sequence of events is not clear, but it seems that it was only with difficulty that Milton escaped exemplary punishment. The proclamation of Charles as king took place on 8 May and he entered

London on his birthday on 29 May. It soon became apparent that there were to be not just executions of surviving regicides – seven were to be named to die – but that also, as was announced on 8 June, twenty non-regicides were to be chosen by the Commons for punishment 'short of death'. Milton had found his writings under increasing attack and on 16 June his works in defence of the rebellion were denounced, and *Eikonoklastes* and the *Defensio* were ordered to be burned by the public hangman. (A subsequent order of 13 August gave people ten days, in which to hand in their copies of Milton's books.) At the same time proceedings were ordered against Milton and John Goodwin, another radical writer, but perhaps as a result of intercessions on his behalf, perhaps of a widely spread feeling that God had already punished and neutralised this rebel with blindness, Milton did not find himself on the list of twenty, though Goodwin did.

During the early part of this period Milton seems to have lived in hiding in London; during the latter part of it, but for how long is not clear, he was actually imprisoned. The first real indication of safety came with the passing of an indemnity bill, on 11 July, pardoning those not included on the lists, a bill which received royal assent on 19 August. But he was evidently held in prison after the issue of this amnesty, for his case was raised in the Commons by friends on 15 December, arguing that he should receive the benefit of indemnity. There was further discussion of his case two days later when it emerged that the sergeant-at-arms at the Tower was charging exorbitantly for the period of his incarceration. The matter was arbitrated, and the official pardon came, and Milton seems then to have resumed private life in a rented house in Holborn, which had been taken for him by this time. Danger, darkness, and humiliating solitude had indeed provided a stark backdrop to a narrative of instructive and delightful discourse with an angel in Paradise.

It is not impossible, then, that the opening to Book VII was written in 1660 when Milton was about half-way through the poem. What indications we have (and these are not many) have led most scholars to think that he began seriously on the poem as we now know it round about 1658, and, according to one particular story it was complete, in draft at least, by 1665, when Milton showed it to his young Quaker pupil and friend, Thomas Ellwood (P 595–8). That it did not appear in print until 1667 may be partially explicable from the disruptions of London life through the plague of the summer, autumn, and winter of 1665 (during which Milton moved

out of London temporarily to Chalfont St Giles) and the Great Fire
(September 1666). There are other indications that Milton composed
slowly, often at night, and best in autumn and winter. The whole
business of constructing an intricate epic must have been made all
the more difficult by his blindness, leading him to rely on
amanuenses to record, correct, and read back to him. But just how
long he spent composing the poem has been open to some debate.

We have the plans for various epics and tragedies recorded in the
Trinity Manuscript in the early 1640s, and of those the four entries
on the story of the Fall (35–6) are the most developed. However, at
that point the poem was to be a tragedy and we have nothing like
the structure of *Paradise Lost* as we know it. Those who have been
tempted to talk of composition long before the late 1650s have also
remembered another story, this one like others from his somewhat
unreliable pupil nephew Edward Philips, that he had seen Satan's
address to the sun of Book IV (32), back when he was living in his
uncle's house.[3] But Milton was full of projects. It is not safe to
assume that a projected tragic poem on the Fall in the 1640s would
have looked anything like the epic published in 1667 and the gist of
the authorial self-representation in the poem is that the reader
should share with him times of notable adversity for his idealistic
causes: a time of composition which spanned the declining years of
the Commonwealth and the danger and advent of new royalist
'tyranny' would make some sense of that suggested reader relationship. It would give a function of the poem, to reinforce the fit, few
audience in times in which they may have thought that Providence
had deserted them. Persecution may well have intervened in
composition and been recorded in the poem, but it seems most
likely that the poet was actually blind when he began *Paradise Lost*,
and that the reference to blindness in Book III is delayed for its
instructional effect, not for any reason of biography.

Understanding the full impact of the Fall, in *Paradise Lost*, then, is
also to be reminded of times of adversity for the godly and the
educated. That positioning provides a mainspring for the poem, a
religious and political engagement. It is, I think, too simple to say
with recent editors, that the poem 'suppresses its politics'.[4] To illustrate how dynamically political analysis, broadly conceived as to do
with the whole spiritual discipline of peoples and founded on a
highly developed historical sense, is built into the structures of
Paradise Lost one might look for example at the first two books of the
poem, in which the institutions of evil gather themselves for the

assault on man, and in which the expectations of the reader are first set. The decision to begin the narrative at the moment at which Satan and his crew pick themselves up from the burning lake and to follow them to the point at which they are ready to prey on man's state of innocence had large consequences, from this point of view. Even by the end of Book I, which develops its action with seemingly irresistible pace, we see instituted tyrannical monarchy built on false religion. This first section of the narrative of the poem already invites the reader to share with the narrator long, militant perspectives on the history of the fallen world.

The satanic powers are defined by reference to powers of godless tyranny or the destruction of civilisation throughout history: Busiris and Egyptian cruelty (305); impious pharoahs at the time of Israel in bondage (330); a great paynim Sultan (348); or the hordes of barbarians (352). Behind this exposition is a sequence of cause and effect, showing how political disorder develops from false religion: it is a grandly allusive illustration of the old fear of privy wolves. The epic roll-call of the chief angels names them as they were known as idols in the Old Testament, representing the infections of false religion surrounding God's people. The list of Satan's disciples is systematic: all the major cultural dangers are there, to be released on godlike man in history. Protestant nations identify with the literature of Israel fighting for its cultural identity in the Old Testament. Even as we are introduced to Satan and his leaders we are being put in mind of that struggle for a true church and the liberty of a nation.

Although most of the references belong specifically to the history of Israel (whatever their generalised significance), there is also a moment in which a reminder is issued that the patterns are current in more recent history. Belial, the most slothful of the satanic princes, aptly 'came last' and at first the narrative is in the past tense, of Old Testament history: '... then whom a spirit more lewd / Fell not from heaven ... to him no temple stood / Or altar smoked ...'. But then, though the examples are still Old Testament, the tense shifts into the present of poet and reader, suggesting recurrent and familiar patterns:

> ... yet who more oft than he
> In temple and at altars, when the priest
> Turns atheist, as did Ely's sons, who filled
> With lust and violence the house of God.

> In courts and palaces he also reigns
> And in luxurious cities, where the noise
> Of riot ascends above their loftiest towers,
> And injury and outrage: and when night
> Darkens the streets, then wander forth the sons
> Of Belial, flown with insolence and wine.
> Witness the streets of Sodom, and that night
> In Gibeah, when the hospitable door
> Exposed a matron to avoid worse rape.
>
> (i 493–505)

The method is continued in the short passage following, in which the pagan gods of Greece and Rome are briefly covered. Then, as Saturn and his followers are banished by Jove, there is a provocative westward movement to Britain and Ireland: 'Fled over Adria to the Hesperian fields, / And o'er the Celtic roamed the utmost isles.' Long ago false religion spread to these shores and set the agenda for the champions of truth.

By the time 'the imperial ensign' (536) is raised an ordered, powerful army, 'Breathing united force with fixéd thought', is in place, its leader hardened in new pride, a power beyond any that earth has known, but also recalling patterns the earth has known. After the creation of such military might as to create empires, the buildings are established such as might be at the centre of such empires. Pandaemonium, which some have seen as a reflection on Rome, is far more broadly based: it has an aggregate design, incorporating the seats of great tyrants and warriors of old, Nimrod, and the rulers of Egypt and Babylon. It is the site of secular power, but it employs for political ends the intimidating features of a temple; it is part temple, part palace, in the combination of religion and state which Milton so distrusted. The architecture and the interior lighting strike admiration, the trumpets announce 'awful ceremony' (753). The conditions are ripe for the subjugation of minds by a tyrant. As the fallen hosts crowd to the council, they are mocked by an authorial irony, noting that they allow themselves to be belittled:

> So thick the airy crowd
> Swarmed and were straitened; till the signal given,
> Behold a wonder! they but now who seemed
> In bigness to surpass Earth's giant sons

Now less than smallest dwarfs, in narrow room
Throng numberless ...

(i 775–80)

and there is withering play on the phrase 'at large': 'Thus incor-
poreal spirits to smallest forms / Reduced their shaped immense,
and were at large ...' (i 789–90). The common host thus subjects
itself to manipulation by a princely caste:

But far within
And in their own dimensions like themselves
The great seraphic lords and cherubim
In close recess and secret conclave sat ...

(i 792–5)

It is no surprise to find that when 'the great consult' begins, in Book
II, what appears to be a public debate has in fact been stage-
managed by Satan and his henchman Beelzebub. Thus easily are
weakened minds, even of great angels, led. Abdiel, confronting
Satan's falsehood with the undeceiving powers of Truth in Book VI,
gets his definitions right as usual, when he calls the false monarch
'idol of majesty divine' (vi 101), one who inspires awe with the
trappings of false religion. And amongst other unmaskings of falsehood in the poem is a great one performed in Book X by God
himself. Satan's return to Pandaemonium is a scene managed as a
theatrical triumph: disguised entry, blaze of light from his throne,
self-aggrandising speech, proposed triumphal procession. These
awing effects are upstaged by God, who transforms the whole self-
glorifying court to snakes at the moment of proposed climax.

What we have here is of course couched in historical generality,
though applications to recent British history invite. One could argue
that the generality is itself a prudent retreat from the possibility of
censorship, though one should also say that there is nothing
guarded about the way in which the connections between idolatry
and tyranny have been demonstrated. There is in fact never any
pulling of punches, with regard to the vital matter of false religion
and the enslaving of minds in *Paradise Lost*: for example, one of the
first irrational acts of Eve after the Fall is one of idolatry. From false
religion most tyrannic enslavements begin. In view of this, it is
ironic that the one story we have (yet another story to weigh) of a
censorship difficulty with *Paradise Lost* concerns attitudes to

monarchs and the issue of superstition: writing in 1698 Toland, who had an interest in Milton as a radical, claimed that the licenser had paused over the passage comparing Satan as 'dread commander' to the sun in eclipse shedding 'disastrous twilight ... and with fear of change / Perplexes monarchs' (i 597–9). Whatever the passing mischief of these lines, greater importance surely attaches to the fact that the whole initial presentation of Satan shows how the institutions of tyrannical monarchy are in Milton's analysis supported by the use of false religion. The reader is given an immense sense not just of the inevitable impact of evil on innocent Adam and Eve but of the continuing infections through all human history, through to the present time.

Not that the depiction of Satan as a tyrant exploiting idolatry has been unproblematical in the history of interpretation.[5] In a poem in which rebellion from God is shown as a recurring phenomenon – the rebellion of angels precedes the Fall and after the first Fall come all the subsequent disobediences of man – Milton, as often, invites the reader to discriminate between true and false causes, as he defines them. Satan presents his case as one of resistance to tyrants, whilst himself taking on the characteristics of a tyrant. Not all readers have been prepared to accede to Milton's educative distinctions, though they are less contradictory than some have wished to find. For example, although the Son is given the anointing of a king, he is not presented as a feudal model such as monarchists might use, but rather as supreme, perhaps because immortal and perfect, a unique example of a 'vice-regent' chosen on merit for the good of the people. Politics are enmeshed in religious formulation. In a carefully ordered sequence at the beginning of Book III, Milton establishes that the anointing takes place only after the Son has manifested unexampled love in being willing to sacrifice himself for the sake of man. As Mary Ann Radzinowicz[6] correctly points out, Milton is careful *not* to allow the Son's kingship to be read as a model for earthly hereditary kings: 'Because thou hast...

>   ... quitted all to save
> A world from utter loss, and hast been found
> By merit more than birthright Son of God,
> Found worthiest to be so by being good,
> Far more than great or high; because in thee
> Love hath abounded more than glory abounds,

Therefore thy humiliation shall exalt
With thee thy manhood also to this throne …
                              (iii 307–14)

Political education does not cease with the cases of Satan and the Son. In particular, the whole closing closing episode, like the opening, fills out an analysis as political as it is religious. In Michael's instructive story of man's constant fallings and the unfolding of the divine scheme of justice and mercy, even into the era of Christ, Adam learns how often and in how many ways the temperate discipline of godly living will fail. Through a series of scenes Michael presents a schematised historical account in such a way as to be of the greatest educational benefit to Adam, who learns the events for the first time and seeks with Michael's help to interpret them aright, so as not to impugn Providence. The benefits are presumably meant also for the reader, who will recognise the patterns with the benefit of analytical retrospection, and who may also be seeking to recognise the justice and mercy of Providence throughout history. A Providence which has acted thus in the past, which has purposes which enfold all human history, must care for present predicaments as well.

Organised into simplified periods each teaching specific lessons, the history depends upon many familiar analyses and touches upon many types with which the reader would have been familiar. After a neatly interconnected series of visions, the first great epoch ends with the Flood, a judgement following excesses of a period of peace, which had in turn followed the barbarities of a period of brutal militarism. The method may perhaps be illustrated with this material. In Milton's account the laxness of the people of Noah's time leads to 'civil broils'. Many a writer had used the myth of the Flood to issue warning to a slack nation: Drayton, for example, had used it in his warning volume of 1627, and less publically Marvell had used inundation at Nun Appleton to figure judgemental purgation after civil strife.[7] Lack of godly discipline was often blamed for the nation's ills, especially after the long period of peace during which the early Stuarts began. Milton's masque, in its themes of temperance and the importance of godly education, had participated in these assumptions. But there is no crude use of typology or historical analogy here in Michael's description of the time of Noah. As we have seen elsewhere, Milton was too much a historian to formulate his lessons from history too simply. It is only in

Michael's subsequent analysis that scholars have sensed the possibilities of contemporary application, and even here the evidence is not of the kind to suggest a crude allegory. The conquerors of the militaristic period revel in their earthly booty: 'Who having ... achieved thereby /Fame in the world, high titles, and rich prey, / Shall change their course to pleasure, ease, and sloth ...' (xi 791–4). The oppressed lose even the pretence to godly virtue and no longer fight for their liberty:

> The conquered also, and enslaved by war
> Shall with their freedom lost all virtue lose
> And fear of God, from whom their piety feigned
> In sharp contest of battle found no aid
> Against invaders; therefore cooled in zeal
> Thenceforth shall practise how to live secure,
> Worldly or dissolute, on what their lords
> Shall leave them to enjoy; for the earth shall bear
> More than enough, that temperance may be tried:
> So all shall turn degenerate, all depraved,
> Justice and temperance, truth and faith forgot;
> One man except, the only son of light
> In a dark age ...
>
> (xi 797–809)

Scholars have been tempted to see a reference to the collapsed sense of purpose in the reformers, Alastair Fowler, for example, in his edition writing: 'The lines about feigned zeal cooling in adversity, which sound particularly *ad hominem*, refer to a problem dealt with more fully in *Samson Agonistes*' (CF 1022). It may be, but the technique is not *ad hominem*, rather the identification more broadly of a state of mind – time-serving – in the context of what should be uncompromised principle – zeal for freedom and true religion. The broad underlying commitments are clear, and the 'fit' audience will doubtless recognise those commitments.

If the ante-diluvian worlds ends in judgement upon a collapse of godly discipline, the post-diluvian world is one in which, after a period of godly fear, tyranny and idolatry are the repeated adversities, in a phase initiated by Nimrod, the type of the tyrant whose self-glorifying endeavours lead to the mockery of Babel. Adam's judgement on tyranny reveals a deep aversion to the lording of some men over others:

O execrable son so to aspire
Above his brethren, to himself assuming
Authority usurped, from God not given:
He gave us only over beast, fish, fowl
Dominion absolute; that right we hold
By his donation; but man over men
He made not lord; such title to himself
Reserving, human left from human free.
                              (xii 64–71)

Michael commends these thoughts, talking of the subduing of
'rational liberty', only adding an explanation for God's purposes,
that tyranny is sometimes allowed by God ('Though to the tyrant
thereby no excuse') in justice for man's own falling into irrational
servitude. Here too is another judgemental idea, which could be
applied to England's capitulation to monarchy, but no specific
application is made, only the basic principles clarified.

And so it is in general through Michael's account. Different stages
in the evolution of societies are recognised, but the general
objectives are clear, those of prosperity based on obedience and
'freedom and peace to men', as Adam expresses it early in the
account, or as in the 'faire equality, fraternal rule' of the rule of the
patriarchs before Nimrod, or under the 'laws and rites' established
under Moses in the twelve tribes, a state in which God marked his
approval by granting his presence in the tabernacle. That last case is
also framed so as to embody a matter of principle which might have
been seen by the contemporary reader to bear upon government at
the time. With some simplification, Milton presents the government
of Israel as formulated in the wilderness as one of a meritocracy,
under the Sanhedrim or 'senate', like that he had advocated at the
eve of the Restoration:

This also shall they gain by their delay
In the wide wilderness, there they shall found
Their government, and their great senate choose
Through the twelve tribes, to rule by laws ordained...
                              (xii 223–6)

This form of government 'might be thought aristocratical', said one
popular book of Milton's time.[8] The republican implications would
have been clear: it was claimed by contemporary republicans that

the republics of Greece and Rome took their pattern from a form of government first given to the Israelites in the wilderness.

What is in question, then, is not political engagement, but the ways in which it is mediated in the poem. However, to attribute the mode of these formulations to codes of censorship alone seems too simple, partly because the methods are not dissimilar to those in other works by Milton. What we have in Michael's episode is in many ways like what we have in other historical writing: the drawing of lessons by the identification of general principles, without forcing analogies too crudely. The nice matter of the fictional integrity of the poem might also be considered: there is almost certainly a distinction between what is taught to Adam, the man who learns of history for the first time, and what might be remarked from narrator to reader, living in times of experience in the fallen world. Adam does not need an education in the details of English seventeenth-century politics, but an understanding of the great principles by which the discipline of nations may be judged; the educated reader can supply the connections with contemporary history for himself. For that reader to see Adam's mind trying to encompass the great issues of fallibility and justice and grace, for men and for nations, for the first time is in itself a matter of no small imaginative interest.

It follows from that, that there might be moments in the poem, outside the two large episodes with the angelic visitors, in which the narrator addresses the reader directly in more blatant, challenging fashion, bringing the lessons home more clearly to the reader's own time. Such a moment might be identified, for example, in Book IV, in which Satan's jumping over the wall is simultaneously the spoiling of the true church:

> Due entrance he disdained, and in contempt,
> At one slight bound over leaped all bound
> Of hill or highest wall, and sheer within
> Lights on his feet. As when a prowling wolf,
> Whom hunger drives to seek new haunt for prey,
> Watching where shepherds pen their flocks at eve
> In hurdled cotes amid the field secure,
> Leaps o'er the fence with ease into the fold:
> Or as a thief bent to unhoard the cash
> Of some rich burgher, whose substantial doors,
> Cross-barred and bolted fast, fear no assault,
> In at the window climbs, or o'er the tiles;

So clomb this first grand thief into God's fold:
So since into his church lewd hirelings climb.
Thence up he flew, and on the tree of life
The middle tree and highest that there grew,
Sat like a cormorant...

(iv 180–96)

The simile of the thief and the robber derives from well-known New Testament texts in John (10.1). But this is more than a glancing, bitter aside. Paradise *is* the church, in figure, something godly to be fenced, a whole God-praising way of life. The moment Satan breaks into Paradise there is instituted for the future the spoiling of the true primitive church by those who do not reverence its meaning. The rapacious sit on, even 'use for prospect', the means to everlasting life. Wolves at least prey for hunger; window-climbing domestic thieves have pettier minds, bent on lucre. What is instituted by this first grand thief is the career-minded priesthood of lewd hirelings which Milton, like many a reformer before him, thought he saw so clearly through biblical and recent history. To the 'fit' reader these dimensions would be amply plain.

Such a reader might also have appreciated how that seemingly digressive passage functions persuasively in the narrative art of the poem, for it is in fact no heavy intrusion. Like the great invocations, it has to do with the pacing and counterpointing of the narration: the time spent on reminders of the baleful significance of Satan's illicit entrance into the 'church' of Paradise serves to intensify the reader's sense of dread and expectation, as the Destroyer approaches innocence. There are many such persuasive features in the poem.

Nor are the historical and political analyses confined to the church, for all the centrality of religion to the discipline of the nation. One could take another obvious example of historical cross-reference from Book IV, which praises the felicity of domestic discipline in marriage:

Perpetual fountain of domestic sweets,
Whose bed is undefiled and chaste pronounced,
Present, or past, as saints and patriarchs used.
Here Love his golden shafts employs, here lights
His constant lamp, and waves his purple wings,
Reigns here and revels; not in the bought smile

> Of harlots, loveless, joyless, unendeared,
> Casual fruition, nor in court amours
> Mixed dance, or wanton mask, or midnight ball,
> Or serenade, which the starved lover sings
> To his proud fair, best quitted with disdain.
>
> (iv 760–70)

Milton's readers may not have omitted to notice that he included in his list of false loves, illustrated with mischievous conciseness from literary culture, the social habits of courts such as that which England had dismissed and gained once more at the Restoration. Here and elsewhere, a whole cultural critique is on hand. The beauty of his subject, which involved describing the *whole* discipline of life before and after the Fall of man (as well as an equivalent for the fall of angels), was that it provided many points of contrast with known later cultures which the instructional, sometimes satirical voice of the narrator could exploit.

Again, the seeming digression plays a part in the art of narration: the sharp reminders about false ideas of love give much greater celebratory yet poignant power to the picture of Adam and Eve in peaceful slumber, to which the narration returns – 'These lulled by nightingales embracing slept.' That is to point to what has been lost.

As a result of these methods, the most important moments of definition of life in Paradise are punctuated with clarifications and reflections which bear upon post-lapsarian knowledge. Sometimes these moments are, to the modern ear, almost comically directive, as in the pedantic aside about the status of pagan myth against biblical truth, not unimportant to the Christian educator, but an odd way of creating a suspension at a celebratory high point:

> Groves whose rich trees wept odorous gums and balm,
> Others whose fruit burnished with golden rind
> Hung amiable, Hesperian fables true,
> If true, here only, and of delicious taste
>
> (iv 248–51)

But often the definitions seem less peripheral, for in the act of imagining paradisal life a whole mode of reflection has been created, bearing upon the fallen world. So in the crucial definitions of Adam and Eve as first seen by reader and Satan:

Two of far nobler shape, erect and tall,
Godlike erect, with native honour clad
In naked majesty seemed lords of all,
And worthy seemed, for in their looks divine
The image of their glorious maker shone,
Truth, wisdom, sanctitude severe and pure,
Severe, but in true filial freedom placed;
Whence true authority in men; though both
Not equal ...

(iv 288–296)

What binds the passage is the idea of the divine image in Adam and
Eve, and that is what strikes the envious Satan, too. It is an
insistently religious formulation. Their authority is defined by their
godliness (the wonderful figure 'native honour clad' is based on the
formulation of Psalm 104.1 and refers also to divine image), but the
insertion of the word 'true' – 'Whence true authority in men' –
encompasses a passing corrective to other earthly claims of
domination: all claims of men to have right of authority over others,
except on the basis of their godly behaviour, are to be rejected.
Eminence is thus freely earned and freely recognised. So the story of
Eden can inform subsequent moral and political discourse in the
most fundamental ways. The poem is an education in such basic
principles.

A second insistence in the passage occurs in the clarifications
about the image of 'severe and pure' saintly demeanour: lest his
readers think that man was made in rigid 'puritan' or regimented
neomonastic mode, subduing the full personality, Milton issues a
reminder that he was created to be in a state of freely loving, ration-
ally self-determining obedience, using all his capacities to God's
praise. Without such a model, true Reformation, based on reason,
cannot be. Nothing is not political, in the end.

It is of course a modern shibboleth, to find political functions for
all literary texts, whether those functions are overt and pronounced,
or whether they are constructed by scholars who place the texts in
wider cultural readings. The Genesis story, filled out in such copi-
ous detail as Milton provides, furnishes almost endless opportunity
for kinds of political reading, because the myth engages so many
issues of cultural perception. In the limited functions of this chapter,
it may be enough to notice, as I have said, that the poem abounds in
moments which explicitly connect with the fallen world of poet and

reader, and that political issues are subsumed into a broader language of Christian humanism, whatever one's attitude to it. In that sense politics is not subjected to censorship so much as taken into a larger, if outmoded, linguistic scheme.

Such may be illustrated in many ways. One could, for example, point to a structure in the poem which denotes the difference between what it means to have the presence of God and what it means to be in a state of exile or alienation from the divine. Such a structure is an obvious component of the story of the Fall, with its comparisons of existence in Paradise and after the expulsion. It also encompasses the idea of the care of Providence, the divine presence which is never absent from the godly, and it is articulated in the whole epic design of the poem, which inherits from cultural history schemes of exile and restoration. To see how such a structure might function, in a way which includes spiritual, moral, and political definition, we need only begin at the end of the long educational scheme, with the state of Adam's final, reconciled understanding of Providence before being exiled from Paradise:

> Greatly instructed I shall hence depart,
> Greatly in peace of thought, and have my fill
> Of knowledge, what this vessel can contain;
> Beyond which was my folly to aspire.
> Henceforth I learn, that to obey is best,
> And love with fear the only God, to walk
> As in his presence, ever to observe
> His providence, and on him sole depend,
> Merciful over all his works, with good
> Still overcoming evil, and by small
> Accomplishing great things, by things deemed weak
> Subverting worldly strong, and worldly wise
> By simply meek; that suffering for truth's sake
> Is fortitude to highest victory,
> And to the faithful death the gate of life;
> Taught this by his example whom I now
> Acknowledge my redeemer ever blest.
>
> (xii 557–73)

Milton's major poems are specifically educational in the sense of strengthening the spirit for action in the world, action understood to be imminent. 'Lycidas', having re-enacted with considerable affective power negative thoughts about Providence, takes singer and reader into calm resolution towards 'pastures new', new vocational responsibilities; *Paradise Regained*, the poem directly about Jesus, chooses the preparatory and elucidating episode of the temptation in the wilderness, where the redeemer would emerge from trial ready to play his great part in the world; and *Samson Agonistes*, having like 'Lycidas' raised and stilled passionate doubts about Providence, ends with an implicit challenge to the faithful, to learn from the great example of Samson's trial of faith and to realise how God awaits their part in the struggle against tyranny and idolatry. *Paradise Lost* takes Adam, the reader, and, arguably, the presented poet to the same strengthening but challenging point of instruction. Adam, by his own efforts of repentance and by new instruction recovering from despair, learning from Michael the pattern of future history for the faithful, and being relieved of his many doubts by seeing the constant overarching presence of God in judgemental and merciful acts towards man right into the era of Christ, walks in a state of preparation into the same kind of world which poet and reader share. It is not a quiescent world: in the history of nations small things will be seen to overcome great, the meek will have power over the worldly, and in the fight for good there will be true spiritual heroism. There are causes always to be espoused. But divine presence is promised even in seeming exile, and the loss of Eden is understood to lead ultimately to the restoration of the blissful seat. The pastures new are now the 'world before them', and the resounding psalmic phrase with which the poet ends, 'their solitary way', is to be understood as modified by the provision of a 'paradise within' and 'rest' and continuing divine guidance.

Reaching that point of clarification has been a process of being subjected to many kinds of persuasion, including something like cathartic experience, that is, of the raising and stilling of disturbing emotions and questions, for the Fall is a tragic subject, though contained within epic form. 'Lycidas', *Samson* and *Paradise Lost* all share something of this kind of tragic dynamic, in their affective designs. Having fallen, despite being freshly instructed by Raphael, Adam suffers with his wife the experience of despair and must with her work through repentance, and then be further instructed by Michael, before he can clear his mind of doubts and fears, in order to enter prepared into his new world. The reader, though never short of instruction, is subjected to a longer series of disturbing emotions, for as we have seen from the very first book the powers of evil are fully conveyed, so that there is an immense sense of vulnerability built up about the unfallen state even before it is described. If pity and fear are passions which Milton gives as an example in his preface to *Samson* concerning catharsis, then those emotions seem intended to be invoked in the reader long before the experiences of Adam and Eve are shared. And the understanding of Providence, which Adam has learnt, has also been further demonstrated to the reader, because the sequence of episodes is such that the powers of evil are always followed in the narration by the reactions of the powers of good, so that the project of Satan is always seen to be encompassed by the divine plan. As for the poet, left in solitary darkness at the opening of Book VII, his experience as another kind of exile who need not lose divine presence must be presumed to be taken into the final spiritual strengthening.

There is a curious power to Milton's use of phrases about God's presence, which are often biblical, with cultural assumptions attached. The presence of God is comforting, yet awing; it seems to recover some sense of true majestic kingship, even sometimes of a court. To be a Uriel, a high-ranking angel, is to be 'one of the seven / ... in God's presence, nearest to his throne' (iii 649). There is a necessity for humility in his presence, when acts of grace are extended, a humility which Belial cannot manage: 'with what eyes could we / Stand in his presence humble ...' (ii 239–40). More broadly, beyond the 'court' of heaven, to be in the presence of God and not alienated, implies being in the eye and favour of the Almighty, hence the vision of eternal bliss given by the Son, when 'wrath shall be no more / Thenceforth, but in thy presence joy entire' (ii 265). A people denied that eye and favour may even be cast out, as in the time of the Flood:

> ... till God at last
> Wearied with their iniquities, withdraw
> His presence from among them, and avert
> His holy eyes ...
>
> (xii 106–9)

Adam's fears about losing Paradise are expressed memorably, if primitively in religious understanding, in terms of loss of divine presence:

> ... here I could frequent,
> With worship, place by place where he vouchsafed
> Presence divine, and to my sons relate;
> 'On this mount he appeared; under this tree
> Stood visible, among these pines his voice
> I heard, here with him at this fountain talked ...'
>
> (xi 317–22)

Denied physical presence, Adam must understand subtler forms of divine communication, although the dispensation of princely grace still defines the actions, as Michael explains:

> God is as here, and will be found alike
> Present, and of his presence many a sign
> Still following thee, still compassing thee round
> With goodness and paternal love, his face
> Express, and of his steps the track divine.
>
> (xi 350–4)

Adam's determination to go into the world 'To walk as in his presence' wonderfully expresses the state of godly living to be replicated in new circumstances in the fallen world. In Paradise heavenly visitations had been amply described, and the structure of epic amply exploited to define an amazing liberal education from the two archangels. Direct presences are now denied: Adam walks *'as in'* the divine presence; yet there are still the same feelings of obedient fear mixed with reassurance of grace and comfort, that in more mysterious ways there will be communication with the divine.

The definition of states of life according the sense of divine presence is absolutely structural to the poem, as the organisation of the metaphysical 'universe' in which the action takes place makes clear. What places Heaven, Hell, and the newly created world is not so much a single cosmological scheme, Ptolomean or Copernican, as a symbolic idea, that the devil's place is 'utter', outermost, in a darkness remote from divine light. The new world hangs between, as the place of contention. Journeys through this symbolic universe tend to express relationships with the divine, so that Satan, for example, finding Jacob's ladder to heaven (iii 510), sees the way towards the light yet cannot climb to that light, self-exiled; indeed, the cruel predator seems to be cruelly goaded by his 'sad exclusion'. Distance from the divine presence is often expressed in terms of alienation,

and alienation in spirit leads to actual fall from grace, as Abdiel tells
Satan, as he declines from godly behaviour:

> O alienate from God, O spirit accursed,
> Forsaken of all good; I see thy fall
> Determined, and thy hapless crew involved ...
>   (v 877–9)

Whole nations may alienate themselves, like Judah through
idolatry (i 457), and God may justly alienate himself, as is
rehearsed in turning the poem to 'tragic' notes at impending Fall,
where again the relationship between faithless man and his
divine ruler and benefactor sounds almost in the mode of feudal
social bonds:

>   foul distrust, and breach
> Disloyal on the part of man, revolt,
> And disobedience: on the part of heaven
> Now alienated, distance and distaste,
> Anger and just rebuke, and judgment given ...
>   (ix 6–10)

The whole poem asks the reader to consider states of spiritual and
moral discipline: nearness to God is used as a measure and judgement of events in the past and as the hope for the period of time
beyond the end of the poem, as the only way forward towards true
restoration in a fallen world. The story of Fall, with the assumption of repeated fallings off through history, had immense power
to those who saw their own nation as exemplifying a pattern to be
traced throughout history, of God-given opportunities being
renewed and being repeatedly lost. In the beginning man had been
given in his enviable state of life great liberty and powers of
rational self-determination, but had failed in the matter of self-
discipline. Even angels in heaven had failed to form a lesson to
Adam:

> ... let it profit thee to have heard
> By terrible example the reward
> Of disobedience; firm they might have stood,
> Yet fell; remember, and fear to transgress.
>   (vi 909–12)

So Adam, though in the constant presence of the divine and the subject of divine guardianship and education, failed in the one symbolic and seemingly easy act of service his master required:

> ... he who requires
> From us no other service than to keep
> This one, this easy charge, of all the trees
> In Paradise that bear delicious fruit
> So various, not to taste that only tree
> Of knowledge ...
>
> (iv 419–24)

So men and nations, even favoured men and nations, had constantly fallen away from God.

In time of disaster, in the religious seventeenth century even more than now, men often sought explanations, seeking to apportion blame, so that Providence should be more understandable. *Paradise Lost* makes sense of the past both by offering to praise the larger ways of Providence, showing its care from Creation through to the Restoration and regaining of 'that blissful seat' by one man far 'greater' than any earthly monarch, and by analysing the ways of men according to the basic criteria of a godliness which is both moral and spiritual discipline. The ultimate goodness of God is demonstrated (with whatever success), in an attempt to allay doubts and fears, and by creating a fundamental measure of explanation about the conduct of men in the past a way is also cleared for positive action in the future. *Paradise Lost* faced its historical moment by getting back to basics, to heal and strengthen the mind.

As to the way forward, there is both encouragement and challenge. It is understood, through the example of Abdiel in the war in heaven and through the roles of such as Noah and Enoch in the Old Testament, not to mention the mission of Christ and the self-presentation of the poet in his poem, that the trials of obedience may involve solitary heroism in times of persecution and adversity. Readiness for such trial is shared by Adam and the reader at the end of the poem. Not all of this is new. Milton had always rehearsed the biblical commonplace that God might work great things through instruments seeming small and weak, that acts of spiritual strength should eventually overcome earthly might. As a younger man, as we have seen (above, p. 60) he had liked to write a text from Paul – 'my strength is made perfect in weakness' (II Cor.12.9) – into visitors' books, and he had always thought, more broadly, of the leadership of the spiritual and moral elite. The vision into the possibilities of a prosperous future given in the pastoralism of the end of the masque had shown godliness and chastity at the centre of land favoured by God. The difference now is not in the basic ideas of the priority of discipline but in the implication, given in the examples in *Paradise Lost*, that the times are not those in which it is easy to talk of pious prosperity for nations: rather, the formula is for patient, perhaps isolated virtue, and a waiting on Providence to show its mighty hand. In that sense, *Paradise Lost* is therapy for saints, for those who persevere as a disciplined godly, educated, saving remnant in dark times.

The problems of trying to describe the meaning and methods of Milton's analysis in *Paradise Lost*, in relation to the Restoration context, may be neatly illustrated by quoting the diametrically opposite reactions of two scholars to the story of how a north German pastor, H. L. Benthem, characterised Milton's poem after Milton's friend, the international educationalist Theodore Haak, read his version of the poem in German blank verse to him in 1686–7 (P 661, 1186). Pamela K. Bartlett, writing a monograph on Haak,[9] treats Benthem's conclusions about political functions with dismissive amusement, signalled by her exclamation mark:

> [Benthem] seems to have been interested in the translation primarily as a source of information about Milton's purpose in writing the poem: his impression, from the version which Haak read to him, was that the English poet was really lamenting not the loss of Eden but the loss of England's 'paradise' at the Restoration!

Christopher Hill, ears pricked at this potentially very interesting piece of evidence, dug behind Bartlett's sentence to come up triumphantly with the opposite attitude, to use the story as a clinching piece of evidence as to how to read encoded politics in a text produced under conditions of censorship:

> From this reading and from talking to Haak, Benthem gathered the impression that Milton's poem was really about politics in Restoration England. When Milton's friends were told the title of the poem, they feared that it would be a lament for the loss of England happiness with the downfall of the revolutionary

régime. But when they read it they saw that the prudent Milton had dealt only with the fall of Adam; reassured, they withdrew their objection to publication. But ('so far as I understand from what Haak told me and what I read for myself'), although at first sight the epic's subject was indeed the fall of our first parents, in fact 'this very wily politician ("dieser sehr schlau Politicus") concealed under this disguise exactly the sort of lament that his friends had suspected.' Some have thought that this story shows how silly Benthem (or Haak) was; but by now we may think otherwise. Haak was as likely to know what Milton was up to as anyone.[10]

There are clearly dangers both in Bartlett's unpoliticised humanism and in Hill's assumptions about political encoding, but both are reacting to real features of the poem. Milton's poem deals in an analysis which is far less parochial then English politics in the 1660s, yet that analysis encompasses, and sometimes expresses, a continuing political commitment. But the flexibility and variety of Milton's method must not be unstated.

To explain everything by assumptions of encoding under censorship clearly will not do. For all that the poem abounds in glancing references into the poet's own time, and that caution about censorship may be read into the relative indirectness of some moments, the resort to a radical examination of Providence and of man's responsibilities of godly discipline over the ages are too central to be accounted for as a mere cover for ultimate political intent. That is the way in which the past has been accommodated and that is the way action for the future may be planned. There is no reason to doubt that reason has been applied to the argument of theodicy, for its own persuasive sake, or that the poet and historian has not used many of his wonted, overt educative methods in his analytical and therapeutic task. It is precisely the general principles of divine and human conduct which would be sought in an educative poem: that is, meditation, not just prudent retreat. There can be no doubting either that Milton sought to engage the reader in his poem, affectively, by subjecting him to the conflicting reactions of lament and despair and final resolutions of doubts and fears, and Socratically and instructively by making the reader, though never without authorial guidance, discriminate between true and pretended values in the poem. Those educative methods cannot have much to do with enciphering.

To realise the analytical breadth of Milton's therapy for fit spirits in the England of the 1660s one need only think of the irony of the fact before he had published his poem, perhaps before he had quite finished it, London had seen what most regarded as the divine judgements of plague and fire. Every such cataclysmic affliction called forth the analyses and dire prophecies of divines and moralists. George Wither, sometimes seen as Milton's populist shadow, took the opportunity to publish an anthology of all his right prophecies to the nation issued through a long career.[11] Milton's poem also concerned itself with getting the mind straight, in times of judgement and alienation. A lesser poet might have quickly capitalised on recent events for publication in 1667. Although some have seen glancing allusions to the omen of comets in the poem, on the whole Milton does not go in for such local evidence. Amongst all the other prophets who took the stand at that time he would distinguish himself as the poet and historian, and perhaps the divine, of huge scope. He would seek to put his experience, and the reader's experience, into the perspective of all history. His poem, doctrinal to a nation, educates clearly enough on matter of principle and is genuinely about the fundamentals of godly discipline and the long providential view.

Notes

1. Annabel Patterson, *Censorship and Interpretation: The Conditions of Writing and Reading in Early Modern England* (Madison: University of Wisconsin Press 1984), pp. 20, 47, 179; Michael Wilding, 'Regaining the Radical Milton', Chapter 9 in *Dragons Teeth: Literature in the English Revolution* (Oxford: Clarendon, 1987).

2. Wilding, 'Regaining the Radical Milton', p. 244.

3. D 72; P 224–5.

4. *John Milton*, ed. Stephen Orgel and Jonathan Goldberg (Oxford and New York: Oxford University Press, 1990), p. xx.

5. Because Cromwell could be seen to have slipped into pseudo-monarchy, some have been tempted to see him included in Satan's tyranny in *Paradise Lost*. The boldest argument on these lines is David Armitage, in *Milton and Republicanism* (forthcoming).

6. Mary Ann Radzinowicz, 'The Politics of *Paradise Lost*', in *Politics of Discourse: The Literature and History of Seventeenth-Century England*, ed. Kevin Sharpe and Steven N. Zwicker (Berkeley, Los Angeles, and London: University of California Press, 1987), pp. 204–29.

7. See Mother Redcap's Tale from 'The Moone-Calfe', in Drayton's *The Battaile of Agincourt* (London, 1627), ed. J. William Hebel in vol. III of

The Works of Michael Drayton (Oxford: Blackwell, 1932); Marvell, 'Upon Appleton House'

8. Thomas Godwyn, Moses and Aaron: Civil and Ecclesiastical Rites used by the Ancient Hebrews ... (10th edn, 1671), p. 2.

9. Pamela K. Barnett, Theodore Haak (1616–1690) (Hague, 1962), p. 163.

10. Christopher Hill, Milton and the English Revolution (London, 1977), pp. 391–2.

11. George Wither, Echoes from the Sixth Trumpet. Reverberated by a Review of Neglected Remembrances ... (London, 1666).

9

Last Days: Patience and Monuments

Noticing that Milton published a lot of apparently miscellaneous books in his last few years, scholars have been tempted to some unelevated explanations, such as that the old blind poet was in relatively straitened circumstances and therefore glad to fall in with various booksellers in order to turn a penny or two by issuing things which had been lying about for a long time.[1] It is true that Milton was unabashed about realising money from books he had authored, regarding them as his property to trade, and it is true also that he had no great means and contracted his style in his last years, moving from a substantial house in Jewin Street to a smaller one in Bunfields. Here, his daughters having relinquished their duties of reading and writing for their blind father and moved on to independent lives, dwelt only Milton and his third wife, his beloved Betty (Elizabeth Minshull), with a woman servant. He also set about selling his library.

Willingness to earn money could be invoked to explain, for example, his taking on of a translation job in his last year (1674), Englishing the official *Declaration* from Poland of the election to the throne of the military leader John Sobietski (Y viii 441–53). Yet even this was a fitting task for one who was no hack but took his responsibilities as a man of letters seriously: the example of an *elective* monarchy was significant to a nation which had unwisely perpetuated hereditary monarchy, and who more suitable for the task than the man who had dealt with foreign communications in Latin for the Council of State?

Was it, again, in service to education, rather than commercialism, which prompted Milton to publish at a competitive price of a few pence his little textbook on teaching Latin to schoolchildren, *Accidence Commenced Grammar* (Y viii 84–128), in 1669? Presumably that was written back in the years when he was engaged in tutoring boys and busy developing his own reformed educational practices.

He seems also at this time to have given occasional help to individual boys who needed to prepare their languages for entry into university, and he published in 1672 his logic textbook in Latin, *Artis Logicae* (Y viii 206–407), another reforming educational work almost certainly written much earlier. This was actually a compendious work, beginning with the *Dialectic* of the French sixteenth-century reformer Ramus and adding other explanatory materials of his own and derived from commentators, chiefly the Cambridge logician George Downham, and ending with a logical analysis derived from Downham and a life of Ramus abridged from the German scholar Johannes Freige.

His enemies in print sneered at his schoolmasterly activities, for mere schoolmasters had little status then as now, but good education was evidently a cause which John Milton was happy to be seen to serve. It was probably as a sample educational text, too, showing how instructive history might be written (as I have discussed below), that he had printed his incomplete *History of Britain* in 1670. In that context might be placed as well his decision to reprint his little tractate Of *Education* of 1644 in the same volume as the revised, expanded version of his 1645 collection of shorter poems, in 1673. To compare the content of 1673 with those of 1645 is interesting. The poems added since 1645 were mainly sonnets, further developing the comprehensive self-imaging and cultural projection of the volume, encompassing satire (the *Tetrachordon* sonnets and the tailed sonnet on Forcers of Conscience), the commemoration of a disaster in European Protestantism (the Piedmont sonnet), two sonnets (XIV and XIX) in praise of virtuous women, two sonnets (XIII, XVII and XVIII) of cultured convivial friendship, and one (XVI) of dramatised self-examination. The new sonnets advertise the maturing of a man of principle, engaging matters of political and domestic discipline, whilst the many Horatian touches promise an exemplary cultivated style. It may be, as I have suggested,[2] that the extraordinary Englishing of Horace's fifth ode fits such a context, and it may also be no accident that the two social sonnets are to formable young men from an older man, one established in personal example, like the mature Horace in his fourth book of odes. This demonstration of maturing is underlined by the decision to include more of his juvenilia (the 'Fair Infant' written aged seventeen) and of verses from his university days (the Vacation Exercise verses). So we see the growth and rounding out of a career, and education is accompanied with the voice of authority.

Scholars have been less sure about Milton's decision to release for print his familiar letters (*Epistolae Familiares*) and academic exercises (*Prolusiones*) from his university days, in a volume which appeared in July 1674. This has indeed looked like the money-spinning act of a man who threw nothing away. One might also assume that, as he showed more of the range of his occasional writing over a long career, presuming on a certain fame, he also thought that these writings might be regarded as exemplary in their kind. Throughout his literary life, as we have seen, Milton often constructed a sense of his own career for the public to see, showing what he wanted to show and often rationalising retrospectively. So, all in all, we might acknowledge several kinds of explanation for the spate of publishing in the last years, and surmise that he was 'setting his literary house in order', as Parker put it (606), leaving a proper memorial to posterity of the career of John Milton, educationalist and reformer.

Meanwhile, *Paradise Lost* must have been selling quite well. A second edition was registered on 17 April 1674 and advertised for sale in July. The poem was redivided into the twelve-book form in which we now chiefly know it, thus making it correspond better to the pattern of a Virgilian epic. It would be hard to assign this decision to revise simply to his desire to make money out of a fresh product on the market. As we have seen from many instances, Milton liked to refine his works, and he had not ceased to think creatively in these years. Whether there is a strong meaning in the revisions is a matter of debate: textual changes were not great, but Books VII and X split to form the new Books VII and VIII, XI and XII, respectively. The latter division tends to highlight the moment at which Adam rejoices that 'one just Man' (Noah) had redeemed degenerate mankind from destruction by God's just anger, inaugurating a new epoch and by the sign of the covenantal rainbow prefiguring the Redemption itself, towards which the last book of the poem is now solely bent. The former division leaves as a single narrative of praise the creation of the world, and similarly isolates, perhaps therefore draws more attention to, Adam's recounting of his memories and the instructive discourse of Raphael about necessary knowledge and discipline, concerning godly obedience. At the same time, the new divisions put nearer the felt centre of the poem the celebration of the ultimate triumph of Truth through the Son, with the plea to the heavenly muse (before the creation) by a poet who will sing 'more safe' 'unchang'd / To hoarse or mute, though fall'n on evil days / ... yet not alone ...' Whether these reinforcements were made to chime with the affirmations of the *Paradise Regained* volume of 1671 must remain a matter of speculation.

That Milton was still actively engaged with his vocation as a writer at this time, rather than resting on his laurels or perfecting his self-presentation to the public can be illustrated from major new writing which he released in these years. Before we turn to his last great volume of verse, in which *Paradise Regained* and *Samson Agonistes* appeared, I would like to take some terms of reference from the one polemical prose tract of the period, *Of True Religion, Hæresie, Schism, Toleration* (Y viii 408–40), published in March or April of 1673.

This tract has received little attention until recently,[3] because it is short and very plain in style, without any of the rhetorical fullness of the tracts of the 1640s and 1650s. It has also been treated with mixed enthusiasm for its argument. Although the plea for toleration for schism amongst Protestants sounds a sympathetic note to modern ears, the other side of the argument is a repeated condemnation of Catholicism as a kind of religion *not* to be tolerated. Nevertheless, these matters are important for understanding the religious and political underpinning of the late poems.

Despite hopes of religious toleration at the Restoration, the so-called Clarendon Code, which was gradually imposed by a series of measures seeking to control puritan radicalism through the 1660s, had put fetters on dissenting Protestants, ejecting ministers, banning meetings, stopping academies, and forcing conformity on lay officials as well. In an irony which Milton probably savoured, the King was known to be keener on toleration than many of his ministers: after his years in France, he wanted toleration, but for Catholics, and in practice managed to protect them, despite the new measures. His Portuguese queen was Catholic, and royal and court connections with Catholic France were many, more than under Charles I. All this was a new bondage of conscience to reforming spirits, Israel in a new idolatrous tyranny, but it was not until the early 1670s that popular feeling had good opportunity to flair up about the issue of Popery.

Having achieved a measure of financial independence from his parliament by signing the Treaty of Dover with France in 1670 (a secret clause of which, probably cynically intended, promised his own conversion and the promotion of Catholicism in England), Charles felt free to issue a new Declaration of Indulgence in March

1672, just two days before the outbreak of the second Anglo-Dutch War. Toleration of religion, far from being a simple relief to non-conformists, was thus severely problematised: the cost of their greater freedom would be the legitimising of Catholicism in England. Such was the popular fear of Popery, liable to produce wild rumours at any crisis in the country, that some non-conformists were willing to suspend their own freedoms in the cause against false religion.

Parliament and king were thus clearly at odds in the early months of 1673. Parliament refused to accede to the royal decree and initiated in turn its own series of measures, introducing toleration in favour of Protestants but not of Catholics. It was in this context – exactly when we are not sure – that Milton joined the pamphleteers. It was just the kind of occasion to which he had always risen: fortifying the resolve of Parliament at a crucial juncture. His tract encouraged Parliament in their efforts to discriminate firmly between Catholic and Protestant schism, recalling memories of the Gunpowder Plot and Catholic infiltration into the court before the Civil War (Y viii 430).

As Keith Stavely has shown (Y viii 413), Milton tailored arguments he had used earlier in *Of Civil Power* to this new situation of capitalising on anti-Catholic sentiment and Parliament's position against the king. Milton's tract is controlled, but also direct and clear on principle. 'True Religion is the true Worship and Service of God, learnt and believed from the Word of God only' (419). As long as they are 'painful and zealous labourers in his Church' and base their thoughts upon the evidence of the Word, rather than the word of others, Protestant schismatics should be tolerated, for all men err. But 'Popery is the only, or the greatest, heresy' and the state of superstition is a judgement upon its adherents (421). Catholicism is tainted with worldly power, and its idolatry should be absolutely removed. If only Englishmen had been made to study the Bible themselves, if only the conscienceful searches for the Truth had been made open to all, if only England had mended its morals (seen to be sliding further into laxness in these years), then it would not have invited the judgements of plague, fire, and war.

The measured concision of this document earned one admirer at the time, recorded in Parker (681): 'J. Milton has said more ... in two elegant sheets of true religion, heresy, and schism than all the prelates can refute in seven years'. *Of True Religion* preserved that image of strenuous enquiry in the faith which he had promoted earlier in his career: it is incumbent upon good men 'to take the pains of understanding their Religion by their own diligent study' and it is to a constituency of such men that he will speak yet again:

> Every member of the Church, at least of any breeding or capacity, so well ought to be grounded in spiritual knowledge, as, if need be, to examine their Teachers themselves. (435)

The heroic spirit of reformation is not dead, and grounding in spiritual knowledge will be reiterated as the basis of all other things. That this may happen in times of adversity and bewilderment about God's purposes is made evident from this quotation, which comes to rest in the Book of Job:

> But so long as all these profess to set the Word of God only before them as the Rule of faith and obedience; and use all diligence and sincerity of heart, by reading, by learning, by study, by prayer for Illumination of the holy spirit, to understand the Rule and obey it, they have done what man can do: God will assuredly pardon them, as he did the friends of Job, good and pious men, though much mistaken, as there it appears, in some Points of Doctrin. (424)

In this context Milton reports not the seeming unkindness of the three comforters, who accused Job of secret wickedness, but the fact that they were mistaken in doctrine. This follows God's own accusation in 42.7: 'for ye have not spoken of me the thing that is right, as my servant Job hath'. The fault, in otherwise godly men, is that, having insufficient understanding of the mysteries of God's providence, they must not presume to explain. As Elihu put it (32.3), 'they have found no answer, and yet had condemned Job.'

The aptness of the story to his argument in *Of True Religion* apart, the reference expresses a general situation in which, as in *Samson Agonistes*, men find it hard to understand the 'unsearchable dispose' of God, and yet must for all that trust in divine justice and benevolence. On such bases of obedience and searching, even in times of trial, and on the necessity of such total trust, the actions of *Paradise Regained* and *Samson Agonistes* rest. Right action must be grounded in spiritual knowledge. These works show no simple retreat into a less political world: they make statements, perhaps in constrained circumstances, as freedom of conscience was being debated, about the fundamental disciplines of the mind.

It has been a cornerstone of this book, that Milton rarely published any major work without a due sense of the causes which he espoused and that therefore we might consider every major publication carefully for the ways it seems to speak to its times. Thus, I have wanted to think primarily of *Paradise Lost* as it might have impacted upon 1667, rather than speculating about Milton's earlier plans with the story of the Fall. As we approach the volume of 1671, which printed first *Paradise Regained* and, secondly, *Samson Agonistes*, the same kinds of issue arise, because some have speculated as to when *Paradise Regained* was begun, thinking that it may have been a long while before, and a good few have committed themselves to a date of composition for *Samson Agonistes* in the 1640s.[3] It is true that Milton often pondered projects and kept them on the stocks for a long while, but I find it inconceivable that in finishing and publishing these great works some ten or so years into the restored British monarchy that he did not mean them to reflect upon the spiritual discipline and political institutions of that time. The sense that God gives occasions for true poets and prophets to speak is always strong in him, and indeed the two poems are partly about achieving readiness for occasion.

I shall also assume that he thought about the relationship of these two works in the volume of 1671, for in the context of speaking to the times they seem, despite reservations in some quarters, to have a wonderful interplay. It is true that the title-page of 1671 seems to add *Samson* as an afterthought – '*Paradise Regaind. A Poem. In IV Books. To which is added Samson Agonistes*' – and some have therefore surmised that it was a makeweight for a slim volume; but study of the poems seems to indicate that Milton meant the closet tragedy to be read after *Paradise Regained*, to provide a challenging but strengthening address to true Protestants in these times.

One reference which gives structure to both works I have already mentioned: the *Book of Job*, that semi-dramatic narrative, partly in verse (heroic hexameters, they thought), about the trials of faith and the understanding of Providence. Both of Milton's 1671 poems study the keeping of faith, patience, and the waiting on the hand of Providence. The connections are at several levels. Not only did

Milton himself in *The Reason of Church Government* (Y i 813) rehearse the commonplace of the period that *Job* provided a chief model for a brief epic, thus informing the genre of *Paradise Regained*, but also the workings of the 'discourses' or dialogues in *Job* provided an obvious model for the testing conversations of Samson with his various visitors in Milton's poem. Moreover the part of Satan in *Paradise Regained* bears a relationship to the allowed role of the devil in *Job*: in *Job* God allows the devil to present the hero with a severe trial of faith and then, finally, after Job has learned to submit patiently to God, in the hope of clarification of his miseries, rewards him with understanding as well as material restoration. *Paradise Regained* presents a more perfect testing of faith in the wilderness, in which clarifications ensue. But it is Samson who undergoes a testing of his faith in dialogue with friends, like Job, and like Job clarifies his thoughts and gains strength of spirit to the point where he is ready to be used as God's instrument in a heroic martyrdom for Israel.

Although the poems in their depiction of spiritual wrestling in extreme circumstances inevitably recall *Job* and as it were divide its inheritance between them, it is also true that both are more obviously politically embedded in their considerations of past, present, and future than *Job*: the adversity in Milton's poems is located in situations in which those seeking the Truth also suffer tyrannical oppressions which invade the whole culture including religion. The works of Satan are more politically understood, and in their reaffirmation of the primacy of spiritual discipline Milton's poems include some stern strictures of degenerate values and false ideas of kingship and leadership.

I have said that it is helpful if the reader encounters *Paradise Regained* before *Samson Agonistes*, and that is partly because of the kind of reaffirmations that are made in it of causes espoused from the beginnings of Milton's poetic career. The brief epic can be seen to reaffirm what the young poet had celebrated in his early vocational poem, the *Nativity Ode*. Both poems display the triumph of Truth, though the distance travelled between them in experience is also instructive to contemplate.

Such an affirmation is figured in the cessation of the oracles, which comes with the flight of the pagan gods in the youthful poem in the face of the mission of the Son of God. The whole action of *Paradise Regained* concerns the power of the final revelation of Truth. Book I is peculiarly concerned with advertising the separation of truth from falsehood. After taunting Satan with the memory of his self-defeating assault on the faith of Job, the Son accuses him as being the source of lies and falsehood, and attaches to him all the dubious witnesses of false religion:

> Yet thou pretend'st to truth; all oracles
> By thee are given, and what confessed more true
> Among the nations? that hath been thy craft,
> By mixing somewhat true to vent more lies.
>
> (i 430–33)

The idolatrous nations have justly been subjected to these lies, but

>   henceforth oracles are ceased,
> And thou no more with pomp and sacrifice
> Shalt be inquired at Delphos and elsewhere,
> At least in vain, for they shall find thee mute.
> God hath now sent his living oracle
> Into the world, to teach his final will,
> And sends his spirit of truth henceforth to dwell
> In pious hearts, an inward oracle
> To all truth requisite for men to know.
>
> (i 456–64)

With unique distinction, but not without instructive example for other men, since he is incarnate 'in all points like we are' (Heb. 4.11), the Son witnesses to Truth through the spirit in the action of the poem, until Satan like the oracles is mute, and a blinding simplicity of faith in obedience has vanquished a peal of dubious words.

That this happened, and that it is possible for other men possessed of the inward oracle to imitate to their own capacities, trusting to a redemptive providence, is the central strengthening reaffirmation of the poem, and the reassurance of present strength is coupled with a promise of a time when temptation itself will cease. Satan's

>   snares are broke:
> For though that seat of earthly bliss be failed,
> A fairer Paradise is founded now
> For Adam and his chosen sons, whom thou
> A Saviour are come down to reinstall.

Where they shall dwell secure, when time shall be
Of tempter and temptation without fear.
But thou, infernal serpent, shalt not long
Rule in the clouds ...

(iv 611–19)

'When time shall be.' In the *Nativity Ode* the vision into the final Golden Age had been given with rapture, before the corrective to premature youthful enthusiasm was admitted: 'But wisest fate says no, / This must not yet be so'. Yet, after Passion and Last Judgement have been faced, what 'now begins' is triumphant enough, in that nativity Pindaric, the victory of true religion in the era of Christ, which is also the victory of Protestantism over Catholicism. After so many years seeking reform and experiencing revolution, Milton's reaffirmation of the victory of Truth in *Paradise Regained* is more hedged about with a bitter sense of difficulty. Yet, for all that, *Paradise Regained* remains an affirmation of a cause and of the ultimate victory of that cause.

The earlier epic, *Paradise Lost*, had also reaffirmed the triumph of Truth. The actions initiated by Satan and allowed by God as a trial of man are counterpointed through both poems by another set of actions of the agents of heaven. The reader is kept in sight of heavenly deliberations and good angelic offices enough to be invited to understand that there is a providential frame, set to produce yet greater good out of Satanic evil. This line of action bears its own symbols of the power of Truth to unmask deceptive evil, like the effect of the spear with which Ithuriel prods the squatting toad Satan in Book IV of *Paradise Lost* (810). And the War in Heaven had figured not just the conflict which led to the fall of Satan but also, in the triumphant entry of the Son on the third day, the ultimate victory over the forces of evil at the end of time. Such features are vital to the structure of *Paradise Lost*, for without them the providential argument cannot hope to hold. Yet loss of Eden, rather than recovery, remains the central subject, and the most memorable depiction of false gods in this poem is of the ominous spread of idolatry, recounted in the roll-call of fallen angels in Book I, rather than the flight of gods or cessation of oracles. *Paradise Regained*, on the other hand, has the triumph of Truth for subject.

Both *Samson Agonistes* and *Paradise Regained* include celebrations of victory in the form of similes given after the moment of triumph. In *Samson* (1687) one of the semi-choruses figures the miraculous arousing of Samson's spiritual strength in a succession of images of snake and bird – evening dragon, eagle, and Phoenix. In *Paradise Regained* the two great similes (iv 563–75) offered immediately after Satan's fall from the pinnacle illustrate the kind of triumph of which I have been speaking. The second simile, of the Sphinx, celebrates Oedipus' triumph over the 'Theban monster' as of plain truth over a riddle; and the first, of Hercules finally throttling Antaeus in the air after endlessly throwing him on to the earth, where he always revived, employs a myth which had frequently been used in Christian reference to signify the triumph of the spiritual over the fleshly. The heroic victory of Christ is often figured as Herculean in Milton's poetry: in the *Nativity Ode* the infant, like Hercules, overcomes snakes (227–8) and in the uncompleted *The Passion* we have representing Christ the Hercules of the labours: 'Most perfect hero, tried in heaviest plight / Of labours huge and hard, too hard for human wight' (13–14). In the more dialectical *Paradise Regained*, where the wrestlings are of the mind, the labours are precisely not too hard for human wight. The unthinkable has happened: a man has been capable of overcoming Satanic deceptions and has thus made possible the conquering of deceptions by later men, through the help of the 'spirit of truth', the 'inward oracle' given to all the faithful, which is his constant guide. The poem celebrates an enabling in the mind of man and, thus, it seeks to give renewed encouragement even in times of obscurity.

Because the context of all the action of the poem is the discovery of falsehoods, there is a shaping of the story of the temptation in the wilderness unlike most traditional accounts. Many commentators have noted that in following of the order of the temptations as given in Luke (4.1–13), rather than in Matthew (4.1–11), Milton is doing something unusual. We shall have cause to think about the significance of the last 'temptation', standing on the pinnacle, which Milton not only placed last like Luke but also treated in a distinct fashion. In examining the shaping of the action we also need to attend the way the first temptation has been treated, not here by being placed differently in the sequence but in being separated out in other ways.

Like Matthew and Luke, Milton puts the temptation of turning stones into bread first, but he assigns this part of the action to a separate day, and makes Satan present himself in different disguise here from that which he uses on the second day. For this first encounter Satan appears as 'an aged man in rural weeds', in a line of hypocrisy recognisable from Comus as a poor villager or Archimago presenting himself in false humility in the first book of *The Faerie Queene*. Satan suggests that Jesus could not only turn stones into bread, but also relieve the poor inhabitants of the wilderness. The moment the hypocrisy is voiced, the Son knows his antagonist and penetrates the disguise. When Satan persists, to suggest that he may share with the Son 'fellowship in pain', it calls forth from the Son the denunciation of Satanic lies and the announcement of the end of pagan oracles, which we have already seen. Milton has separated out the first temptation and used it primarily as a preliminary exposition of the triumph of truth over falsehood. It was a bold decision. The Bible suggested that the context for the temptation was the accumulated hunger of forty days – 'he was afterwards an hungred', as Matthew put it (4.2). Taking it over to different purpose. Milton has created a new luxurious feast temptation in the second book, not in the Bible, for the real test of fortitude in hunger.

This whole first encounter (also in a sense Spenserian) shows the primacy of religious faith in the forming of virtue. *The Faerie Queene* had begun with a book in which Una, Truth, overcomes Duessa, Falsehood, and the true church is separated with difficulty from its false counterpart. So, too, in *Paradise Regained*. Recognising falsehood for what it is is the condition of Milton's Protestant heroism, its strenuous effort, at which all will fail to some extent, like the virtuous Lady in the masque, and as all men and angels are said in *Paradise Lost* to be deceived by hypocrisy (iii 682–4). Uniquely in Milton's stringent writing, in which there are no easy illusions about godlike immunity in men, the Son in this poem is not deceived by hypocrisy. In his final speech in Book I, Satan acknowledges that his part has been like 'the hypocrite or atheous priest' (I 487) who nevertheless has been permitted access to the church. Even at this early point in the poem, the control is wholly with the Son, and Satan, 'bowing low / His grey dissimulation' as he departs, is on the edge of making his cunning seem foolish.

The episode also sets up a repeated effect of irony in the poem: every move of Satan exposes himself rather than the Son, and serves, counter-productively, only to elicit a clearer sense of purpose in the man he would confuse. Thus, the action progressively reveals both parties, and the rash fallen angel suffers constant diminution, whilst the Son grows in understanding of himself and his role, his trial preparing him for his mission. Obedience and trust are unshakable in him, and his very humility produces authoritative strength. By the time of the action on the third day, when Satan has rashly determined to have a trial of strength, his imperious attempt to taunt the Son and cow him into fearful submission after the storms of the night – 'Fair morning yet betides thee Son of God,/ After a dismal night' – is met with a stoical coolness which renders him also comical, as the Son walks on: 'Me worse than wet thou find'st not ....' That in turn drives Satan to impetuous rage, complete self-revelation, and the desperate last trial, in which he himself will fall. Power and control remain with the studied words of the Son schooled in a complete discipline of rational obedience, and he who tends to humble reticence finally takes on himself the power of the Word, which triumphs through him:

> Tempt not the Lord thy God, he said and stood.
> But Satan smitten with amazement fell ...
>
> (iv 561–2)

The analogy from the masque would be (in the enlarged text of 1637) the moment in which Comus, hearing scriptural wisdom and prophetic authority from the Lady's mouth, acknowledges a superstitious fear of 'words set off by some superior power' (800). But the divine injunction quoted in *Paradise Regained* has a far stronger effect: so perfect are the obedience and the trust that the words of Father and Son have become one: to make trial of the Son is to be pitted against the power of God himself, through the Word. It is Satan who has presumed; it is Satan who falls. Then, in the final irony, the angels whom he dared the Son to summon come by divine command and give a banquet less corrupted than that offered before.

Although the ultimate power is revealed in the speaking of the Word of God, the final episode is like a trial of strength between Satan and the Son. In this context, the meaning of 'tempt' needs some interpretation. For this climactic part of the action Satan wears no disguise but appears in 'his wonted shape'. For the other temptations, he had adopted two different appearances: his hypocritical dress for the first we have already seen; for the second day he appears as one from city or court, tempting in other words with kinds of worldliness. For the third day there is no attempt to deceive. Satan has given up deceptive temptations the night before, after the offering of learning. Instead, he subjects the Son to dreams and a badly broken night, with storm, ghosts, and furies, and the next morning challenges him to a trial of strength in the pinnacle test. When Satan falls, his fall is likened to being thrown at wrestling.

It would seem that Milton has taken the final biblical rebuke –
'Tempt not the Lord thy God' – partly at least in the Latin sense of
tentare: do not make trial of God's strength. This may make greater
sense if one refers to Protestant glosses on the episode. This is
Diodati on Matthew 4.3:

> It seemeth the Devill had two ends in these temptations, the one
> to draw from Christ some proofs and trials of his deity – of which
> he had but an obscure knowledge: which was denied him, as
> miracles were to unbeleevers and profane men. The other was
> to draw his human nature to sin ....[4]

The second of those options, the drawing to sin provides the most
obvious (modern) sense of temptation; the Son is tempted to fall, as
Adam before him, in *Paradise Lost* and Satan's dressing on the first
two days expresses those kinds of deceptive temptation. But the
pinnacle episode of the third day chiefly expresses the first category.
Like the 'atheous priest', Satan has rashly sought trial of the Son's
strength, found the power of God, and been overwhelmed. The third
day of the War in Heaven in *Paradise Lost* had seen a similar rout.

The whole episode of the temptation in the desert has been given
a binding dramatic significance, establishing who is the true 'son of
God'. 'If thou be the Son of God ...' is the repeated biblical formula,
and the action of Milton's poem is framed to settle that 'if' by trial.
At the baptism the spirit was said to descend in the form of a dove:
'and lo a voice from heaven, saying, this is my beloved, in whom I
am well pleased' (Matt. 3.17; Luke 3.22). On the pinnacle Satan himself signifies this unity in the action, by recalling the moment at
which he hears the divine voice at the baptism:

> Thenceforth I thought thee worth my nearer view
> And narrower scrutiny, that I might learn
> In what degree or meaning thou are called
> The Son of God, which bears no single sense;
> The Son of God I also am, or was,
> And if I was, I am; relation stands;
> All men are Sons of God, yet thee I thought
> In some respect far higher so declared.
>
> (iv 512–21)

In the proving of Sonship by acts of pure submissive obedience 'Tempt
not the Lord thy God' does not have to mean, as some have taken it,[5]

that Milton is not consistent here with his insistence elsewhere on the essentially human nature of Jesus; it need only mean that in perfect obedience he will by the gift of the spirit take on the power of the divine, through consummate trust in the divine word. Satan has revealed a mystery of godliness which he perhaps can no longer understand.

With the first day's encounter used for primary definition of the exposure of false religion, and the third day used for the ultimate trial of strength, it was therefore in the long second day of tempt-ations that the 'drawing to sin' was chiefly elaborated, in what is in effect Milton's systematic expansion of the one biblical temptation left, of temptations of the world. At the centre of his poem of 1671 Milton explored worldliness such as might also make sense to the time. As I have said, such is signified by Satan's worldly dress as one from city or court.

In this middle part of the action, also, the political conditions are most clearly shown, and some groundwork had been covered to this purpose in the first book and in the opening parts of the second. Here as in *Samson* God's people are in bondage of tyranny and irre-ligion. In the first book Jesus is shown considering but rejecting the idea of becoming a political Messiah, leading Israel as a nation against Rome. At the opening of Book II the fishermen disciples Andrew and Simon are shown to have a political sense of Jesus' role – 'God of Israel, / Send thy Messiah forth, the time is come; / … free thy people from their yoke, …' (2.42–3; 48). Mary also wonders about her son as a heroic public figure: she has been expecting some great change in his private, contemplative life, with the public acknowledgement at the baptism. That these expectations of a glori-ous, public Messianic role will be re-educated during the course of the poem into a reaffirmation of the unworldly beginnings of the kingdom need not mean that Milton eschewed the political world in the close of his career. It might be interpreted to mean that both poems published in 1671 offer to share with their readers a recog-nition of adverse circumstance, but that as in *Paradise Lost* the first thoughts are for the fundamentals of renovative action, which lie with the discipline of true obedience. What is prescribed in both Job-related poems is repentance, preparedness, and the discipline of trust and waiting. There will come a time when the Son will assume the throne of David and 'shall to pieces dash / All monarchies besides throughout the world' (iv 149–50). It is thus possible to read Milton's telling of the Son's rejection of worldly glories in a spirit more affirmative than that in which the poem has often been received, as a product of a withdrawal in his last years into a puritan asceticism which denies the richer humanistic engagements of his earlier writing. It is of course the last of the four stages of temptation on the second day which critics have taken as symptomatic, the seeming rejection of learning itself.

Milton elaborated worldly glory by creating four incidents. First, the banquet, occupying the rest of Book II, proves temperance and also establishes that heroic virtue may come in poverty. (One is tempted to think again of *The Faerie Queene*: just as Spenser followed a first book of Holiness with a second of Temperance, so Milton unmasked religious hypocrisy in his first book, and engaged worldly intemperance in the second.) Next, after a long preliminary debate about worldly ambition, testing Jesus' political motivation as inheritor of the throne of David, there is the offering of the glory of empire as seen from the mountain in Book III. The Parthian empire is chosen as best exemplifying military glory. It is a political temptation to use foreign arms to liberate a people. Then in Book IV they move to the western side of the mountain and view Rome, which exemplifies the utmost luxury in city and worldly power. For all the historicity of the poem, the mention of that city 'with the spoils enriched / Of nations' (iv 46–7) is likely to have appealed to a Protestant–nationalist spirit in Milton's readers. Then, in a fresh invention not obviously adapting a biblical base, they view Athens and the world of learning.

Although Milton's reading (using others' eyes) in his years of blindness must have been less various and more centred on the Bible, that last temptation is not simple evidence of retraction in the humanist writer. The Son provides the pattern to the most hardworking godly reformer, in finding within the resources of the Bible all and more of the arts of the world, but this poem appears in the same years as Milton is publishing and republishing educational works, the good fruits of learning.

What is more, it signals a realism absolutely in tune with a career of political writing. Satan himself, as often, makes the point without really meaning to:

> Since neither wealth, nor honour, arms nor arts,
> Kingdom nor empire pleases thee, nor aught
> By me proposed in life contemplative,
> Or active, tended on by glory, or fame,

What dost thou in this world? The wilderness
For thee is fittest place...

                                        (iv 368–73)

In dividing worldly glory into his four elements, Milton identified
arenas of activity celebrated through history and in his own
Renaissance world, from which learning cannot be absent, and he
acknowledged at the same time how all these activities, contemplative as well as active, have been, for him, contaminated by
wrong use. The man who had studied politics in history and the
uses of the arts in ancient and modern Europe thought he understood how the arts themselves could be manipulated by governments. These were the lessons of modern Italy, learned at first
hand; these were the discriminations he had made and invited
others to see in the culture of the Caroline court. The inclusion of
learning in the temptations of Satan in *Paradise Regained* shows how
learning and politics have become inseparable. Many may feel that
this Son sometimes speaks as more of a political analyst than
expected. His portrait of the vulgar people comes from a Roman
patrician as much as the New Testament Christ:

> For what is glory but the blaze of fame,
> The people's praise, if always praise unmixed?
> And what the people but a herd confused,
> A miscellaneous rabble, who extol
> Things vulgar, and well weighed, scarce worth the praise,
> They praise and they admire they know not what;
> And know not whom, but as one leads the other ...

                                        (iii 47–52)

Milton's Son demands a strenuous audience sharing such sceptical
understanding. The blockish vulgar is blind. Political realism under-
pins a text which, nevertheless, seeks to reaffirm the faith which
informs the cause. False monarchies will, indeed, one day disappear
and Truth, in which Englishmen must still trust, will ultimately
prevail.

If Satan's tests in *Paradise Regained* merely create a revelatory action
in which the Son is exercised into preparedness for his ministry,

then in *Samson Agonistes* we have an action much more like Job, in which hero and friends move darkly towards an understanding of the necessary trust in providence. Thus, the experience of doubt in Milton's readers is more directly engaged, and fears are imitated in a drama cathartically designed. The reader is in fact drawn into discriminations in more actively engaging ways than in the Book of Job, for there Elishu comes in to correct the thoughts of both Job and the three friends; no such 'correct' mouthpiece enters Milton's dramatic poem, which exposes the reader to the task of critical understanding and to the experience of the ways of Providence, as they are finally revealed.

For his readers to have come to an understanding of *Samson Agonistes* was however no comfortable matter. Anyone knowing the Book of Judges, as Milton's readers would, might remember that the grand opportunity for liberation from Philistine oppression created by Samson's killing of the Philistine hierarchy at the Games was not in fact capitalised upon by the Israelites. This is not like using a story from Exodus, where it is known that after backslidings and trials the Promised Land would indeed be entered. Judges shows division and irresolution, a lack of discipline flowing from lack of leadership, and the action of Milton's closet drama seems to indicate that lack of disciplined faith in both champion and people, after years of servility, is in focus. Samson blames his countrymen for not taking the opportunities he has created in the past and his role is as some kind of special deliverer. Yet it is obvious that his own indiscipline has compromised his efforts and that he struggles to come to terms with the need for a new mental discipline during the course of the action.

The reflections on Milton's own revolutionary times would seem to be considerable. It is not so simple as to blame the slack irresolution of the people: the lack of disciplined religious thinking may also be in those leading the fight for liberation. Milton had often noted about Englishmen in history, as he did in the *History of Britain*, that they showed themselves fitter in physical bravery than in moral discipline. By implication, *Samson* glances at this English disease.

There has been new debate in recent years, following the reading of Joseph Wittreich,[6] about whether Samson himself errs even to the end. *Samson Agonistes* is certainly about erring, but so is Job. I shall take it that Samson comes to a painful understanding which is then confirmed and adopted by God, through the Spirit, and that this speaks to the strengthening function of the poem as published in 1671, but that nevertheless the difficulties of discrimination are fully played out, that each party retains its partiality, and that the poem comes to rest in a situation, for the rest of Samson's countrymen, of typical Miltonic strenuousness and realism in which as much remains to do as has been achieved. Published with *Paradise Regained*, the poem seems to offer agonising reflections about liberty from oppression. It is an unforgiving analysis and a severe challenge, but not without the possibility of recovery and glorious result.

Samson Agonistes has always been acknowledged as encapsulating lifelong preoccupations of the poet, so that almost any perspective one puts upon it is bound to seem partial and incomplete. The following materials are offered in recognition of that fact. In order to suggest how the spiritual searching is located in a complex of social and political situations, I begin with the issue of marriage and divorce, recalling a story told about Milton in Parker's *Life* (612–13) from the anonymous biography:

> It was almost certainly in March of 1670 that 'an eminent member' of the House of lords visited Milton in the hope of receiving help on a matter of national importance. The Portuguese Queen of Charles II was still childless, and fearing that no legitimate heir to the crown would ever be born of this unhappy marriage, some of the royal councillors had decided that Charles should ask Parliament for a special Bill of divorce rather than let the succession go to his brother, the Duke of York, suspected of being a Roman Catholic. While this extreme remedy was being discussed, John Manners, Lord Roos, eldest son of the Earl of Rutland, did ask Parliament to allow him to divorce his wife, Anne Pierpoint, daughter of the Marquis of Dorchester ...

Romish infiltration at court had of course bothered Milton and many 'puritans' before. Quite apart from fears about James, Duke of York, known to be a Romanist, Catholic watchers of Charles II's court had already wondered about a replaying of the situation of Charles I's queen proselytising for Rome through the court (as she had promised the Pope her godfather and Cardinal Barbarini that she would do). The new queen, who arrived in 1662, also had her Catholic chapel, if not the same mission as the old.

It is quite clear from Milton's writings that he expected wives to follow husbands in matters of religion, at least in most cases, where the man's intellect was supposed to lead. This would be according to the positive model of Ruth, celebrated in Sonnet IX, Ruth the Moabite woman who in effect married into Israel to help form the house of David; whilst some of the negative possibilities were registered through Eve, when she is without Adam in *Paradise Lost*, tending to fall to attitudes of superstition. Eve repents and joins with her husband in new piety at the end of the poem, but Milton's argument in the divorce tracts is that despite customary opinion a partner ought to have grounds for divorce if there is no longer the possibility of converting the other to right religion, for to live without the sharing of spiritual discipline is a denial of free charitable bonding itself:

> where the religion is contrary without hope of conversion, there can be no love, no faith, no peacefull society, (they of the other opinion confess it) nay there ought not to be, furder than in expectation of gaining a soul.   (Y ii 682–3)

Furthermore, there is danger that the right-thinking partner might be drawn into false religion – 'the danger of seducement', he calls it, using a favourite word of Protestant militancy – further eroding the familial foundations of the state.

We do not know what Milton might have said as an expert on divorce in 1670 about the idolatrous queen and idolatrous heir to the throne, if indeed the story is true. We might guess his interest. But in 1671, coincidentally or not, he published a poem which actually dramatises the putting away of an idolatrous consort:[7] *Samson Agonistes* demonstrates what Milton had defended in middle life, the rightness for Samson and for the state of putting away the seductive consort of a false religion.

The episode with Dalila is pivotal to the action of the poem and it is written to convey great tension. Samson's misogyny (picked up and uncritically amplified by the Chorus) is probably not in any simple sense Milton's – it is dramatically determined, and Samson is at this point in the action in no reconciled state of mind – but what seems to be meant in his confrontation with Dalila is that everything is stripped away until one fact asks to be recognised: however culpable both Dalila and Samson have been, in the end their loyalties to different cultures, different nations, and religions, deny the possibility of peacable, harmonious marriage. She confesses that '... the priest / Was not behind, but ever at mine ear.' She responds as a Philistine to her 'civil duty / and of religion'; he has a mission to respond to Israel and the God of Israel.

What is recognised is what should have been understood much earlier, if Samson had read Milton's divorce tracts, that 'thou and I long since are twain'. Dalila's rich exotic dress, her sense of place in her society, her weakness for Judas-like payment, her wish to keep her husband in tamed connubial idleness, all these things are finally contextualised by the fact that marriage to idolaters is, as Milton put it in the Commonplace Book, dangerous (Y i 399), and that such a marriage can only persist as a true marriage if the idolatrous partner adopts the true religion of the other – 'for me thou wast to leave / Parents and country' (885–6).

The religious spirit of a nation, which is also the heroic national identity, is in Milton's mind founded on right religious marriage. The analysis is especially important with one who is in some sense a leader amongst his people. In Milton's poem Samson is not only a military deliverer but also, as he is not in the Book of Judges, a potential spiritual leader, one who has obvious authority. Thus, the mind has once more been written into the script of heroic combat.

Once the matter has been clarified and the putting away has happened, Samson goes from strength to strength in his new encounters, and the action takes a turn, a bondage having been removed from his mind. The first two episodes present dialogues between Israelites, not only resuming past action but also tending to be introspective and backward-looking, seeking to explain Samson's divinely appointed role thus far and to apportion blame for the failure. As in Job the parties are not irreligious men, but all three show bewilderment and are liable to err. Although his own honour is engaged and he sometimes deflects blame on to his less resolute countrymen, Samson recognises early, as Job does not, that divine dispensation must not be questioned, and that the fault must lie in himself – 'Sole Author I, sole cause' (376). And he, his father, and the Chorus recognise the ultimate duties are to the One God. Whatever the differences, these are the conversations of friends sharing a cause. Strangely, Manoa's part comes closest to that of Job's comforters, tending to put Samson in mind yet again of what he will forget, the present victory of the oppressor celebrated on the very feast day of the action and precipitating in him the greatest statements of despair. The introspection and despair have a double effect –

Samson is led to an understandable but culpable sense that heaven has deserted him, and yet by acknowledging his own fault he shows that he is nevertheless a man capable of renewal and fresh adoption by God.

From the episode of Dalila onwards, as Philistines come into view, there is a rousing of spirits, because the possibilities have been created of new action. The unmasking and putting away of Dalila first releases him from his bondage. The facing of Harapha then gives him an opportunity to express new trust in his God. When the invitation comes to the Games, he is ready for action, and sees light from darkness. Following his own exercise in spiritual discipline, concerning the need to learn patience and to reaffirm his trust in God, heaven is again with him and the blind man no longer has the sense of lacking a guide.

Dalila, then, is represented as an agency which threatens to unman a heroic spirit which is destined to champion Israel and the One God of Israel. Samson himself analyses his life as having been touched by the kind of 'foul effeminacy' (410) with which his countrymen have been afflicted. Men have been deceived by bad women through history, but Samson had allowed himself to be deceived twice. Samson sees his own life with Dalila as softened with pride, pleasure, and voluptuousness: 'The swoll'n with pride into the snare I fell / Of fair fallacious looks, venereal trains, / Softened with pleasure, and voluptuous life' (532–4). That is the pre-condition for temptation to disobedience, and in this he is as culpable as the faint hearted in the tribe who capitulate to the easy life among the Philistines. Interestingly, and typical of the subtler distinctions in the dramatic poem, the Chorus (at several points vulgarising issues) credits Samson with divine impulsion in the second marriage; Samson himself had held to that conviction with regard to his first marriage, to the woman of Timna, but does not put it so strongly concerning Dalila. Even special champions, like England itself perhaps, fail to learn from experience.

Also concerning failures of spiritual discipline, perhaps, is the matter of obedience by which the story of his hair is understood. Samson's own bitter remark early in the poem looks almost like a superstition: 'God, when he gave me strength, to show withall / How slight the gift was, hung it in my hair'. That looks like a culpable blaming of divine dispensation, and it prompts questions as to other kinds of strength beyond the physical. That strength of mind and spirit, celebrated by the end of the play, is what is needed on

Samson's part if he is to use his gift of physical strength properly. But also, beyond the physical strength with which it is associated, the hair tokens a pledge of obedience, for Samson is enjoined not to divulge its secret. Telling Dalila of the hair is therefore disobedience of divine command, as he reiterates: 'But I God's counsel have not kept, his holy secret / Presumptuously have published, impiously...' (497–8).

A chief issue in his discipline is belief in the One God. The doctrinal faults of Job's friends are now the spiritual faults to which all Israelites in captivity are liable. The Chorus analyses a possible collapse in belief (295): when Providence is hard to read, there will be some atheists, but more puzzled believers. Samson regrets (453) that the mouths of atheists and idolators have been opened (perhaps speaking also to the experience of reforming spirits who have lived through the mid-seventeenth century), and this sense of uncertainty is transmitted to the reader in various ways. The spiritual discipline of a whole nation is engaged, and if, again, we measure *Samson Agonistes* against Job, we have to recognise how far the action has been politicised: 'Promise was that I / Should Israel from Philistinian yoke deliver.' This is not just a rich man down, but a whole nation and lapses in belief reflect upon the honour of the One God. Beyond depression, the poem depicts guilt about political and religious causes, and the occasion is the feast day of Dagon, a superstitious sabbath not to be respected but usurped by heroic labour of mind and body.

The true God will overwhelm the false: as well as its introversions and labourings of the spirit, the action will have that revelatory effect. Samson himself sees the ultimate issue as a trial between the true and false God and comes implicitly to trust in the power of the true during what would be otherwise extreme presumption in confrontation with Harapha. That demonstration has large implications for the shape of the action of *Samson Agonistes*, which like *Paradise Regained* finally shows evil revealing and frustrating itself.

Such a thing happens many times locally: Dalila, revealing her Philistinian rewards in dress, progressively reveals her mind in her speeches; Harapha is exposed as lacking courage (evidently false gods do not inspire the same confidence as true ones). Most importantly, the Philistines are seen in the end to have lost their senses and brought upon themselves their own destruction. Samson's behaviour with the messenger looks superficially mad, first risking displeasure, then seeming to take an extreme risk in a wild kind of gamble that God will provide the opportunity he is looking for at the Games. But paradoxically it is the Philistines who have madly brought about their own downfall, by daring the powers of the God of Israel. As in *Paradise Lost*, where Satan's ultimate proud triumphal return to his people is turned to ashes, so here the triumphal procession bringing Samson as a champion of Israel into the idolatrous celebratory feast turns suddenly into judgemental death on the luxuriating. They have been blind, not he. And like Satan in *Paradise Regained*, they have 'tempted', that is to say, made trial of, the Lord. Both poems of 1671 end in celebrations of victory for the powers of the true God.

Paradise Regained seemed set to give ultimate reassurance of the final triumph of good over evil; *Samson Agonistes* seemed set to show that evidences of God's hand will be found even in the darkest circumstances, of bondage, tyranny, and temptation to cease in trust, provided that God's champions keep themselves in a state of disciplined readiness. When even God's champions cannot see a way out, God himself will let his enemies bring themselves into madness and destruction: they will 'hurt their minds' (1676). If England has drifted towards effeminacy, seduced by a culture of false religion, if it has in effect, in the radicalised formulation of the poem, put itself into bondage to a foreign culture, then it should take note of the inevitable judgemental result.

This is not, however, to imply that *Samson Agonistes* is an unreflecting prophecy, or a call to arms. Its power is also in the searching and critical quality of its analysis of the state of mind of those who would think of themselves as God's champions. A poem which imitates Job, even if on a larger political stage, shares with the Old Testament a cathartic rehearsal of conflicting confusions in a community amongst those who are nevertheless pious men. The fact that there is communication between the Hebrews is as important as that there is disagreement in the understanding of the mysteries of Providence.

In this connection it may be worth recalling that *Of True Religion*, which has its own reference to Job, would in 1673 show more than tactical wisdom in its advocacy of tolerance between Protestant parties. It is more important for Protestants to seek together, in debate, than it is to labour divisions and define heresies, in the adverse circumstances of the Clarendon Code. All men err. *Samson* witnesses especially to the dangers of pride, and one may notice how Milton has interwoven a sense of honour into the parts of his characters, in such as a way as to show that the best of men partake in dificulties of orientation. The matter is clear with the Philistines: Dalila is finally concerned with the honour and fame she might have among her countrymen; Harapha obviously exposes the hollowness of one concerned with his social self-image. But Manoa also has to heart the honour of his house, and he and Samson cannot forget the honour due to their God. Although self-blaming, Samson is not immune from moments of difficulty with his own sense of self-image, for it is the fact that he was God's 'nursling once' (633) which makes most difficult his self-examination. That it is so difficult to separate out one's own sense of honour from the honour due to God is, I take it, an analysis of the need of all who would be thought God's champions in 1671 to examine their own cases and think not uncharitably of other seekers of truth. God's hand will only be felt against his enemies, when Protestant Englishmen, like Job and his friends, have been through such examination.

The poem seems to speak, then, not only out of a situation which can be radically fictionalised as that of idolatrous oppression, but also more broadly of the experience of a long struggle in the cause of godly reformation. It shares with its readers feelings of division, and cultural confusion, and of the difficulty of reading hopes and disappointments in the godly cause. But it seems that the one thing never to be forgotten in times of bewildering adversity is the prior necessity of keeping religious and moral discipline. Labouring for that discipline, not to be seduced from that discipline, seems the only way forward. Minds must be schooled and the trials of despair must themselves be turned into healthful labours. Not all men are separated out for such special witness as Samson, but unless at least a section of the nation is able to school itself into that discipline, it will not be ready to hear the calling when it comes.

So we have in the Restoration period three great poems which seem to be addressed in spiritual healing to those who seek to strive in reforming causes. If *Paradise Lost* set out to reaffirm Providence in an action by showing the repentant how large was the ultimate restorative plan of God, *Paradise Regained* was added to this therapy for saints, seemingly designed to renew faith in ultimate victory. *Samson Agonistes* seems to speak in shared contemplation with and prophetic hope for the bewildered and oppressed – if there is renewed trust in Providence among the champions of the True God, God's enemies will surely destroy themselves. It is a poem peculiarly concerned with states of mind amongst God's champions, who are fortified, as true shepherds had been in 'Lycidas', with hope of some perhaps quite imminent divine judgement. That there was to be an accession of a Catholic king in 1685 Milton might have foreseen; that there was to be a relatively unbloody revolution in 1688, rather unlike the violent destruction of the Philistines, he could not be expected to foresee, but of prophecies of divine intervention spiritual fortifications are often made.

Notes

1. See for example, P 606.
2. 'Milton and Civilised Community', 336.
3. The major advocate of an early date for *Samson Agonistes* is Parker (see P 903–17). The most extreme case for an early composition of both *Paradise Regained* and *Samson Agonistes* is made by John T. Shawcross, *Paradise Regain'd: Worthy T'have Not Remain'd So Long Unsung* (Pittsburgh: DuQuesne University Press, 1988).
4. John [Giovanni] Diodati, *Pious Annotations upon the Holy Bible* (2nd edn, London, 1648), p. 7 (second pagination).
5. See the debate reported at VC IV 239–40, where the claim of A. S. P. Woodhouse is discussed, that 'it is Christ's first claim to participate in the Godhead'.
6. Joseph Wittreich, *Interpreting 'Samson Agonistes'* (Princeton: Princeton University Press, 1986).
7. The next section shares some common ground with 'Milton and the Idolatrous Consort', pp. 435–7.

Further Reading

This book is not a general critical introduction to the works of Milton, so a selection of general critical books does not seem very appropriate. What is more, the Milton bibliography has become so huge that a reading list covering not just the well-known writings but something approaching the whole range, as this book does, is a plain impossibility in this space. Mentioned below, therefore, are some basic reference works, some recent bibliographies which the student may explore, and a brief selection of collections of essays of different critical character, from which the student may seek directions. (Abbreviations are as shown on p. vii)

The only exhaustive edition of verse and prose is C. For study of the prose, with full apparatus, the student now generally refers to Y. For a fully, if sometimes a little eccentrically annotated edition of the verse, the usual source is CF. Lightly annotated volumes of the complete poetry in paperback form include *The Complete Poetry of John Milton, Edited with an Introduction, Notes and Variants*, by John T. Shawcross (revised edition, 1971). Paperback volumes containing the complete or nearly complete poetry and selected prose include *Complete Poems and Major Prose*, ed. M. Y. Hughes (1957), *Complete English Poems, Of Education, Areopagitica*, ed. G. Campbell (4th ed, revised, 1993), and *John Milton*, ed. S. Orgel and J. Goldberg (1990). The last mentioned has the fullest selection of prose, though its annotation is brief. Purchasable editions of much of the prose remain a problem, though the situation is helped by Martin Dzelzainis' edition of *Tenure* and a new translation of the *First Defence* in *Political Writings* (1991).

The basic biographical tool is P (about to be reissued with corrections by Gordon Campbell), though many still like to refer to David Masson's magisterial *Life of John Milton* (7 vols, 1859–94). There are no satisfactory short lives currently in print. *The Life of John Milton* (1983), by the novelist A. N. Wilson is better on readability than scrupulosity. The early lives have been collected in D. Still useful for their setting of the works of Milton into political context, despite their bias towards ideas of the 'radical underground', are the works of Christopher Hill: *Milton and the English Revolution* (1977) and *The Experience of Defeat: Milton and Some Contemporaries* (1984).

Since Milton's works engage many areas of intellectual debate, students may often find themselves needing information on names, contexts, and traditions of thought. A convenient reference tool for this purpose is *The Milton Encyclopedia*, general editor W. B. Hunter (7 vols, 1878–83).

There are various exhaustive bibliographies of writing on Milton, but the most convenient resource for students will soon be the series of paperback bibliographies (general editor, Roy Flannagan) to be issued by Pegasus Paperbacks (MRTS). There are brief bibliographical guides in some of the editions mentioned above: that in Campbell is mainly traditional in outlook; that of Orgel and Goldberg determinedly radical and theoretical.

A general introduction of collected essays in paperback form, covering many aspects of Milton's writing, is *The Cambridge Companion to Milton*, ed. D. Danielson (1989), which also carries a discursive bibliographical guide. A post-modern collection of recent writing on Milton is to be found in *John Milton* in the *Longman Critical Readers* series, ed. Annabel Patterson (1992), where there is also a brief bibliography organised by approach. The most recent collection of writing on the prose is *Politics, Poetics, and Hermeneutics in Milton's Prose*, ed. D. Loewenstein and J. G. Turner (1990).

Index

Academic Exercise, Summer
vacation (1628), 2–8, 18, 52
Accidence Commenced Grammar, 182
Ad Joannem Rousium Oxoniensis ... ,
107–8
Ad Patrem, 40–1
Ad Salsillum ... , 61
Andrewes, Bishop Launcelot, 14–6
Animadversions ..., 75–6
Apology against a Pamphlet, An, 25,
69, 80–3
'Arcades', 40–6
Areopagitica, 94, 96–9, 100–1, 121, 145
Artis Logicae, 108, 183
'At a Solemn Music', 10
'At a Vacation Exercise ...', 4–8, 183

Benthem, H.-L., 178–9
blindness, xv, 111, 119–20
Bridgewater, John, first Earl of, and
family, 41, 43–6
Brief History of Moscovia, The, 94,
99–100, 108, 114
Brief Notes upon a Sermon, 148
Buckingham, Duke of, 18

Cabinet Council, The (attr. Ralegh),
143–4
Cambridge University, 1–8, 13–15,
19, 28, 39–40, 50–3, 74, 131,
147
    Christ's College, 2–8, 11
Catherina, Queen, xii, 185–6, 200–1
Charles I, King, 16–7, 100, 111–14,
118, 124–8
Charles II, King, 148, 158–9, 185–6,
200
Colasterion, 91–3
comestor, Comus, 4, 8, 47–8
Commonplace Book, 37–8, 64,
69–70, 93, 202
Cromwell, Oliver, 111, 118–23, 132,
134–7, 144–5, 147–8
Cromwell, Richard, 144–5

Dante, 25, 59, 82, 103, 138
Dati, Carlo, 110
Della Casa, 25
Declaration, or Letters Patent, A (tr.
Milton), 182
Defensio pro populo Anglicano (*First
Defence*), 118–19, 124, 126–9,
132, 144, 152, 159
Defensio Secunda (*Second Defence*), 1,
35, 61, 113, 129–32, 134
Defensio, Pro Se (*Third Defence*), 130,
132
Derby, Dowager Countess of, and
household, 41–4
Diodati, Charles, 14, 26–7, 29, 38–9,
59, 63–5
Diodati, Giovanni, 63
Doctrina Christiana, De, 69, 89, 108,
139–42
*Doctrine and Discipline of Divorce,
The*, 90–4, 100–1
Drayton, Michael, 5, 165
Du Moulin, Peter, 130

Eikonoklastes, 118–19, 124–6, 159
Elegies (collection), 13–18
    'Elegia I', 1, 14–15
    'Elegia III', 15–16
    'Elegia IV', 17–18
    'Elegia VI', 27–8
Ellwood, Thomas, 159–60
Epigrams on the Gunpowder Plot,
17
Epigrams to Leonona Baroni, 61
Epistolae Familiares (*Familiar Letters*),
184
'Epitaph on the Marchioness of
Winchester, An', 26
Epitaphium Damonis, 15, 64–6, 106–7

Fairfax, Sir Thomas, 104–5, 131

Galileo, Galilei, 59
Gil, Alexander (Sr), 10–1

Gil, Alexander (Jr), 11, 18, 56–7
Grotius, Hugo, 59

Haak, Theodore, 178–9
Hall, Bishop Joseph, 71, 75–6, 80
Harefield, 41–5
Hartlib, Samuel, 96, 99–100
Henrietta Maria, Queen, xii, 17, 42,
  51–2, 93, 126, 200
History of Britain, The, 70, 113–16,
  122, 134, 153, 183, 199
Holstenius, Lucas, 61
Horace, xiii, 29, 30, 60, 63, 65, 84,
  108, 143, 183
  'Fifth Ode of Horace, English'd',
  183
Houses and lodgings, Milton's
  Bread St, 9
  Hammersmith, 38, 40
  Horton, 38
  Aldersgate, 67, 89–90
  Barbican, 110
  High Holborn, 110
  Charing Cross, 119
  Whitehall, 119
  Petty France, 119–20
  Holborn, 159
  Chalfont St Giles, 159–60
  Bunfields, 182

'Il Penseroso', 28–34

James I, King, 16–7, 143
James Stuart, Duke of York, 200–1,
  207
Jonson, Ben, 87
Judgement of Martin Bucer, The, 90–3
Justa Edouardo King naufrago ..., 51

King, Edward, 51–3

'L'Allegro', 28–34, 48
Laud, Archbishop William, 51–2,
  67, 71–2, 98
Lawes, Henry, 45–9, 59, 103, 106
Letters
  'Letter to a Friend' (1633?), 37, 40
  'Letter to a Friend' (1659),
  149–50

letter to Alexander Gil (Jr) (1634),
  56–7
letter to Benedetto Bonmatthei
  (1638), 60
letter to Carlo Dati (1647), 110
letters to Charles Diodati, 27, 38–9
Ley, Lady Margaret, 86–8
*Likeliest Means to Remove Hirelings,
  The*, 135, 146–8
Ludlow, 45–7
'Lycidas', 12, 15, 22, 39, 50–7, 64–5,
  67, 72–3, 95, 98, 106, 108, 172–3

Manso, Giovanni Battista, 61–3, 66
'*Mansus*', 62–3
Masque at Ludlow, A, 8, 45–51, 55–7,
  108, 192, 194
Milton, John (Sr), 8–10, 37–8, 40–1,
  90, 110
Milton, Mary (Powell), first wife, xii,
  89–90, 110, 119
Milton, Katherine, second wife, 138
Milton, Elizabeth, third wife, 182
More, Alexander, 129–30, 132
Mylius, Hermann, 123

Newport, Countess of, xii, 52

Observations on the Articles of Peace,
  118
Of Education, 69, 94–6, 147, 183
Of Prelatical Episcopacy, 74
Of Reformation, 71–4
Of True Religion, 185–7, 205
'On Shakespeare', 28
'On the Death of a Fair Infant ...', 183
'On the Morning of Christ's
  Nativity', 19–23, 34, 36, 189,
  191–2
'On the University Carrier', 26
Ovid, 13–6, 82

Paradise Lost, 23, 48, 55, 61, 73, 83, 90,
  92, 95, 108, 126, 141–2, 148,
  155–80, 184–5, 195–6, 205–6
Paradise Regained, 98, 136, 141, 173,
  187–98, 204–6
'Parlamentum', 123
'Passion, The', 23–4, 107, 192

Petrarch, 24–6, 59, 82
Phillips, Edward, nephew, 67–9
  Life of Milton, 67–9, 88, 160
Pindar, 20, 23, 84
Plato, 22
Poemata ... (1645), 106–7
Poems of Mr. John Milton ... (1645), 13, 19, 23–4, 45, 51, 86, 100, 105–7, 183
Poems, &c. upon Several Occasions ... (1673), 41, 96, 101, 103, 120, 135, 137, 139, 142, 183
Powell, Richard, 89–90, 110
Present Means and Free Delineation ...., The, 150
Prolusiones, 184
'Proposals of Certain Expedients', 150
Psalm paraphrases
  Ps. 1–8 (1653), 135–8
  Ps. 80–8 (1648), 108–10
  Ps. 114, 126 (1623–4), 16–7
  Ps. 114 (Greek; 1634), 57

Quintum Novembris, In, 17

Racovian Catechism, 121
Ready and Easy Way, The, 148–51
Reason of Church-Government, The, ix, 67, 76–81, 189
Rous, John, 107–8

Salmasius, Claudius, 118, 126–9
Samson Agonistes, 70, 92–3, 100, 108, 142, 160, 166, 173–4, 187–9, 191–2, 196, 198–207
Shakespeare, William, 28–32
Skinner, Cyriack, 128–9, 138, 143
Skinner, Daniel, 140
Smectymnuus, 71, 82
Sonnets
  Sonnets I–VI, 24
  'How soon hath time ...', 36–7
  'Captain or colonel ...', 83–4
  'To the Lady Margaret Ley', 86–8
  'Lady, that in the prime ...', 88–9, 201
  'A book was writ of late ...', 100–3, 183
  'I did but prompt ...', 100–3, 183

'To Mr H. Lawes ...', 103, 106, 183
'When faith and love ...', 86, 103, 183
'On the Lord Fairfax ...', 104–5
'On the New Forcers ...', 103, 109, 183
'To the Lord General Cromwell', 104, 119–23
'To Sir Henry Vane the Younger', 104, 119–23
'When I consider ...', xiv–xvii, 120, 124, 183
'Cyriack, this three years day ...', 128–9
'On the late Massacre in Piedmont', 135, 183
'Methought I saw ...', 138–9, 183
'Lawrence of virtuous father ...', 142, 183
'Cyriack, whose grandsire ...', 142, 183
Spenser, Edmund, 5, 20, 24, 28, 47, 76, 98, 192–3, 197
Stock, Richard, 11
Sylvester, Joshua, 17

Tempe Restores (masque), 43
Tenure of Kings, The, 111–5, 118
Tetrachordon, 91–3
Thirty Years War, 16–18
Thomason, Mrs Katherine, 86
Treatise of Civil Power, A, 140–1, 144–6
Trinity Manuscript, 37, 40–1, 43, 55, 70, 86, 101, 103–4, 120, 160

Ussher, Archbishop James, *The Judgement of Doctor Rainolds*, 74
Vane, Sir Henry, 119–23
Virgil, 22, 32, 50, 64–6, 95, 106, 184
Vossius, Nicholas, 127

Westminster Assembly of Divines, 90–1, 97–9, 104, 109
Wither, George, 16, 180
Wotton, Sir Henry, 59

Young, Patrick, 108
Young, Thomas, 10, 12, 14, 17–18, 71